The *landscape house* was never built. Around sixty models relative to this house were made: some in concrete, others in cardboard, ceramic, plexiglas, and styrofoam. Several of them were exhibited at the Museu do Índio in Rio de Janeiro in 2003. An edition binder was compiled that brought together photos, drawings, and research notes on the project. A Devonian Press publication on the *landscape house* was also published in 2013.

The *landscape house* is a reinforced concrete structure in which somebody can live. It consists of a concrete geometric form, welded to an amorphous hump, produced by pouring the concrete rather than casting it. The house is a transition between two states: solid and liquid. It is continuous and discontinuous. A metamorphosis. The concrete gives an account of its potential failure by recording various marks and imprints, and allowing for cracks to appear and underline the passage from one state to another. The resulting silhouette is that of a rock or a small mountain, onto which one can walk or climb. It is a landscape, and it is part of the landscape.

This house takes the shape of a catastrophe.

La *landscape house* (maison paysage) n'a jamais été construite. Une soixantaine de maquettes de cette maison ont été produites : certaines en ciment, d'autres en carton, céramique, plexiglas, et polystyrène. Une sélection de ces maquettes a été présentée au Museu do Índio à Rio de Janeiro en 2003. Un classeur de travail, édité par la suite, rassemble les photos, dessins et notes de recherche du projet. Elle donna lieu à une publication Devonian Press en 2013.

La *landscape house* est une structure en béton armé dans laquelle on peut vivre. Elle est le résultat d'un double processus de moulage, l'un contenu et géométrique, l'autre ouvert et informe. La maison est une transition entre deux états : le solide et le liquide. Elle est continue et discontinue. Une métamorphose. Le béton armé rend compte de sa faillite potentielle en enregistrant diverses marques et traces, et en autorisant l'apparition de fêlures soulignant le passage d'un état à l'autre. La silhouette est celle d'un rocher où d'une petite montagne sur laquelle on peut grimper et marcher. La maison est un paysage et fait partie du paysage.

La maison prend la forme d'une catastrophe.

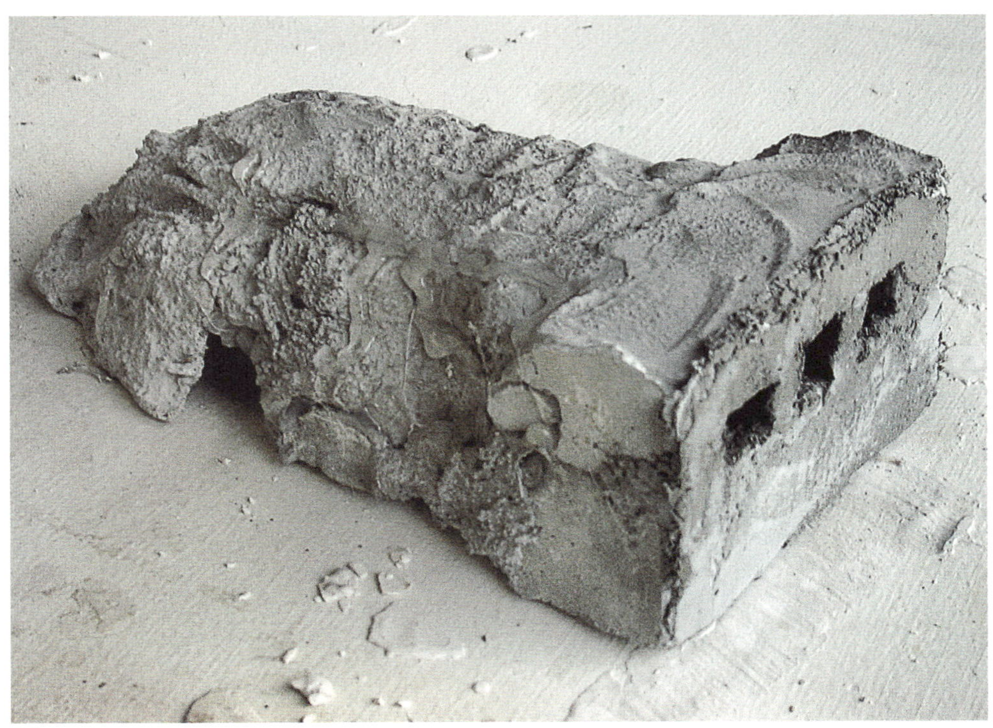

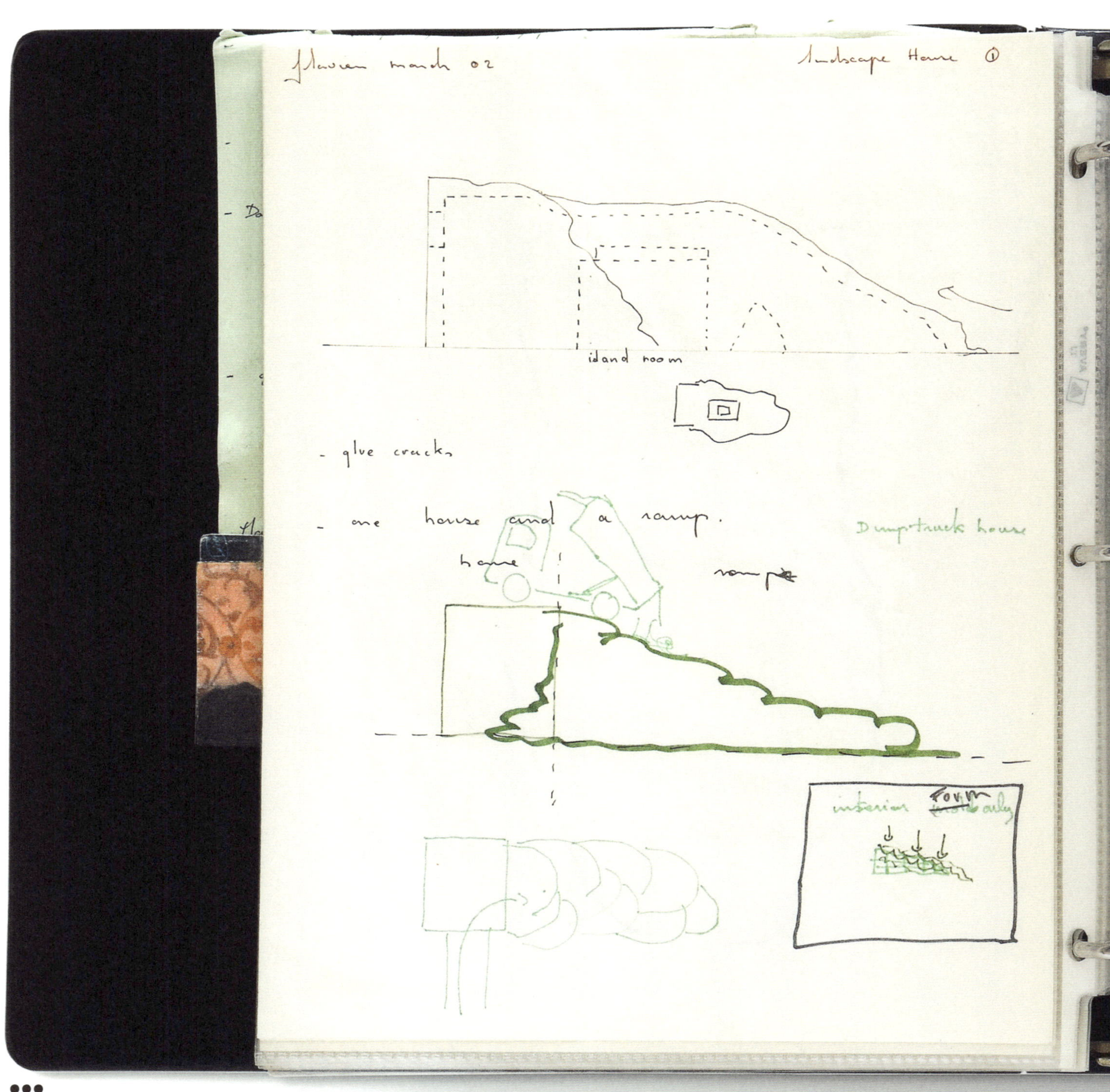
island room
- glue cracks
- one house and a ramp.
house
ramp
Dumptruck house
interior form only

flavin march 02

landscape house ①

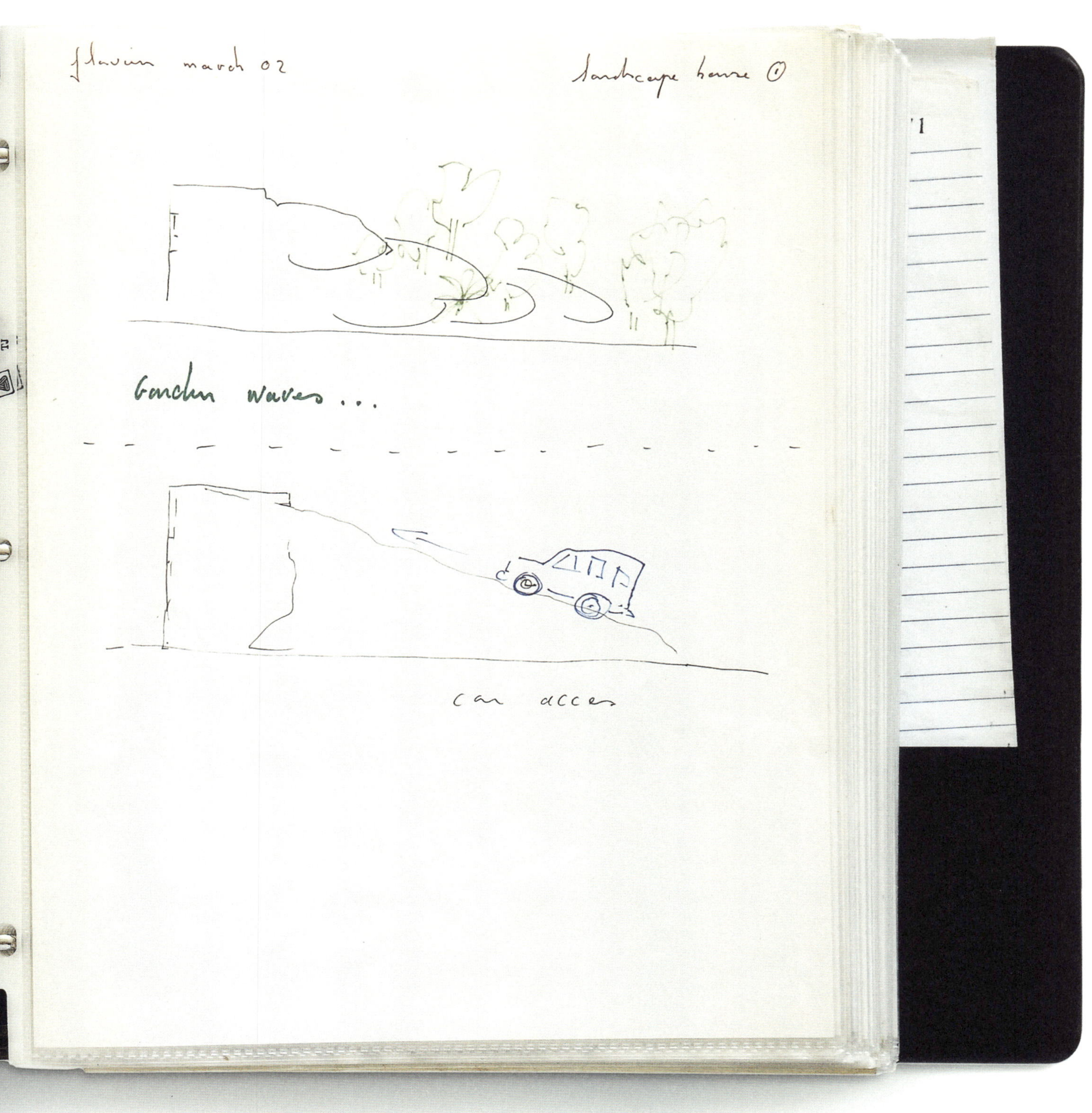

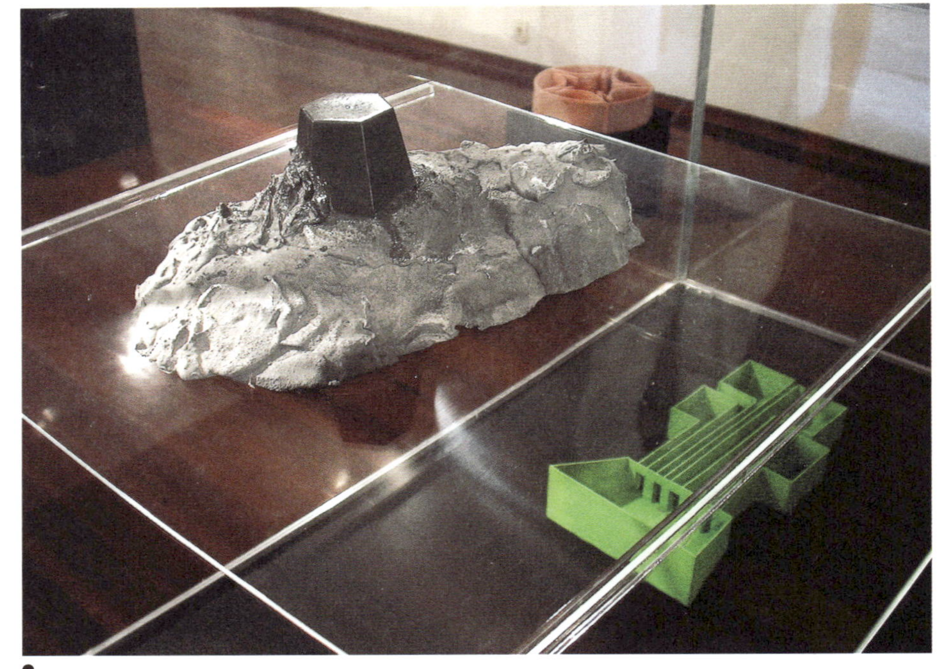

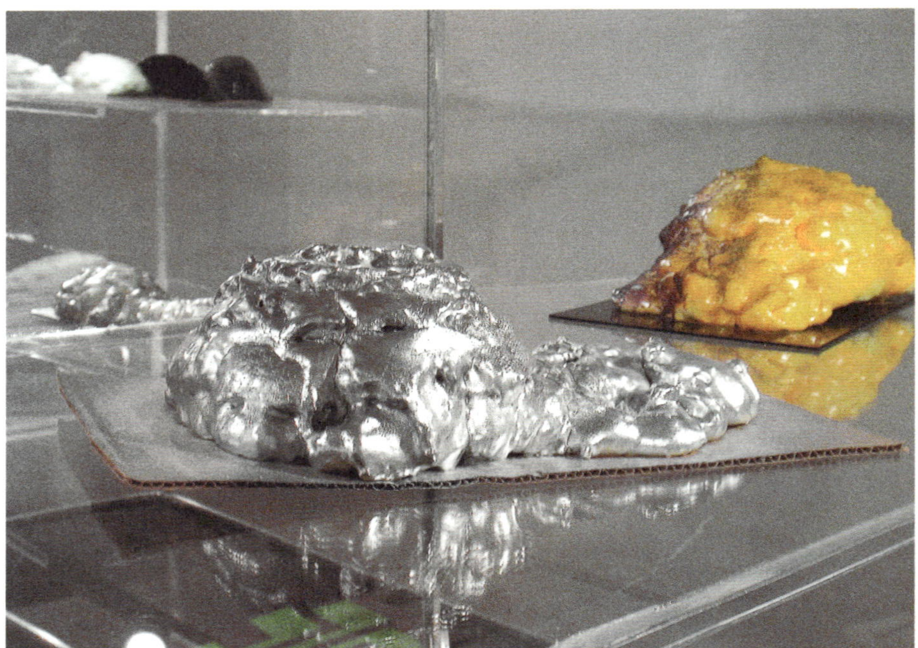

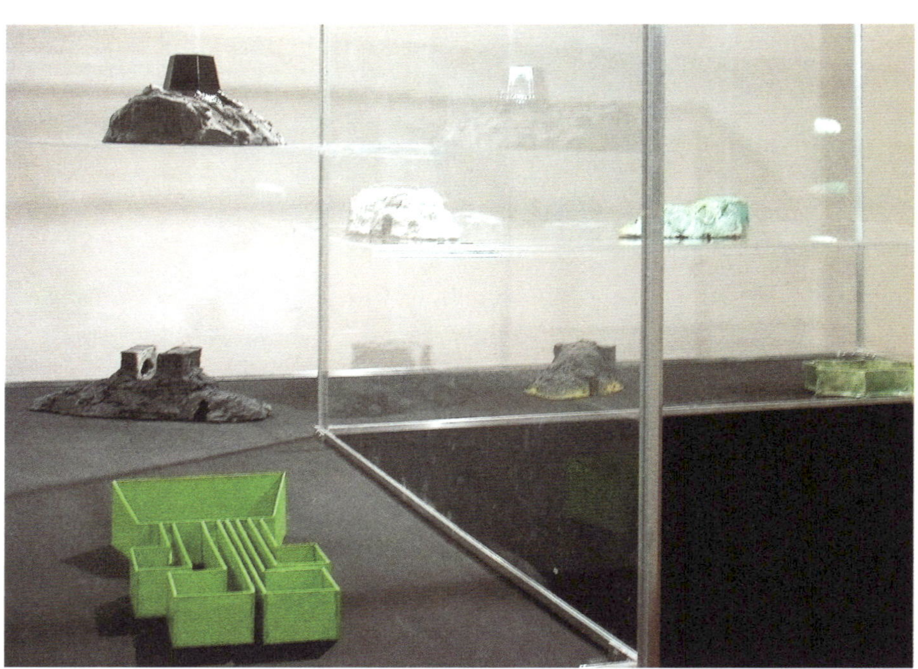

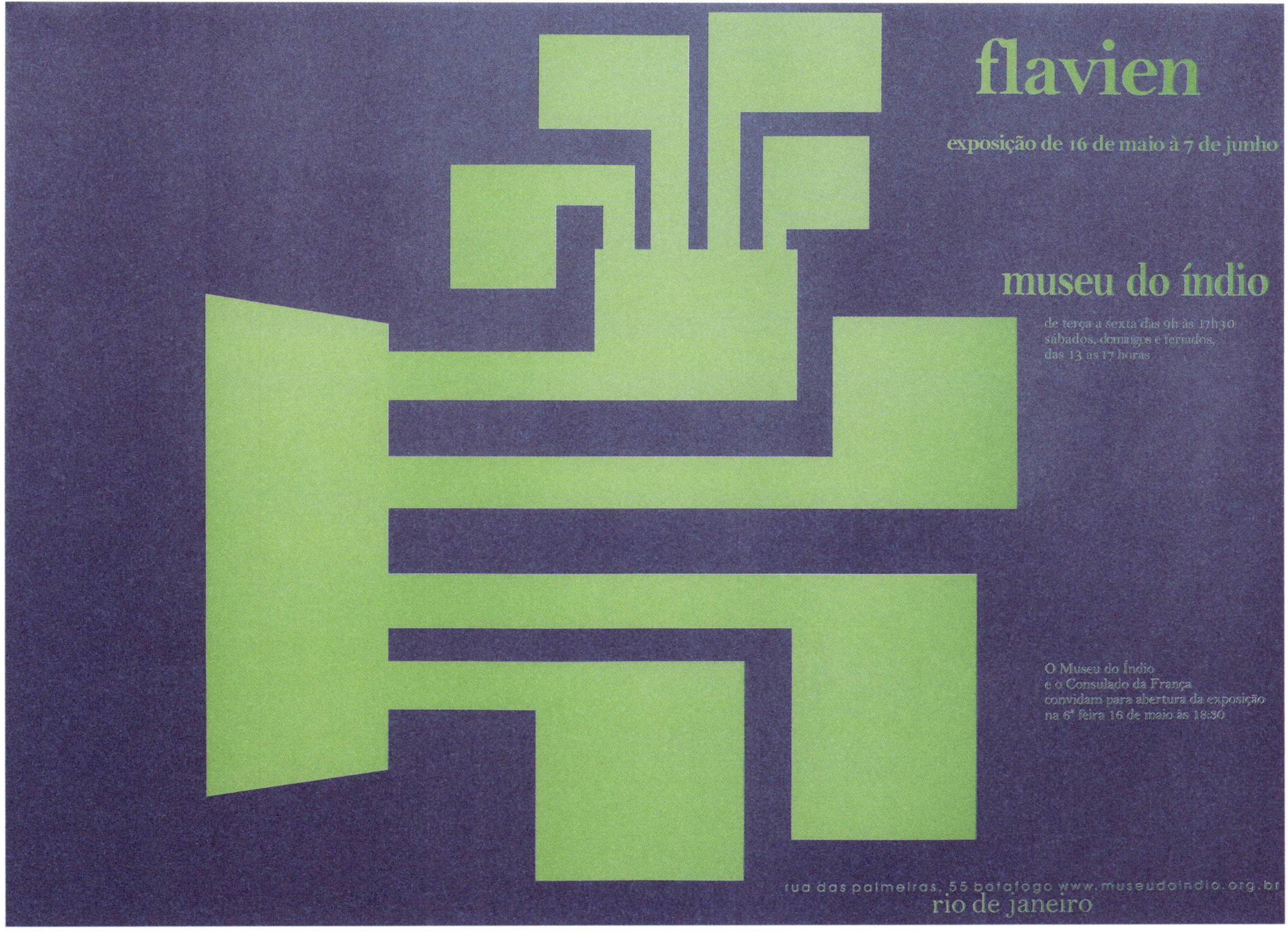

●   Exhibition views, Museu do Índio, Rio de Janeiro, 2003
●● Exhibition poster, Museu do Índio, offset print, 44×59 cm, 2003

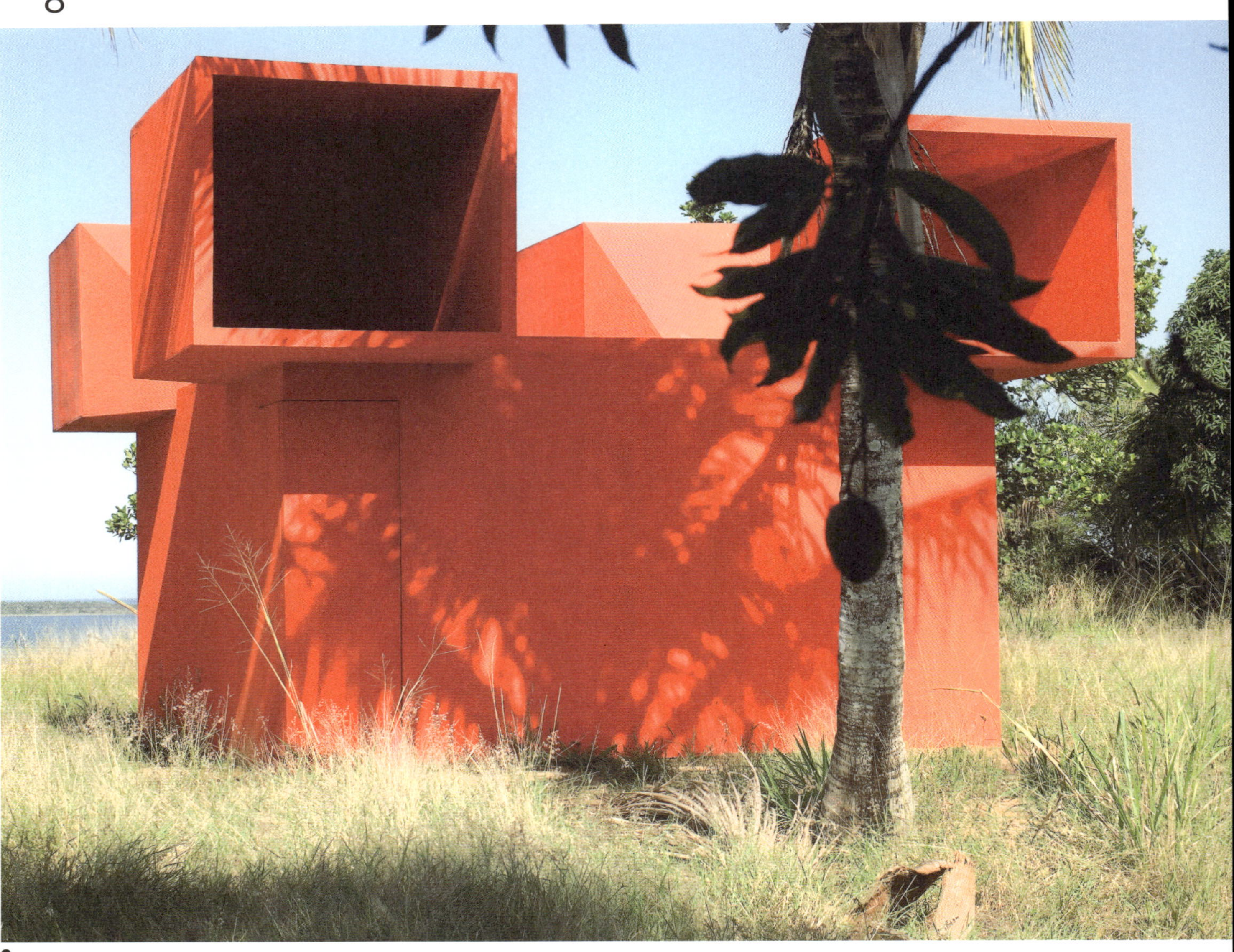

● *viewer* (medium), Maricá, Rio de Janeiro, painted wood, sound system, 4×7,7×4,9 m, 2007
●● The three sizes of the *viewer*

viewer

2007–2009
Rua Itapajé 20, Maricá
RJ 24900-000, Rio de Janeiro

The *viewer* is a construction in three possible sizes, of which two were built: the middle size on a cliff in Brazil in 2007, and the smallest size at Art Basel Statements the following year. Linked to a series of 200 drawings in red pencil, it inspired four Devonian Press publications, a series of microfilms (i.e. very short video sequences), and a video titled *sci-fi film*. The building is also associated with a hard drive, which functions as a separate work for storing and displaying various documents and images associated with this project. I traveled several times to live and work in the *viewer* that was built in Rio de Janeiro.

The *viewer* took shape through a series of drawings of dinosaurs and prehistoric landscapes. It was within this context that the *viewer* defined its scale, its relationships, its sizes, its place in the landscape, its alterity, its allure…It tested its relationship with its environment, devoid of human beings. Its silhouette changed.

This building would exist Before! Before man, before architecture, before adulthood, before language, before consciousness…? We speak of pre-language, but can a type of space correspond to this moment in time where words are not yet separated from one another, phrases are not composed, the world is not organized, and the grammar that exists is in a primary state? If consciousness distinguishes itself from unconsciousness, can there be a space built by means of their interweaving in such a way as to live with what is not said? What would be its forms of forgetfulness, omission, or inattention? Or of concealment? Can the earth be transparent? Where does my sight stop? The building, like the drawings, is made to look behind, that is to say Before! Even if, in that place, neither architecture nor man are possible. This place Before is also a type of space. Can we place ourselves inside of it?

The *viewer* comes in three different sizes. It is a principle that has three terms, each with the same form but distinct properties, depending on whether one can enter into it or not, whether it is big or small, whether the climate is inside or outside. In the room of the Rio *viewer*, there were two switches, one for light and one for sound: I turn on the light, I turn on the sound.

Le *viewer* est une structure à trois tailles dont deux furent construites; la taille moyenne sur une falaise au Brésil en 2007 et la plus petite à Art Basel Statements l'année suivante. Lié à un groupe de 200 dessins au crayon rouge, il a donné lieu à quatre publications Devonian Press, à une série de microfilms (séquences vidéo très brèves), et à une vidéo intitulée *sci-fi film*. Le bâtiment est couplé à un disque dur qui fonctionne comme une pièce à part entière pour stocker et présenter divers documents et images associés avec ce projet. J'ai fait plusieurs voyages pour habiter et travailler avec le *viewer* de Rio.

Il prit forme au travers d'un groupe de dessins de dinosaures et de paysages préhistoriques. Dans ce contexte, le *viewer* a défini son échelle, ses rapports, ses tailles, sa place dans le paysage, son allure, son altérité…Il y éprouva ses relations avec son milieu en absence de l'humain. Sa silhouette se modifia.

Le bâtiment existerait Avant! Avant l'homme, avant l'architecture, avant l'âge adulte, avant le langage, avant la conscience…On parle de pré-langage, mais est-ce qu'à ce moment peut correspondre un type d'espace? Là où les mots ne sont pas séparés les uns des autres, les phrases pas composées, le monde pas organisé, la grammaire primaire. Si le conscient se distingue de l'inconscient, peut-il y avoir un espace fabriqué de leur maillage de façon à habiter ce qui ne se dit pas? Quelles y seraient les formes d'oubli, d'omission, d'inattention? Ou de recouvrement? La terre peut-elle être transparente? Où s'arrête ma vue? Le bâtiment comme les dessins sont faits pour voir vers l'arrière, c'est à dire Avant! Même si à cet endroit, l'architecture ou l'homme n'est pas possible. Cette place avant, c'est aussi un type d'espace. Peut-on s'y placer?

Le *viewer*, en recouvrant trois grandeurs différentes, est un principe à trois termes, avec à chaque fois une forme identique et des propriétés distinctes, suivant qu'on puisse y entrer ou pas, qu'il soit petit ou grand, que le climat soit dedans ou dehors. Dans la salle du *viewer* de Rio, il y a deux interrupteurs, un pour la lumière et un pour le son: J'allume la lumière, j'allume le son.

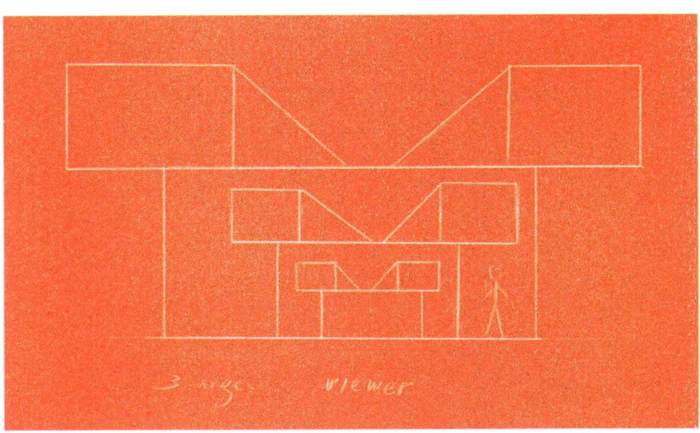

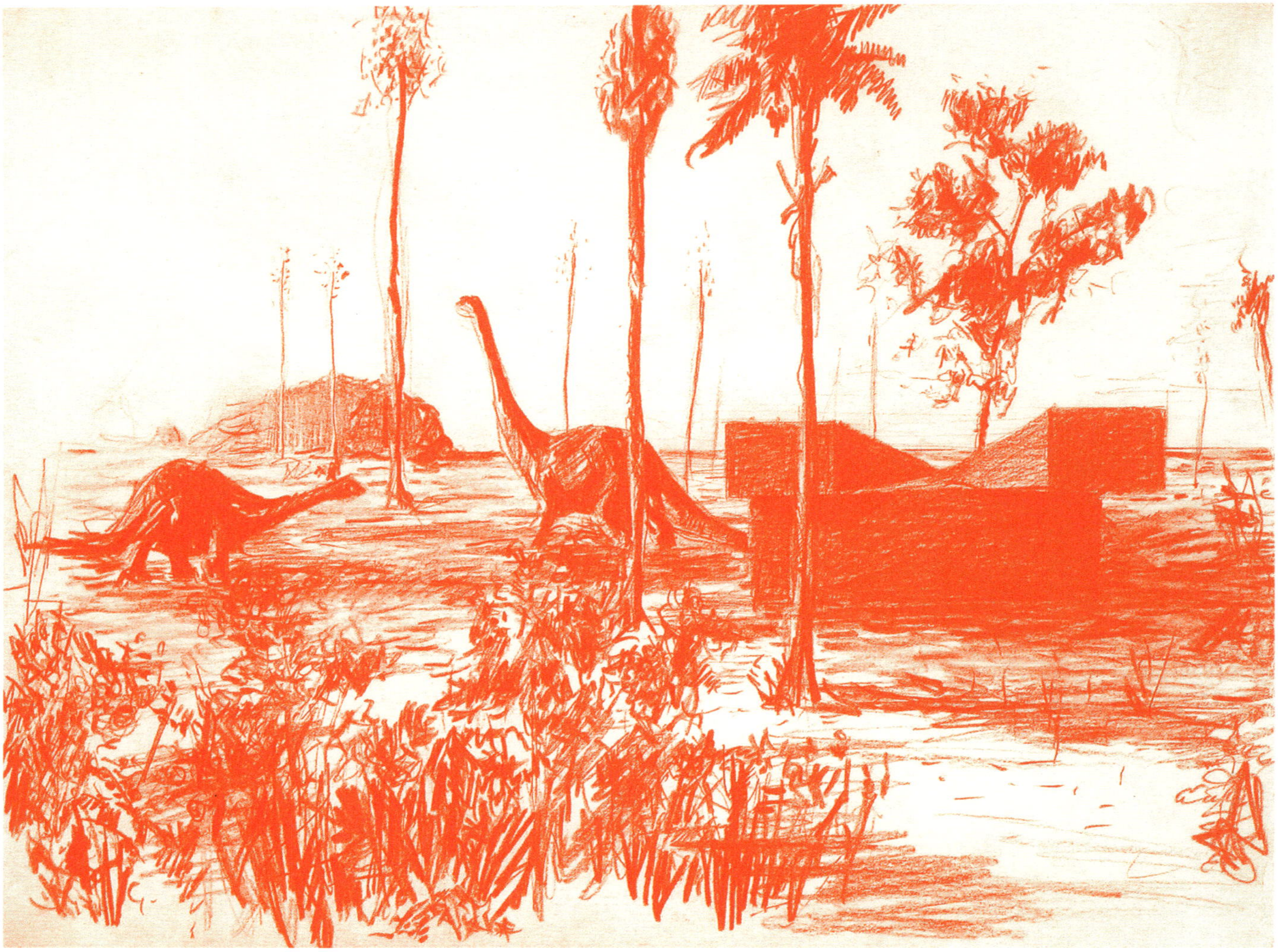

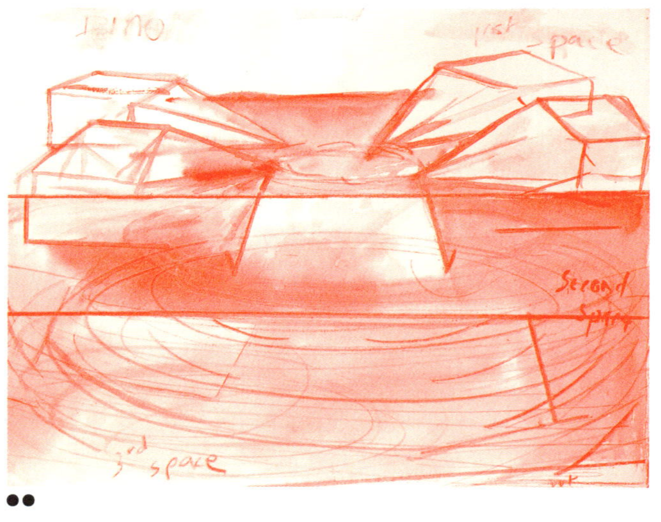

● *Dinosaur drawings*, red pencil on paper, variable dimensions, 2004–2010
●● Sketch of winds inside *viewer* (small), gouache on paper, 25 × 32,5 cm, 2004

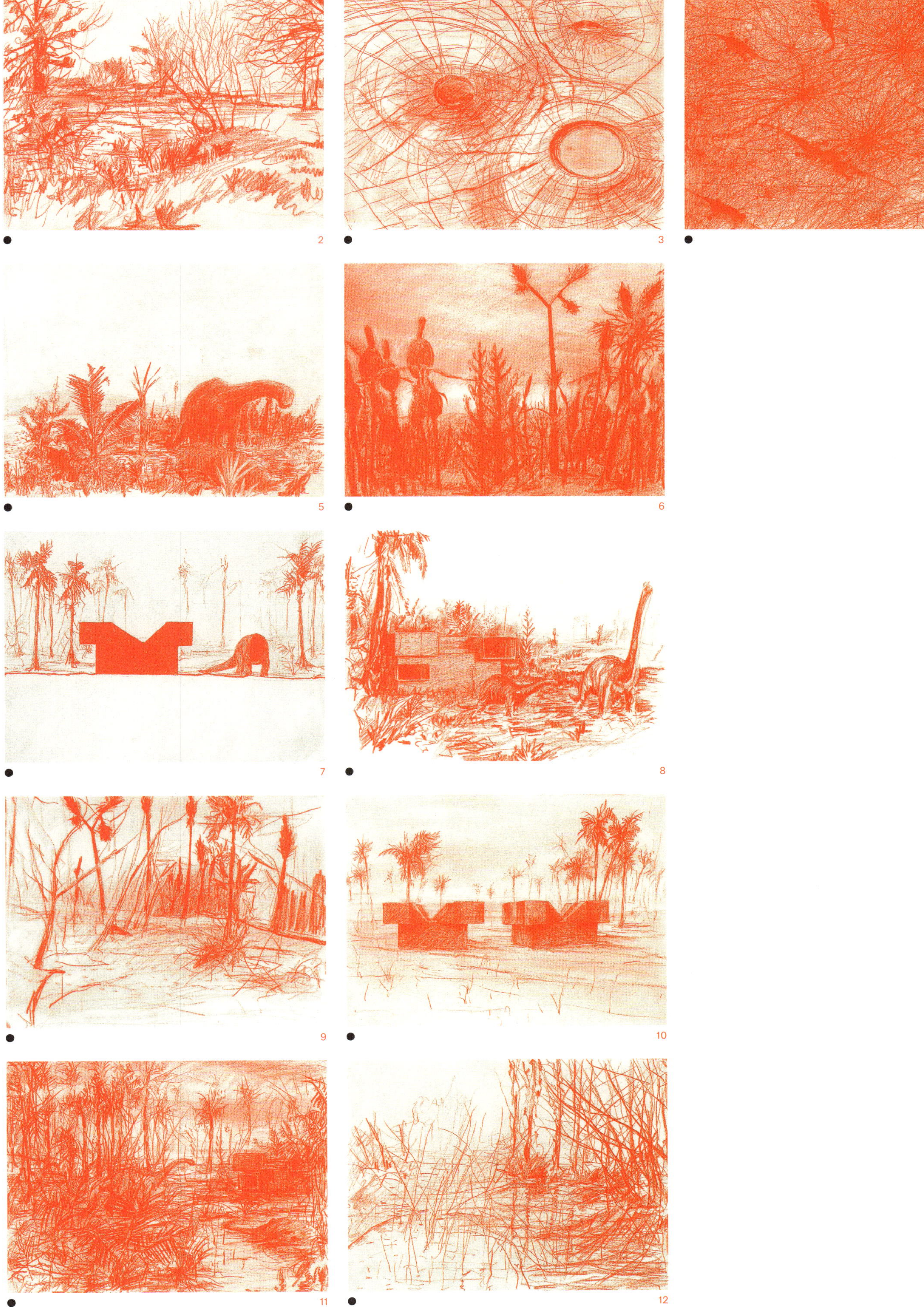

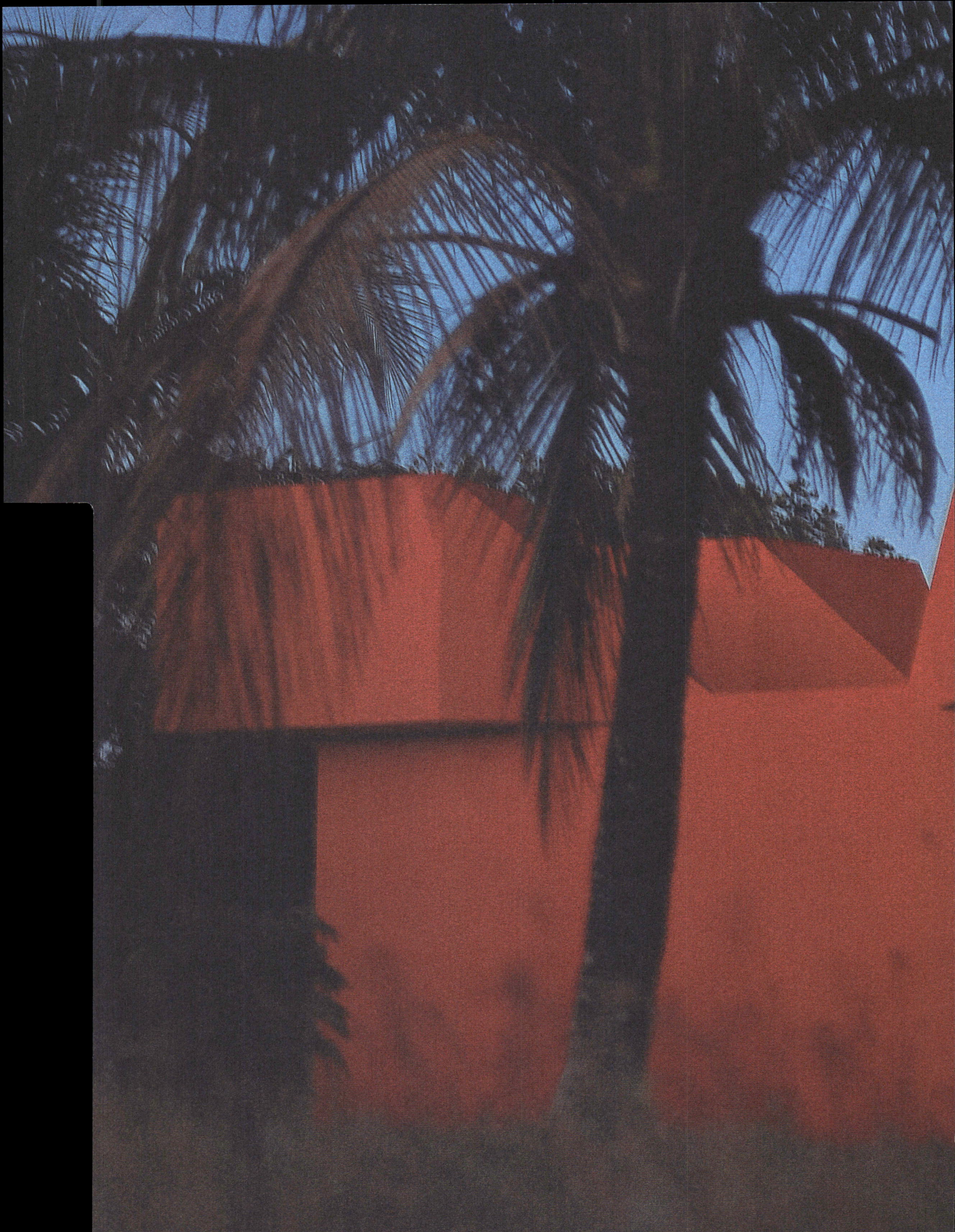

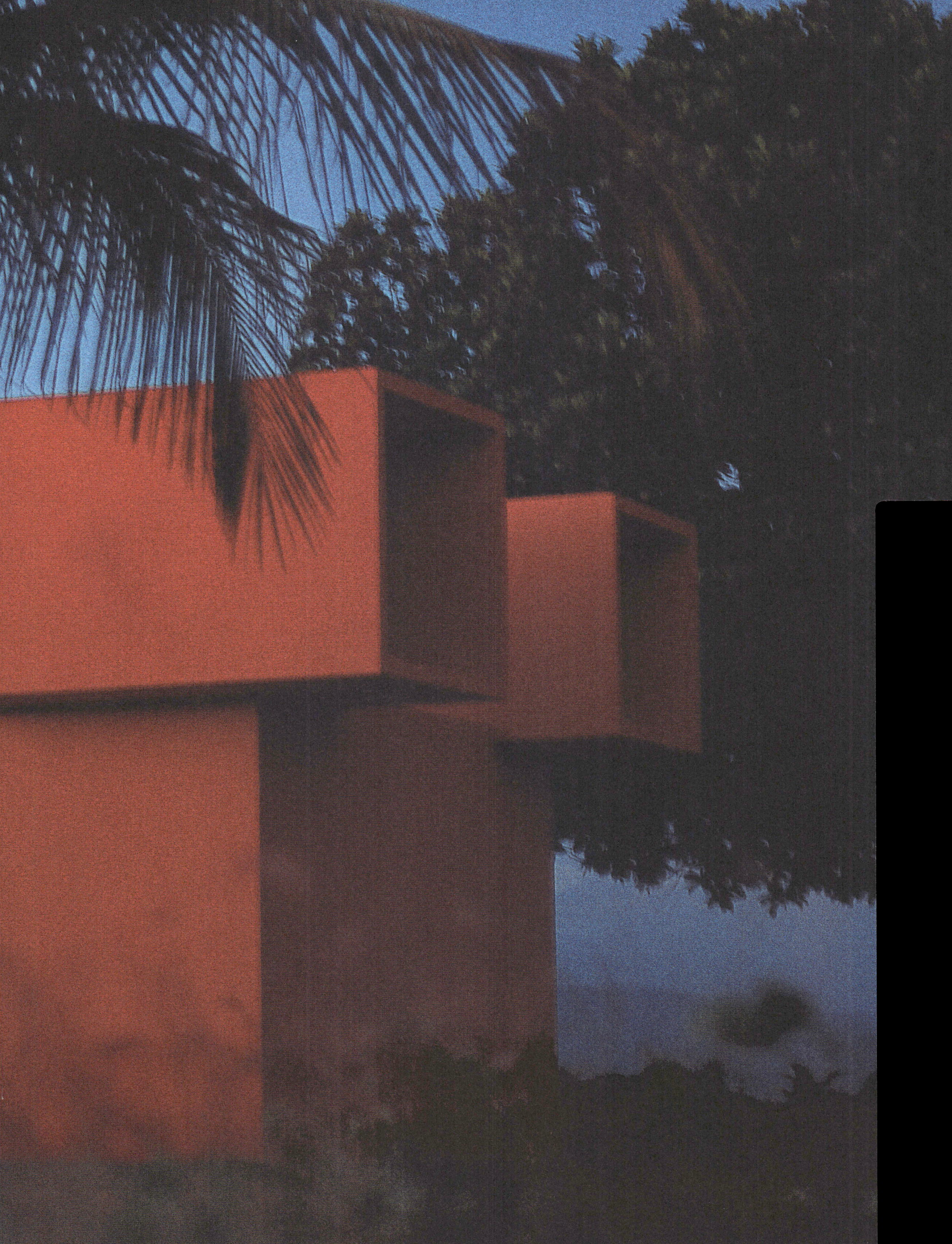

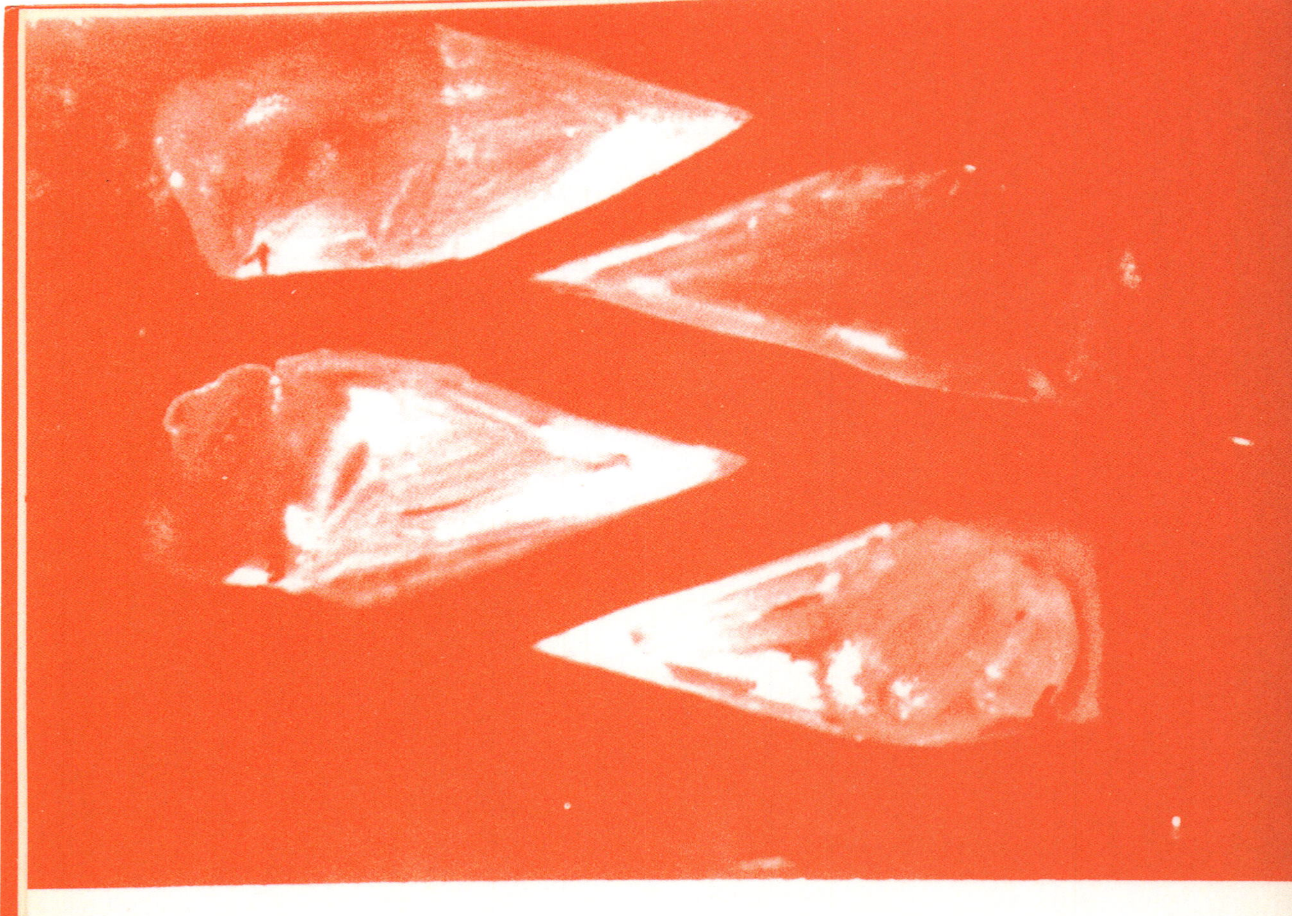

loud noise

the sound of the ground

four heads

compression of events

lack of focus

missing days

blind house

a low roar

dry climate

subconscious light

tumult

low frequency

a door slam

clamor

The viewer can have three different sizes.

The first size is smaller than a room, it is not much higher than a person. It is a place into which you cannot enter. The openings are placed at eye level, so people can look into the viewer from the outside. Each head is like a display. The central space becomes like a belly or an unconscious. There could be objects displayed in each head, as if in a viewing cabinet or a shelf. Some transparent objects, and you could look through them into the dark central room of the viewer. There could also be artificial lights, spinning lights shining from the inside out. If so, perhaps the inside could also be painted red.

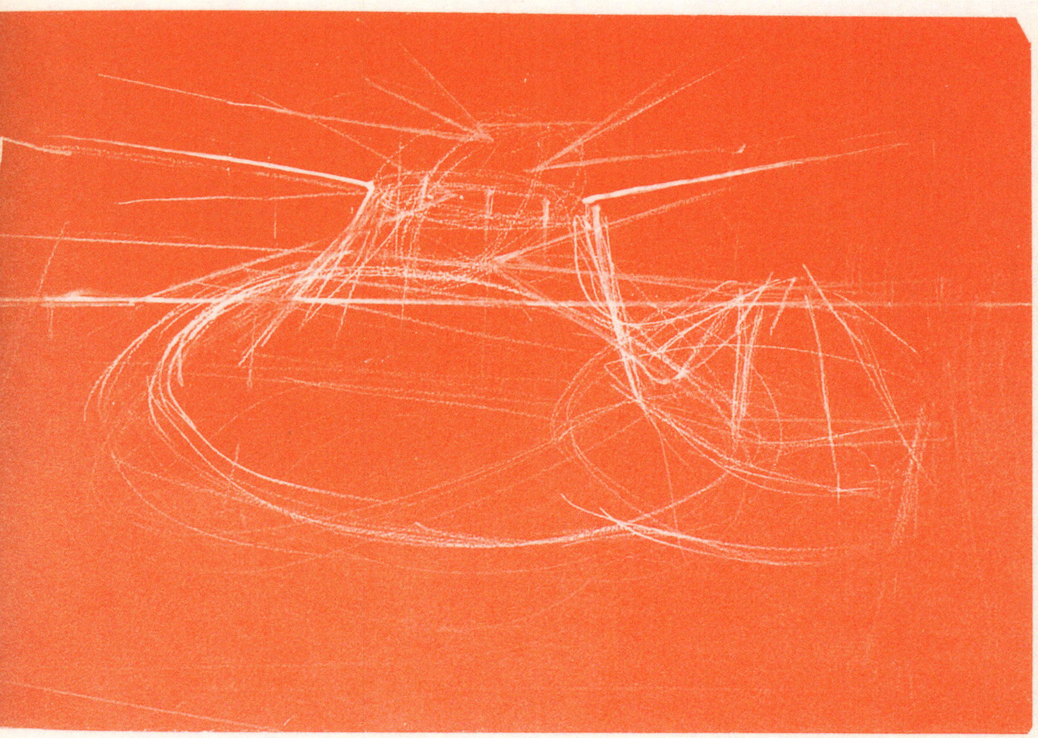

There would be light moving in and out of the viewer, and also movements of air. A sound could be broadcast from inside the space. A sound like a low roar. Movements of air could also be generated from the inside, some would remain trapped inside, others would blow outside like a breeze, a puff of air onto the onlooker's face. The viewer becomes a source of light, of sound, of air… It could also keep them in its internal belly, in an incessant spin.

The viewer could also generate other things, maybe even climatic conditions.

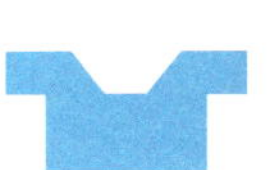

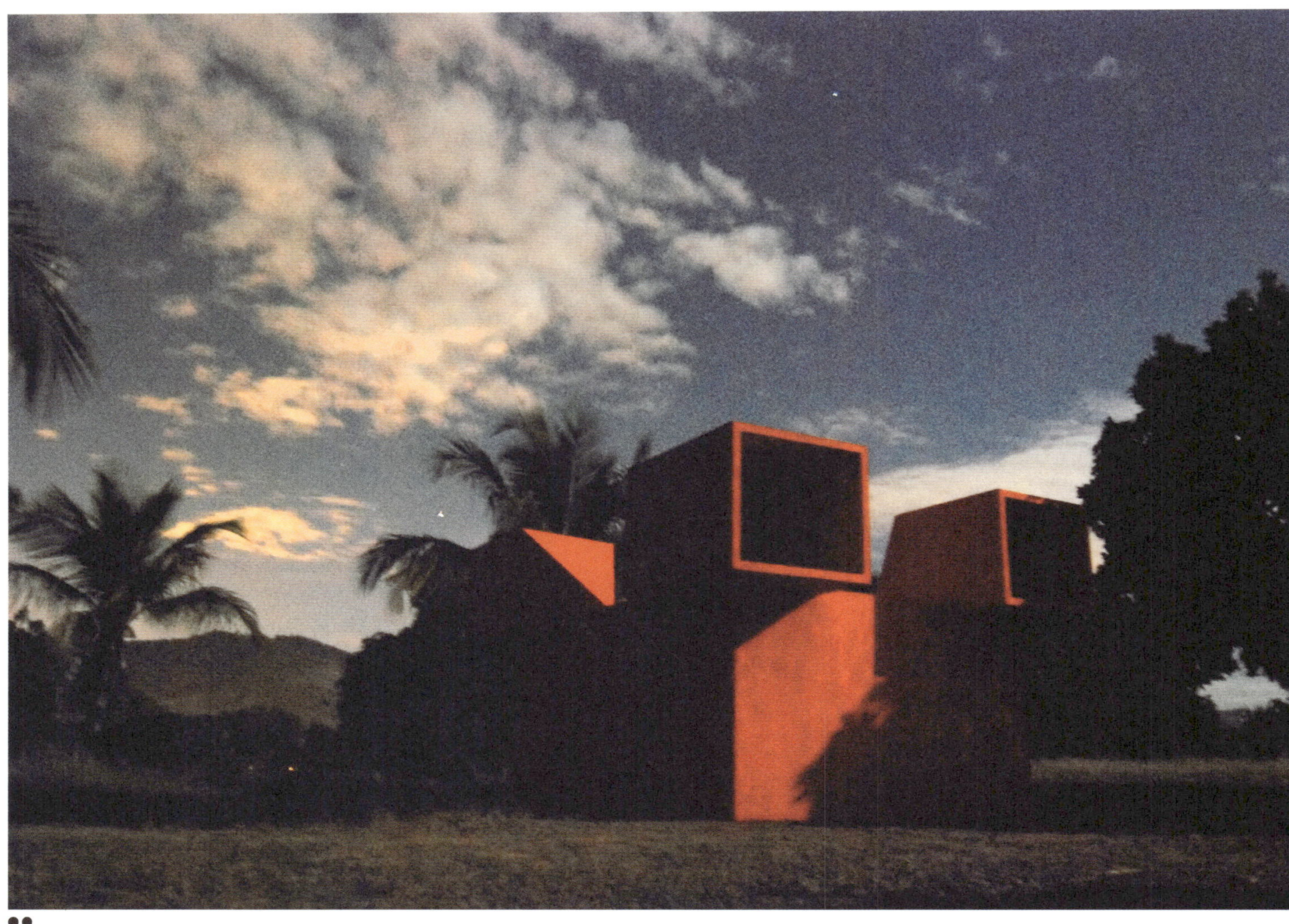

• *viewer*, Devonian Press, 48 pages, 29,7 × 21,5 cm, 2006 (previous spread)
•• *viewer*, Maricá, 2007

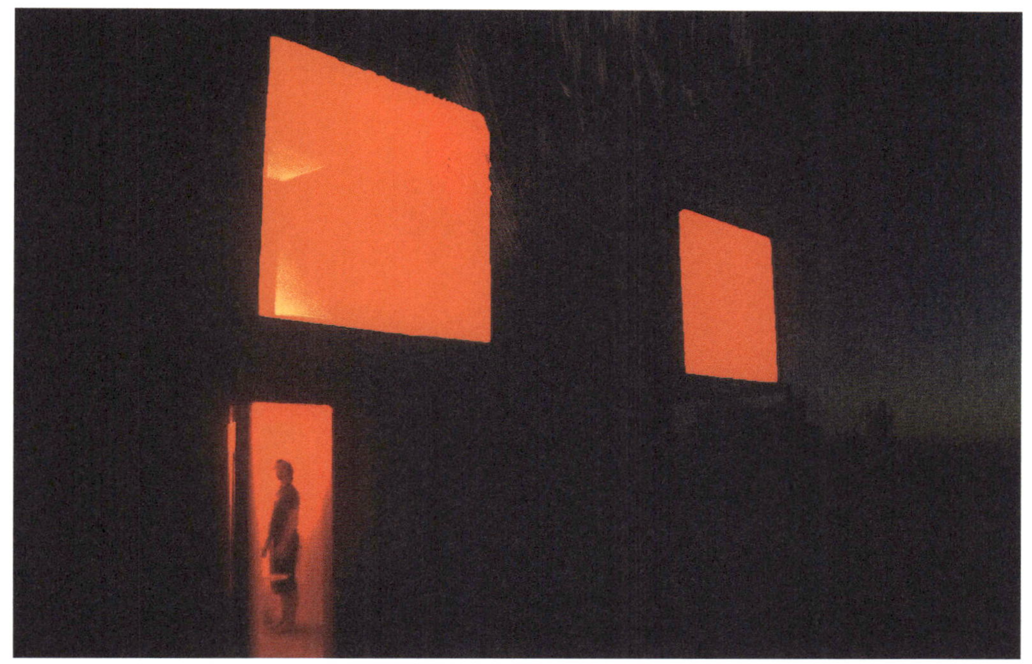

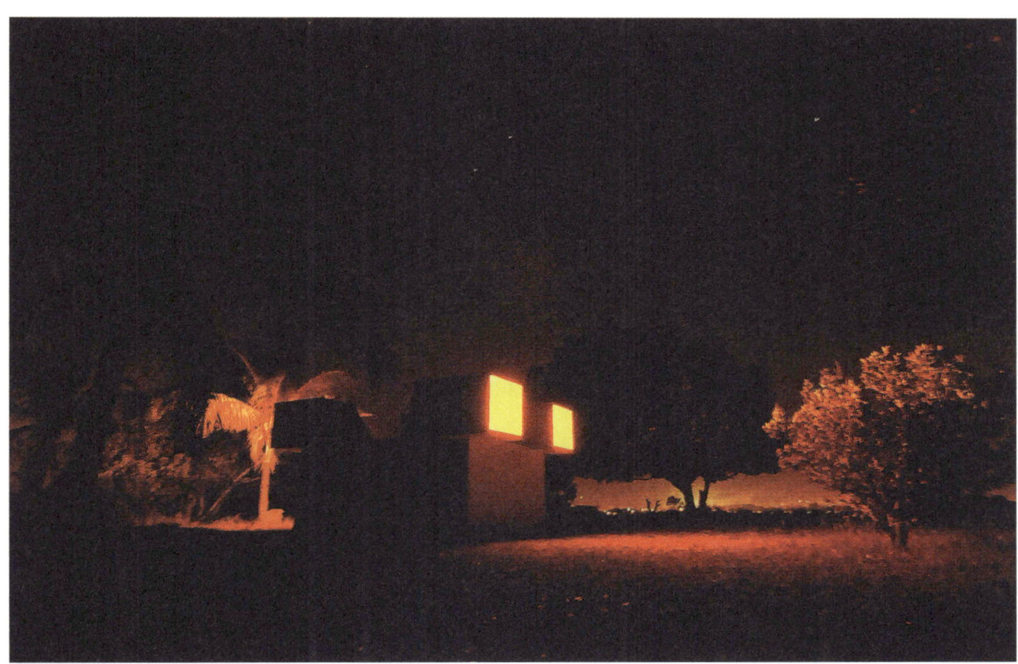

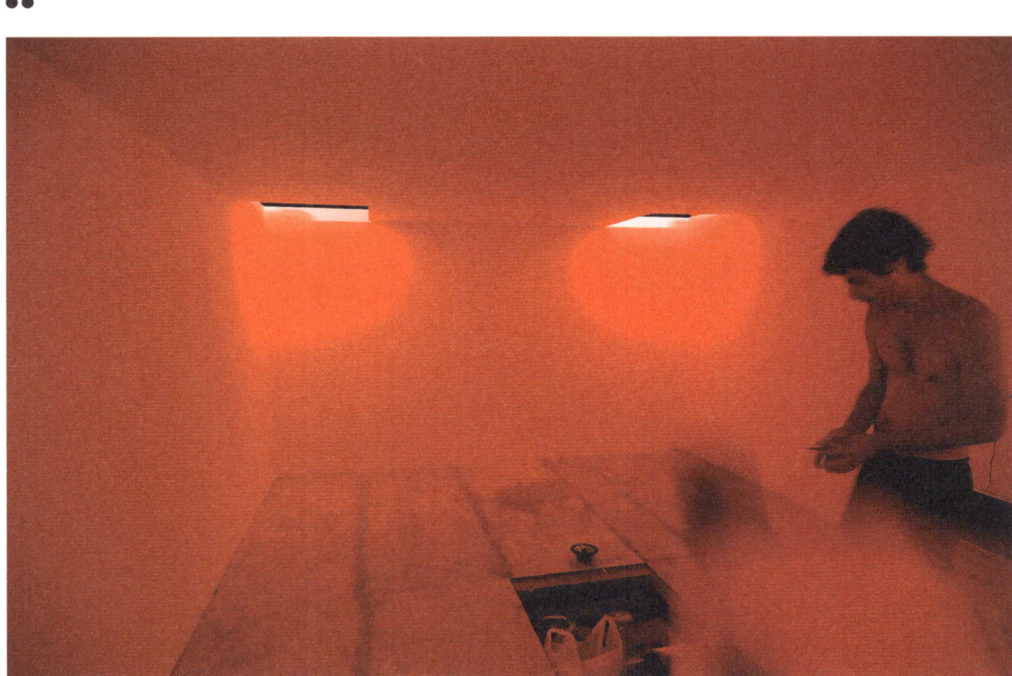

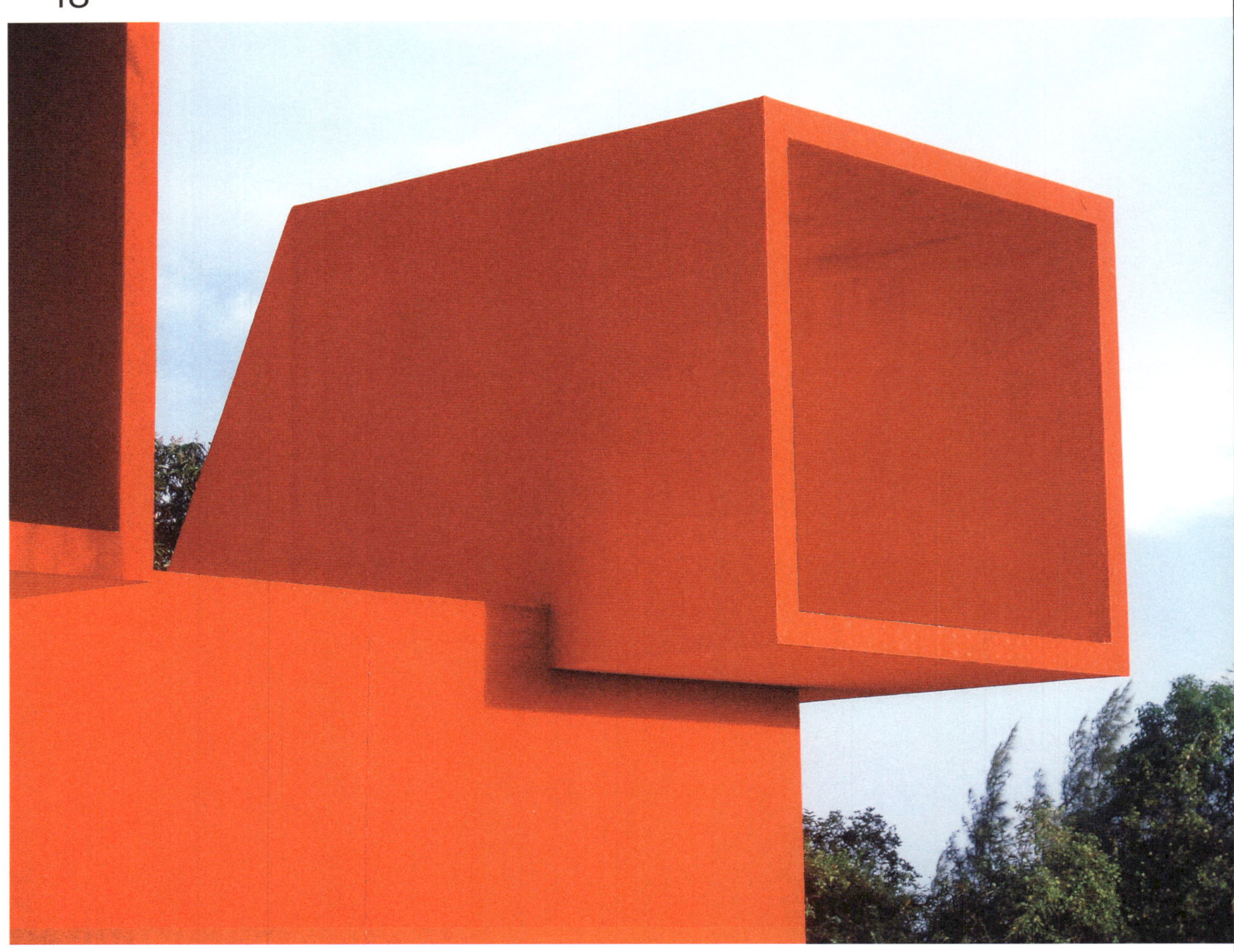

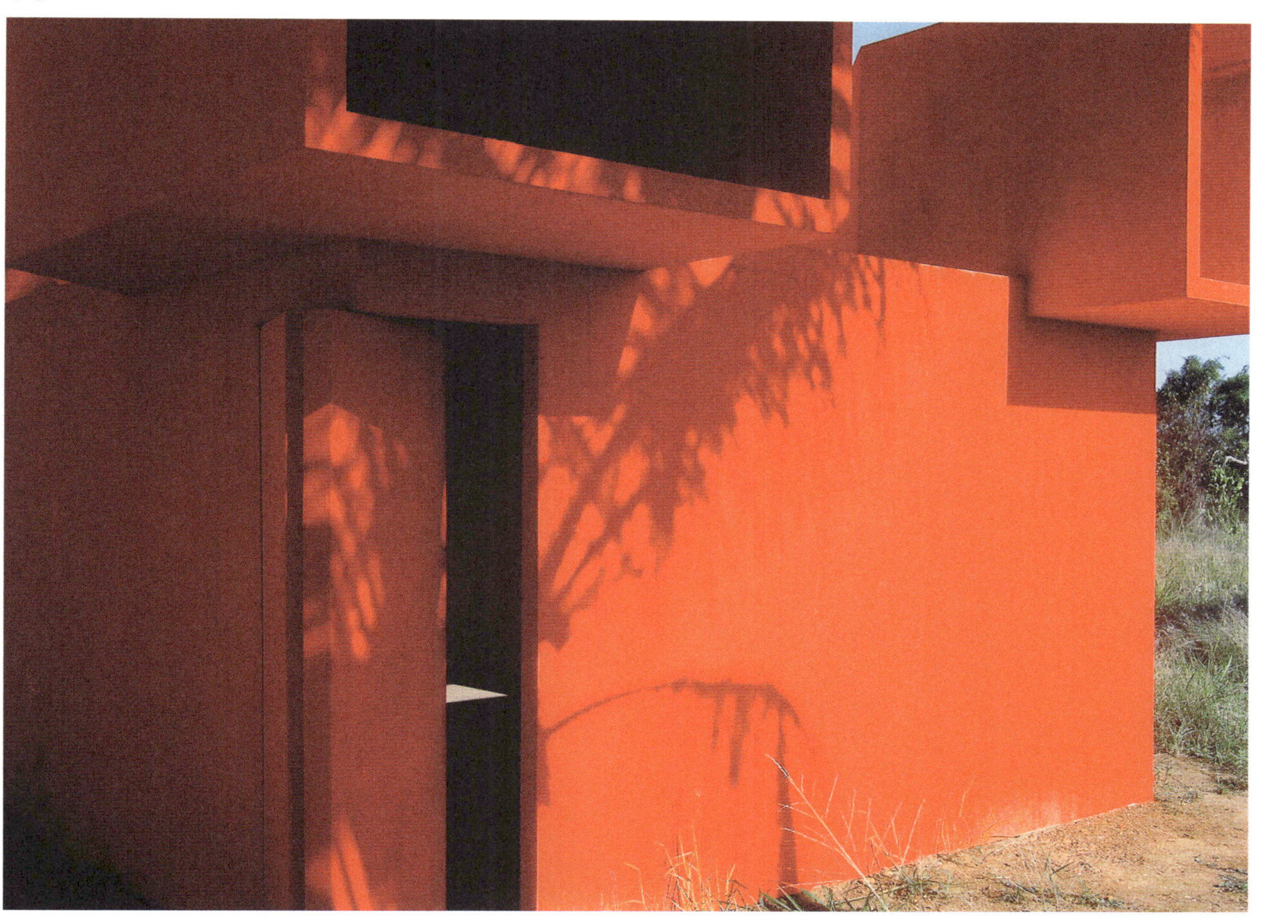

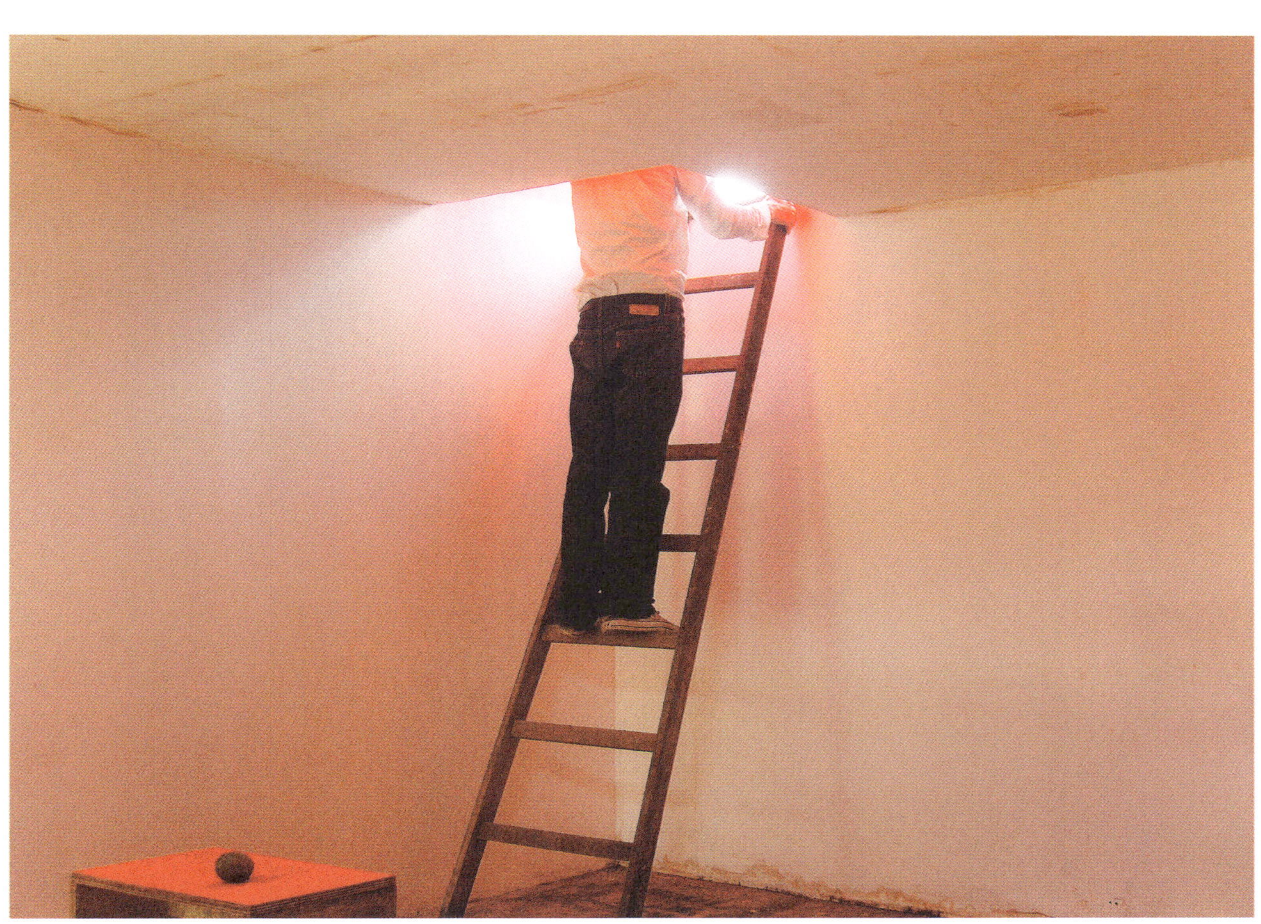

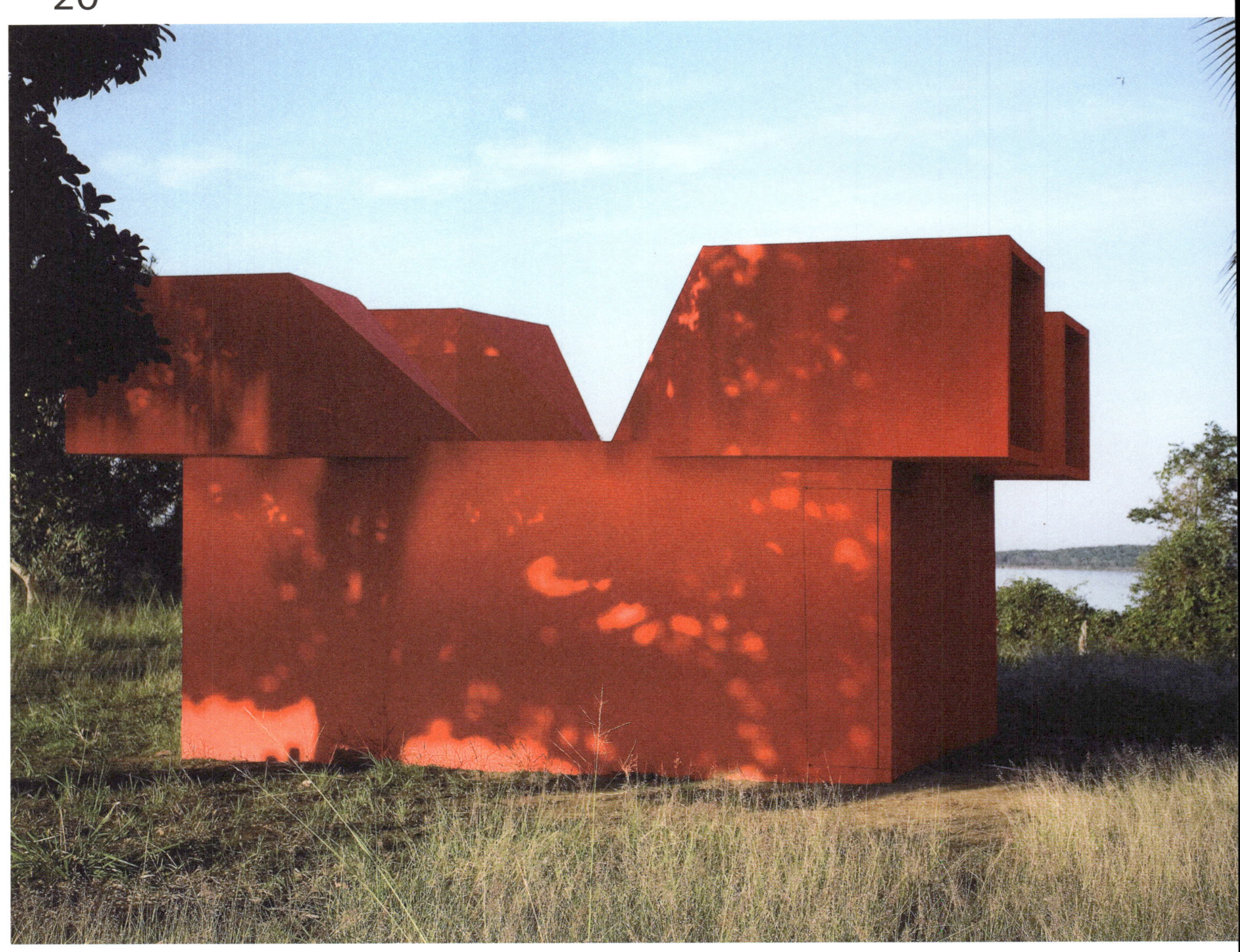

Documentation of the *viewer* in Maricá being used as a Devonian Press office

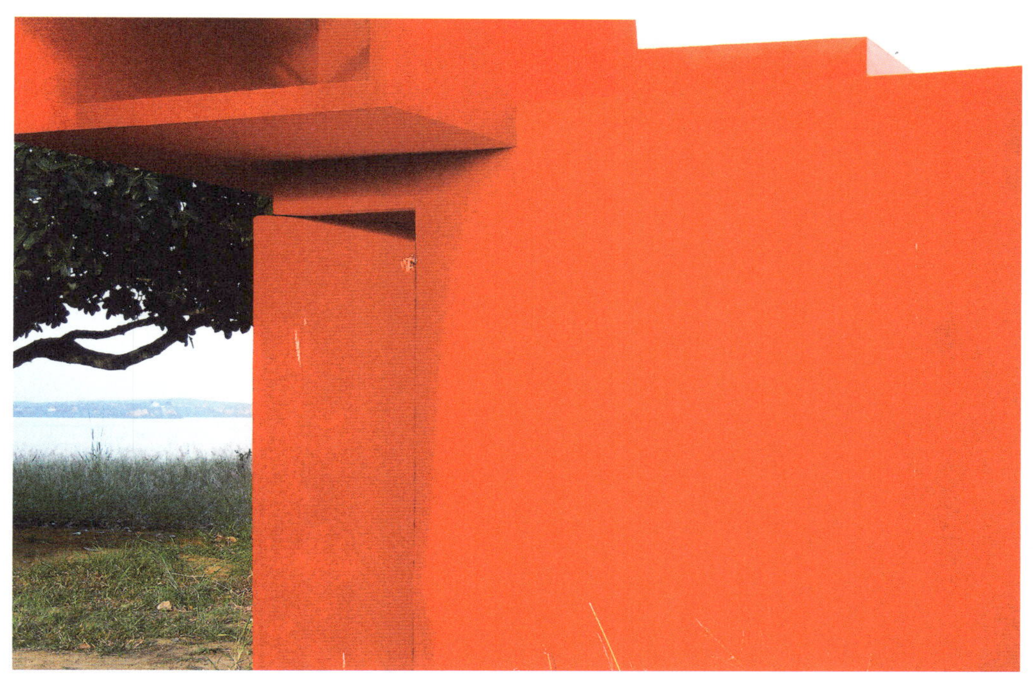

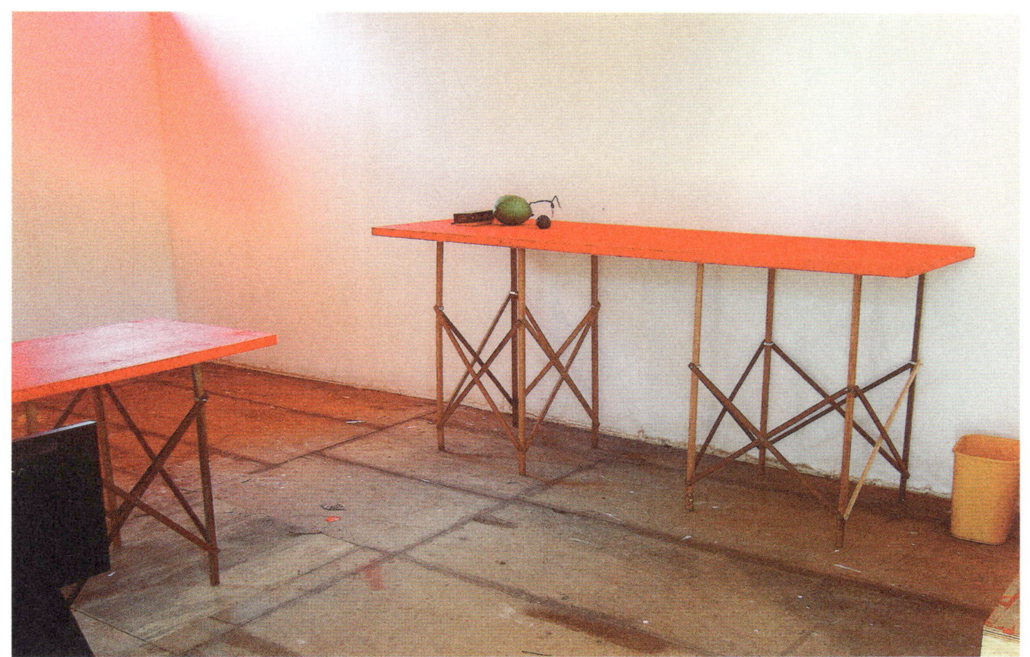

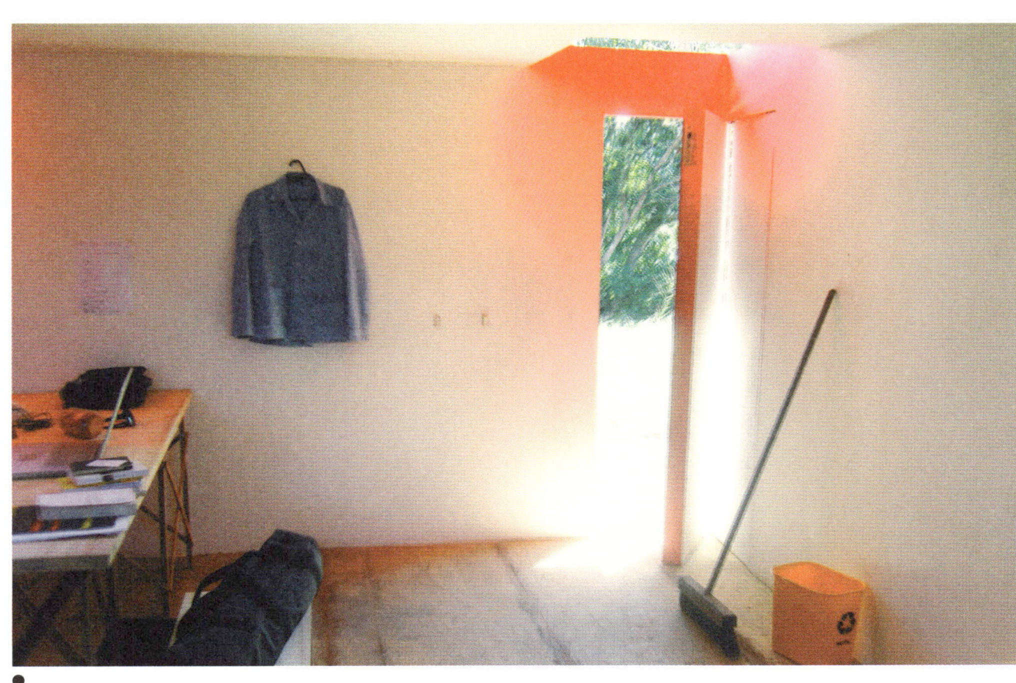

jean-pascal flavien
jpflavien@gmail.com

Devonian Press

Rio de Janeiro

Sítio Bela Vista, Rua Itapajé 20, Maricá Km 22, RJ 24900-000

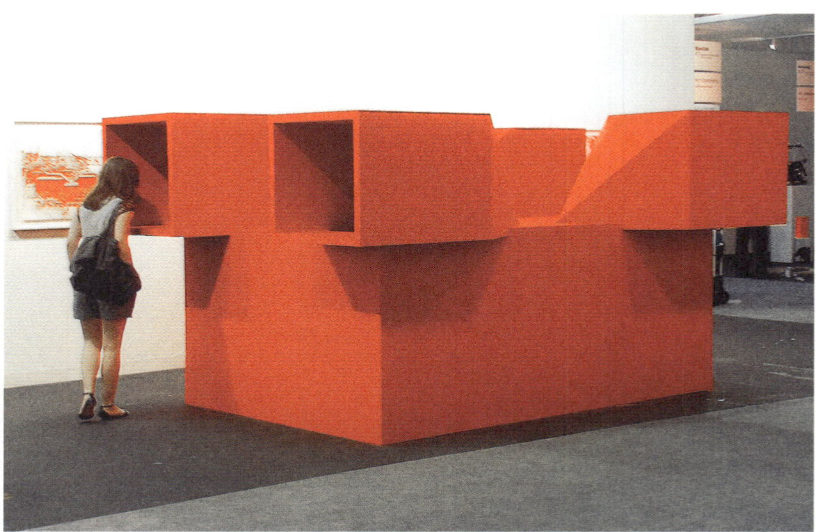

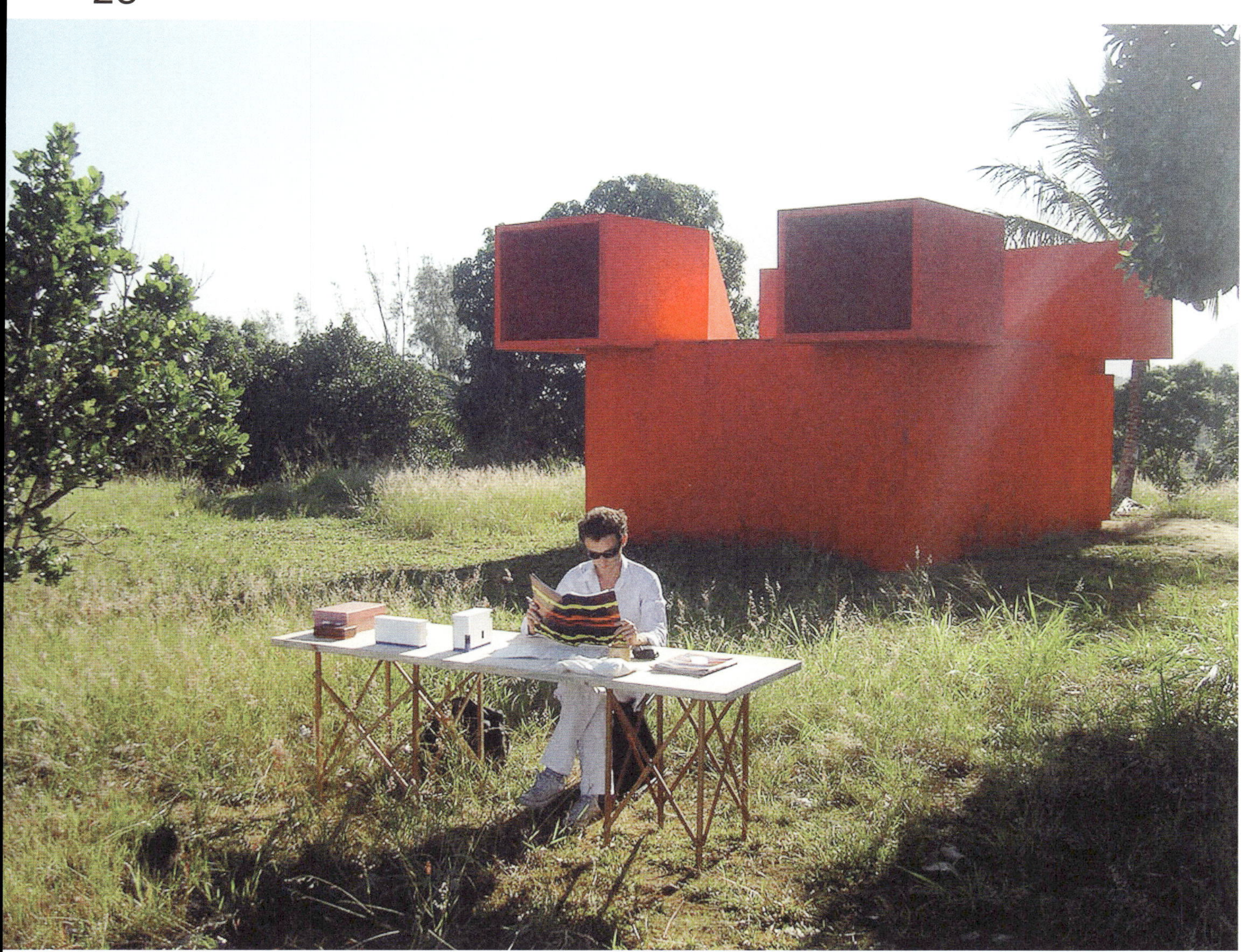

●	Devonian Press business card, inkjet print, 5,5 × 8,8 cm, 2007
●●	*viewer* (small), Art Basel Statements, wood, fan, heater,
	5.1 surround sound system, 180 × 270 × 420 cm, 2008

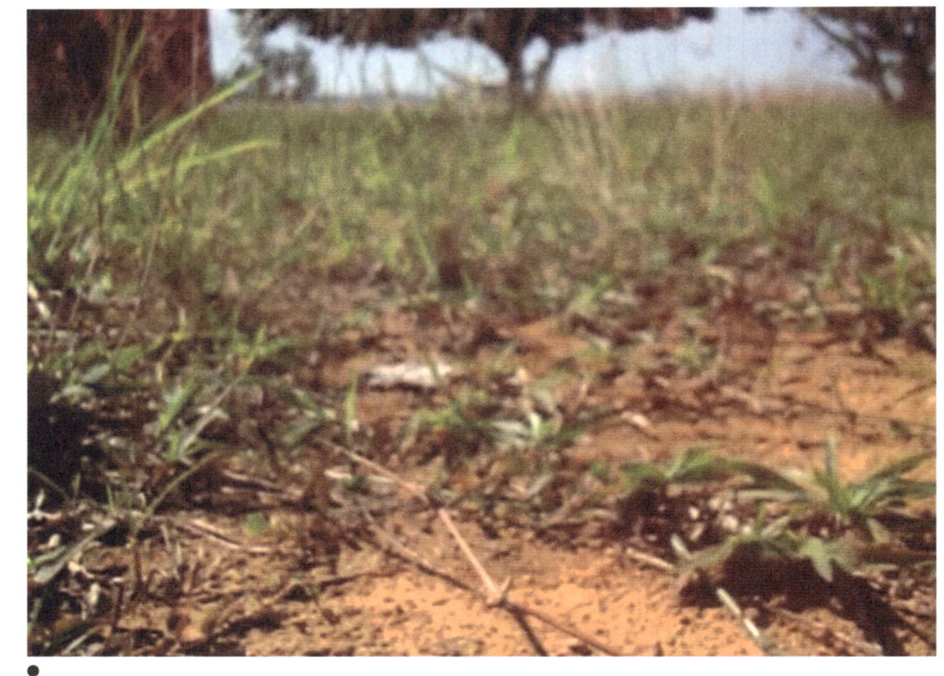

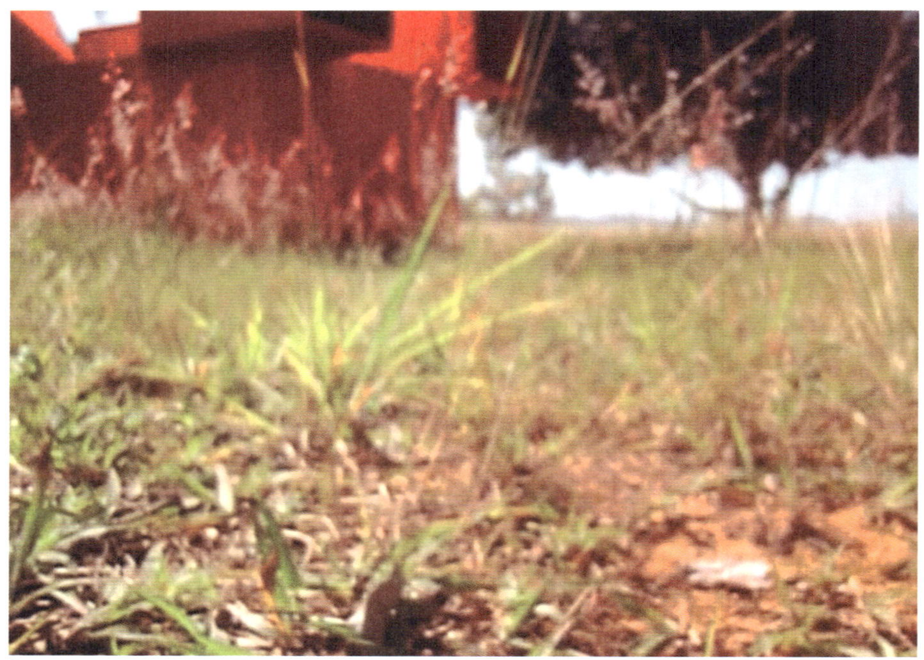

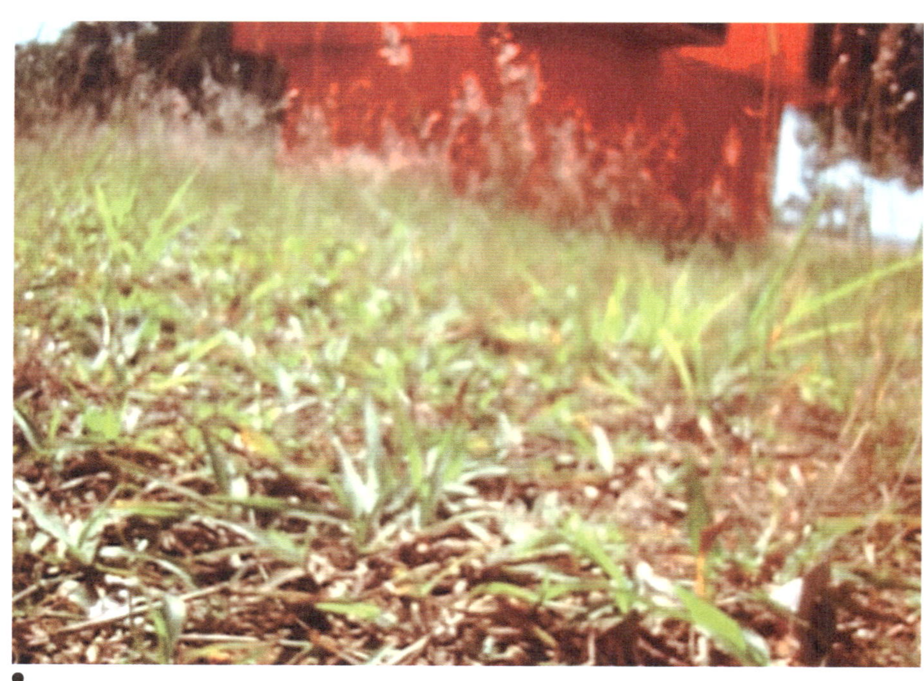

sci-fi film

2007
Video, 7:45 min.

The *sci-fi film* was shot around the *viewer* in Maricá, outside of Rio de Janeiro. It is a science fiction film that has no visible human elements or factors, other than the *viewer* itself. Its time period could be that of a very remote past, or a distant future. Some sequences are filmed as if the *viewer* were seen from a distance, but without being recognized, as if it were seen by an animal preoccupied only with its search for food. This animal could be a dinosaur or an evolution of an electronic species in a far-off future. Shot with a small photo camera, the red color of the building saturates the images. The red of the house intensifies the light and color adjustments of the camera. The recorded sound accentuates these effects, creating saturations, revealing the frame. The film is played in a loop. Each repetition is punctuated by red-tinted electronic noise, rather than the conventional black screen. The film is projected onto a wall, the room is not quite dark. Its sound is asymmetrical, as both speakers are located on the right side of the projection.

Le *sci-fi film* fut tourné avec le *viewer* à Maricá, près de Rio de Janeiro. C'est un film de science-fiction n'ayant pas d'éléments ou de facteurs humains visibles pendant son déroulement autre que le *viewer* lui-même. Son époque pourrait être un passé très reculé ou un futur très distant. Certaines séquences ont été filmées comme si le *viewer* était perçu par un animal occupé seulement par la recherche de sa nourriture. Cet animal pourrait être un dinosaure ou une évolution d'une espèce électronique dans un lointain futur. Filmée avec un petit appareil photo, la couleur rouge du bâtiment sature l'image. Le rouge de la maison exacerbe les ajustements lumineux et couleurs de la camera. La bande-son accentue ces effets, créant des saturations, révélant le cadre. Le film est monté en boucle. Chaque répétition est ponctuée par un bruit électronique rouge, au lieu du fond noir conventionnel. Le film est projeté sur un mur, la salle n'est pas plongée dans l'obscurité. Le son est asymétrique, les deux haut-parleurs étant placés à droite de la surface de projection.

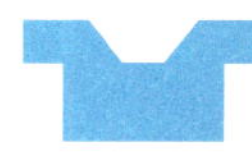

● Video stills of *sci-fi film*, 2007

Vanessa
Desclaux

construire...

building...

Building, Composing, Displacing, Arranging,
Constructing, Playing:
Jean-Pascal Flavien's Grammar of Things

"No nook or cranny, no activity, landscape, or thought
stands outside the pale of poetic subject matter."[1]

I stress the power of abstraction that is characteristic of
Jean-Pascal Flavien's compositions. The power of abstraction
of the house, the book, the chair, the bed, the ladder, like
that of the dinosaur, the sun, or the cowboy. An abstractive
power that, as Roman Jakobson notes, is characteristic
of "human thought, underlying … both geometrical relations
and grammar" and "superimposes simple geometrical
and grammatical figures upon the pictorial world of particular objects and upon the concrete lexical 'wherewithal' of
verbal art."[2] The power of abstraction of architecture when
we consider it, on the one hand, as a composition of fun-
damentally geometrical figures, and if we recognize, on the
other, the essentially linguistic dimension of relationships
between form and function at the heart of architectural constructions.

Grammar appears as a set of rules, conventions, and
norms that regulate language within the context of a clearly
identified objective: that of communication. Architecture,
like language, organizes itself around rules, conventions, or
norms that, within a specific cultural context, determine
what that entity is that we call "a house." Let us now think of
the possibilities of challenging and questioning these rules,
conventions, and norms. With respect to language, revolt
against grammatical composition has opened up—and con-
tinues to open up—a path towards poetic forms. And if
other rules arise there, naming new stylistic devices, metrical conventions and other *enjambements*, it is always this
same instinct for revolt which confounds compositions once
more, and produces a wave of combinations wherein the
mutual relationships between letters, words, punctuation,
spacing and signification start once again to call into question all conventions.

"Beginning again and again is a natural thing even when
there is a series. Beginning again and again and
again explaining composition and time is a natural thing."[3]
In my eyes, Jean-Pascal Flavien's work, which is entirely
architectural and poetic, locates its revolt at a very precise

1 Roman Jakobson, *What is Poetry?*, in: *Language in Literature*,
ed. Krystyna Pomorska and Stephen Rudy (Boston: Harvard University Press, 1987), p. 368.
2 Roman Jakobson, *Poetry of Grammar and Grammar of Poetry*,
op. cit., p. 133.
3 Gertrude Stein, *Composition as explanation*, in: *The Hogarth essays*
(London: L. and V. Woolf at the Hogarth Press, 1926), p. 12.

Construire, composer, déplacer,
agencer, jouer:
la grammaire des choses de
Jean-Pascal Flavien

«Il n'est pas de nature morte ou d'acte,
de paysage ou de pensée, qui soit à présent
hors du domaine de la poésie.»[1]

Je souligne la puissance d'abstraction propre aux
compositions de Jean-Pascal Flavien. Puissance d'abstraction de la maison, du livre, de la
chaise, du lit, de l'échelle, comme celle du
dinosaure, du soleil ou du cowboy. Puissance
d'abstraction, qui, comme le souligne Roman
Jakobson, est propre à «la pensée humaine, qui
est le fondement (…) tout à la fois de la géométrie et de la grammaire» et «surimpose des
figures géométriques ou grammaticales simples
au mot, qui se contente de ‹peindre› les objets particuliers (…)».[2] Puissance d'abstraction
de l'architecture lorsque nous la considérons,
d'une part, comme un agencement de figures
fondamentalement géométriques, et que
nous reconnaissons, d'autre part, la dimension
essentiellement linguistique des relations
entre forme et fonction au sein des constructions architecturales.

La grammaire apparaît comme un ensemble de règles, de conventions ou de normes
qui régissent le langage dans le contexte d'un
objectif clairement identifié, celui de la communication. L'architecture, comme le langage,
s'organise autour de règles, de conventions ou de
normes, qui, dans un contexte culturel particulier, déterminent ce qu'est l'entité «maison».
Pensons alors à la possibilité de révolte, de
remise en cause de ces règles, conventions et
normes. Dans le contexte du langage, la révolte
contre l'agencement grammatical a ouvert
– et continue d'ouvrir – la voie vers les formes
poétiques. Et si d'autres règles s'y inventent,
nommant des figures de style, des conventions
rythmiques et autres enjambements, c'est
toujours l'instinct de révolte qui déroute à nouveau les compositions, et laisse déferler des
combinaisons au sein desquelles les relations
mutuelles entre lettres, mots, ponctuation,
espace et signification recommencent encore
à déplacer les conventions.

«Recommencer et recommencer encore
est une chose naturelle même lorsqu'il y a
une série. Recommencer et recommencer
encore et encore d'expliquer la composition
et le temps est une chose naturelle.»[3]
L'œuvre de Jean-Pascal Flavien, toute entière
architecturale et poétique, situe à mes yeux sa
révolte en un lieu très précis. Ce lieu est l'espace à la fois immatériel, conceptuel, mental,

building…

1 Roman Jakobson, *Qu'est-ce que la poésie?*, in:
Huit questions de Poétique (Paris: Points Essais, Seuil,
1977), p. 32.
2 Roman Jakobson, *Poésie de la grammaire et grammaire
de la poésie*, op. cit., p. 102.
3 Gertrude Stein, *Composition et explication*, traduit
par Marc Eikhenbaum Voline, in: *Luna-Park 4: Cahiers
du GRIF* (Bruxelles: Transédition, 1978), p. 24.

point. That space is the simultaneously immaterial, conceptual, mental, but also effectively viable, physical, material site of this encounter between architecture and poetry.

Composition of the Poem,
Composition of the House

> "When I said.
> A rose is a rose is a rose is a rose.
> And then later made that into a ring I made poetry
> and what did I do I caressed completely caressed and
> addressed a noun."[4]

If I did not know the work of Jean-Pascal Flavien, if I had not experienced it by making the intellectual effort of engaging with his way of working as well as by making the incarnate investment of visiting, working, and sleeping in one of his houses, I would have considered the space produced by the mutual relationship between architecture and poetry to be unimaginable. For we are not talking here about the metaphorically poetic dimension of architecture, but rather of the superimposition of their forms, the sliding of the one into the other until one is unable to distinguish between them and say that this object, this act, or this statement belongs either to architecture or to poetry. It is the totality of the system of materials and references that Flavien sets up in his work that simultaneously belong to these two fields of artistic practice. Architecture, beyond its social and esthetic conventions, has a link to the real; it reminds us of an essential human fact, i.e. that of inhabiting. This simple fact will infinitely nourish Flavien's artistic practice and deploy an extremely complex palette of relationships between people, between objects, and between people and objects, allowing the artist to add in gestures, actions, and texts. Therein lies the intervention of the grammar that the artist has acquired for himself—revealing all of his literary and artistic affinities: a grammar of things, of situations and words that continually proposes new ways of composing things. Unsettling combinations therein affirm their desire to disrupt our ways of thinking.

    For each new house, Flavien produces a series of business cards where he designates himself as an "architect." In one of the notes that he sent me after my stay in the *breathing house*, Flavien describes himself as a "grammarian of things." Flavien conceives of his houses less as constructions than as compositions. In the gap that I perceive

mais également effectivement constructible, physique, matériel, de cette rencontre entre architecture et poésie.

Composition du poème,
composition de la maison

> «Quand j'ai dit.
> Une rose est une rose est une rose est
> une rose.
> Et j'en ai ensuite fait une bague j'ai fait
> de la poésie et qu'ai-je fait j'ai caressé complètement caressé et adressé un nom.»[4]

Si je ne connaissais pas l'œuvre de Jean-Pascal Flavien, si je n'en avais pas fait l'expérience fondée à la fois sur l'effort intellectuel d'engagement avec sa démarche artistique et sur l'investissement incarné de visiter, travailler et dormir dans une de ses maisons, je considérerais cet espace produit par la relation mutuelle entre architecture et poésie comme inimaginable. Car nous ne parlons pas ici de la dimension métaphoriquement poétique de l'architecture, mais bien de la superposition de leurs formes et le glissement de l'une dans l'autre jusqu'à être absolument incapables de les distinguer, et de dire que tel objet, tel acte ou tel énoncé appartiendrait soit à l'architecture, soit à la poésie. C'est la totalité du système matériel et du système de références que Flavien met en place dans l'ensemble de son œuvre qui appartiennent simultanément à ces deux champs de la pratique artistique. L'architecture, au-delà de ses conventions sociales et esthétiques, entretient un lien avec le réel; elle nous rappelle un fait humain essentiel qui est celui d'habiter. Ce simple fait va infiniment nourrir la démarche artistique de Flavien et déployer une palette extrêmement complexe de relations entre des personnes, entre des objets, et entre des personnes et des objets, permettant à l'artiste d'y associer des gestes, des actes et des textes. C'est l'intervention de la grammaire dont l'artiste se dote – révélant toutes ses affinités littéraires et artistiques; une grammaire des choses, des situations et des mots qui propose sans cesse de nouveaux agencements. Des combinaisons déroutantes y affirment leur désir de bousculer nos modes de pensée.

    À l'occasion de chaque nouvelle maison, Flavien réalise une série de cartes de visites sur lesquelles il se donne le rôle d'«architecte». Dans une des notes qu'il m'envoya suite à mon séjour dans la *breathing house*, Flavien se désigne comme «grammairien des choses». Flavien envisage ses maisons moins comme des constructions que comme des compositions. Dans l'écart que je perçois entre construction et composition, il y a tout l'espace du jeu, essentiel au processus de travail de Flavien.

4 Gertrude Stein, *Poetry and Grammar*, in: *Lectures in America* (Boston: Beacon Press, 1985), p. 231, traduit par Julien Bismuth.

4 Gertrude Stein, *Poetry and Grammar*, in: *Lectures in America* (Boston: Beacon Press, 1985), p. 231.

between construction and composition lies a space of play, which is essential to Flavien's work process.

"...composition is not simply an act through which a writer presents a completed conception but a process that displays the growth of the form that the work renders— a process in which statement and observation occur simultaneously."[5]

Gertrude Stein stands as a literary figure whose textual corpus does not fail to produce startling resonances with Flavien's artistic propositions. After all, Stein never ceased to produce very intense relationships between the materiality of her poetic writing and her personal experience of the real world. Stein's writing demonstrates that literature does not constitute an extra-linguistic situation in which language only plays the role of a communication tool; on the contrary, it demonstrates that it is also the process of its own materialization and construction. Bruce Elder notes that in Stein's work "The material system, by way of contrast, presents each iteration as a new item, unconnected to any paradigm. Within the material system, all likeness, whether between the terms in a syntagma or between word and referent, is an illusion constructed on a plane of difference."[6] "Rose is a rose is a rose is a rose,"[7] a poem to which Stein will also give a circular form, demonstrates how, within the apparent repetition of this word, difference spreads within the poem, juxtaposition after juxtaposition. On that subject, Stan Brakhage notes that "...words are no more serving the collective rhetoric or thoughts of the author than they are, each, characterizing each-and-every word's evolution in the course of the poem."[8] And the intervals between words do not serve as markers of a linguistic convention, but incarnate the potential for new configurations, for Stein's language is also made to be read out loud, offering the reader's voice a new freedom of movement, which is to say new directions and new means of producing sense in relation to the sounds of words.

"Very small means smaller very much smaller and very much smaller not as to size but as to intervals.
Intervals can be used to describe space also can be used to describe annoyance and also be used to describe directions. All in all."[9]

5   Bruce Elder, *The Films of Stan Brakhage in the American Tradition of Ezra Pound, Gertrude Stein, and Charles Olson* (Waterloo, Ontario: Wilfrid Laurier University Press, 1998), p. 222.
6   Idem, p. 223.
7   Gertrude Stein, *Sacred Emily* (1913), in: *Geography and Plays* (Madison: University of Wisconsin Press, 1922), p. 187.
8   Stan Brakhage, *Gertrude Stein: Meditative Literature and Film* (Boulder, Colorado: The Graduate School, University of Colorado, 1990), p. 4.
9   Gertrude Stein, *A Novel of Thank You* (London: Dalkey Archive Press, 2004), p. 56.

« (...) composition n'est pas simplement un acte à travers lequel l'écrivain présente une conception complète mais plutôt un processus qui donne à voir le développement de la forme que l'œuvre déploie – un processus dans lequel énoncé et observation se font simultanément. »[5]

Gertrude Stein représente une figure littéraire dont le corpus textuel ne cesse de produire des résonances étonnantes avec les propositions artistiques de Flavien. Car Stein ne cessera jamais de produire des relations d'une grande intensité entre la matérialité de son écriture poétique et son expérience personnelle du monde réel. L'écriture de Stein permet de montrer que la littérature ne se constitue plus comme une situation extralinguistique dans laquelle le langage joue seulement le rôle d'un outil de communication; elle démontre au contraire qu'elle est aussi le processus de sa propre matérialisation et de sa construction. Bruce Elder souligne que dans l'œuvre de Stein, «le système matériel, par le biais du contraste, présente chaque itération comme un nouvel élément, déconnecté de tout paradigme. Avec ce système matériel, toute ressemblance, qu'elle soit entre les termes d'un syntagme ou entre le mot et son référent, est une illusion construite sur le plan de la différence».[6] «Rose is a rose is a rose is a rose»[7], poème auquel Stein donnera aussi une forme circulaire, démontre comment, au sein de l'apparente répétition de ce nom, la différence se répand dans le poème, juxtaposition après juxtaposition. À ce propos, Stan Brakhage note que «les mots ne servent pas plus la rhétorique collective ou la pensée de l'auteur, qu'ils ne caractérisent chacun l'évolution de chaque mot dans le flot du poème».[8] Et les intervalles entre les mots ne sont plus seulement les marqueurs d'une convention linguistique mais incarnent le potentiel de nouveaux arrangements, car le langage de Stein est aussi fait pour être lu à voix haute, offrant à la voix du lecteur une nouvelle liberté de déplacement, c'est-à-dire de nouvelles directions, et de production du sens au gré des sonorités des mots.

«Très petit veut dire encore plus petit et encore plus petit non pas en terme de taille mais d'intervalles. Les intervalles peuvent être utilisés pour décrire l'espace mais peuvent aussi être utilisés pour décrire l'agencement et peuvent aussi être utilisés pour décrire des directions. En tout et pour tout. »[9]

building...

5   Bruce Elder, *The Films of Stan Brakhage in the American Tradition of Ezra Pound, Gertrude Stein, and Charles Olson* (Waterloo, Ontario: Wilfrid Laurier University Press, 1998), p. 222, traduit par l'auteur.
6   Idem, p. 223.
7   Gertrude Stein, *Sacred Emily* (1913), in: *Geography and Plays* (Madison: University of Wisconsin Press, 1922), p. 187.
8   Stan Brakhage, *Gertrude Stein: Meditative Literature and Film* (Boulder, Colorado: The Graduate School, University of Colorado, 1990), p. 4, traduit par l'auteur.
9   Gertrude Stein, *A Novel of Thank You* (London: Dalkey Archive Press, 2004) p. 56, traduit par Julien Bismuth.

The interval is the central element of *no drama house*. The *no drama house* is a narrow house, a house with problems, problems which are in fact simply new situations, states of affairs that have to be negotiated. It has two stories but a staircase does not link them, you need a ladder to go from one to the other from outside. The narrow space—narrower than usual, that is narrower than what is usually required by the conventions of a house—produces marginal intervals between objects, between the pieces of furniture. Life in this house consists in continually re-arranging these minuscule intervals, but in this configuration, the juxtaposition of the three stools—which seems confused if one considers it strictly from a functionalist point of view—can thus be read as the three points of an ellipsis...

> "four stools, three chairs, two tables, the day bed with the blanket, then Vanessa sits on one of the chairs. Vanessa gets up, takes a chair, goes to a corner. Flavien steps over the four stools, one after the other, as in a game of solitaire. Flavien sits on each of the stools, on the chairs, and on the bed respectively. Flavien unfolds the blanket, spreads it on the bed, folds it back up, and lays it back down on a corner of the bed."[10]

The compositions of Flavien's houses are not fixed; they are unstable, wobbly even. The exterior world is itself not fixed, but in movement, so why set down the arrangement of a house? Daily life can be represented as a juxtaposed sequence of events: waking, showering, eating, working, eating, working, walking, reading, eating, sleeping ... Once again, relatively strict norms seem to determine this organization of our time, and in turn impact how spaces are organized. Flavien simultaneously unsettles both the normative approaches of grammar and architecture, undoing the logic of sequences of actions, introducing absurdity, illogic, and irrationality in our use of space. He problematizes hierarchies, habits, and rhythms, inasmuch as the latter petrify situations and exclude other ways of seeing, saying, or doing, defying the logic of continuity and discontinuity for that of juxtaposition, parataxis, and the contiguity of spaces, words, and moments.

L'intervalle est un élément central dans la *no drama house*. La *no drama house* est une maison étroite, une maison à problèmes, des problèmes qui ne sont en fait que des nouvelles situations comme autant d'états de choses à négocier: elle a deux étages mais aucun escalier ne les relie, il faut donc une échelle pour circuler de l'un à l'autre en passant par l'extérieur. L'espace étroit – plus étroit qu'à l'habitude, c'est à dire plus étroit que le veulent les conventions d'une maison – produit des intervalles marginaux entre les objets, entre les meubles. La vie dans la maison consistera à sans cesse agencer de nouveau ces intervalles minuscules, mais dans cette configuration, la juxtaposition de trois tabourets – confuse si on la considère uniquement du point de vue fonctionnel – peut être lue alors comme trois points de suspension...

> «quatre tabourets, trois chaises, deux tables, le lit de jour avec la couverture, puis Vanessa s'assoit sur une des chaises, Vanessa se lève, prend une chaise, va dans un coin. Flavien enjambe l'un après l'autre les quatre tabourets à la façon d'un jeu de solitaire. Flavien s'assoit respectivement sur chacun des tabourets, chaises, lit. Flavien déplie la couverture, l'étale sur le lit, la replie, et la recouche sur un coin du lit.»[10]

Les compositions des maisons de Flavien ne sont pas fixes, mais instables, voire bancales. Le monde extérieur n'est lui-même pas fixe, mais en mouvement, alors pourquoi rendre l'arrangement d'une maison fixe? La vie quotidienne peut être représentée comme une séquence d'activités qui se juxtaposent: se lever, se doucher, manger, travailler, manger, travailler, marcher, lire, manger, dormir... Ce sont une nouvelle fois des normes relativement strictes qui semblent régir cette organisation du temps, qui se répercute aussi sur notre organisation des espaces. Flavien met parallèlement en déroute les approches normatives de l'architecture et de la grammaire, défaisant la logique des séquences d'actions, introduisant de l'absurde, de l'illogique et de l'irrationnel dans l'utilisation de l'espace. Il met à mal les hiérarchies, les habitudes et les rythmes en tant que ces derniers figent des situations et excluent d'autres manières de voir, de faire ou de dire, défiant la dialectique continuité / discontinuité au profit de la juxtaposition, de la parataxe et de la contiguïté des espaces, des mots et des moments.

10 Extrait du scenario conçu par l'artiste à l'occasion de la présentation de *PLAy* à Heddah, Maastricht, mai 2011.

10 Excerpt from the scenario written by the artist for the performance of *PLAy* at Heddah, Maastricht, May 2011.

A Contiguous Flow of Moments

"In a habit and never he had had it here.
Lead it right.
Follow the house.
And save it.
In to use as in a habit and never to decide it after all.
Settled and unsettled."[11]

Time is of crucial importance to Flavien's work. "It is understood by this time that everything is the same except composition and time, composition and the time of composition and the time in the composition." explains Stein in the essay that she published on her approach to composition.[12] What is identical? In Stein's texts, words are identical, the words that language makes available to us. In Flavien's works, the entities which he names "house," "chair," "table," etc. are identical. But what cannot be identical, as Stein points out, is composition, i.e. what Flavien calls his arrangements or configurations, or the mutual relationships between elements, but also time. Why time? The time to do things, the time to rearrange them, the time to take control of the intervals and change direction—we change direction and sense changes of direction as well. A simple gesture— like a simple word, or a phrase fragment that articulates an action in Stein's text—can be repeated and inverted: to do, to redo, to start anew, to do differently, to do once more a few minutes or a few hours later. The point is to become aware of gestures, words, and the relationships between things. Consciousness is a flow of moments, and, by means of her writing, Stein seems to make us share this process of consciousness which continually takes hold of a moment that has just passed so as to bring it back to the present by way of the repetition or juxtaposition of a new moment, a new situation. The syntax or articulation of a text is thus fractured in its linear unfolding so as to liberate us from a sense-driven logic that continually projects us forward without giving us time to grasp the preceding moment, and to extend it into the present moment, or into the future.

"The composition is the thing seen by every one living in the living they are doing, they are the composing of the composition that at the time they are living is the composition of the time in which they are living."[13]

In 2012, Flavien activated the *breathing house*, a house that was built in Pougues-les-Eaux in the Parc Saint Léger, where the eponymous exhibition space can be found. As its

11 Gertrude Stein, *A Novel of Thank You*, op. cit., p. 86.
12 Gertrude Stein, *Composition as Explanation*, in: *The Hogarth essays*, op. cit., p. 12.
13 Idem, p. 13.

«Dans une habitude et jamais il l'avait eu ici.
Bien le mener.
Suivre la maison.
Et la sauver.
Dedans pour utiliser comme dans une habitude et jamais pour le décider après tout.
Réglé et déréglé.»[11]

Le temps a une importance cruciale dans l'œuvre de Flavien. «On comprend à ce moment là que tout est la même chose exceptés composition et temps, composition et le temps de la composition et le temps dans la composition.»[12], explique Stein dans l'essai qu'elle publia en référence à son approche de l'écriture. Qu'est-ce qui est identique? Dans les textes de Stein, ce sont les mots, les mots que le langage met à notre disposition. Dans les œuvres de Flavien, ce sont les entités qu'il nomme «maison», «chaise», «table», etc. Mais ce qui ne peut être identique, comme le souligne Stein, c'est la composition, c'est-à-dire ce que Flavien nomme ses arrangements, ou agencements, ce sont les relations mutuelles entre les termes, et c'est aussi le temps. Pourquoi le temps? Le temps de faire les choses, le temps de les réarranger, le temps d'investir les intervalles et de changer de direction – nous changeons de direction et le sens change de direction aussi. Un simple geste – comme un simple mot, ou un fragment de phrase énonçant une action chez Stein – peut être répété, fait dans le sens inverse; faire, défaire, recommencer, faire autrement, faire à nouveau quelques minutes ou quelques heures plus tard. Il s'agit de prendre conscience des gestes, des mots, des relations entre les choses. La conscience est un flot de moments et par son écriture, Stein semble nous faire partager ce processus de conscience qui se saisit sans cesse du moment qui vient de s'écouler et le ramène dans le présent par la répétition et la juxtaposition d'un nouveau moment, d'une nouvelle situation. La syntaxe, l'articulation du texte, est alors fracturée dans son déroulement linéaire pour ne pas s'enfermer dans cette logique du sens qui nous projette toujours en avant sans nous donner le temps de nous saisir du moment précédent, de le prolonger dans le temps présent, futur.

«La composition est la chose vue par tout le monde en vie dans la vie qu'ils font, ils sont les composants de la composition ce qui au temps où ils vivent est la composition du temps dans lequel ils sont en train de vivre.»[13]

En 2012, Flavien met en œuvre la *breathing house*, une maison qui est construite à Pougues-les-Eaux dans le Parc Saint Léger où se trouve le centre d'art éponyme. La *breathing house*, comme l'indique le titre, est une «maison qui

11 Gertrude Stein, *A Novel of Thank You*, op. cit., p. 86.
12 Gertrude Stein, *Composition et explication*, op. cit., p. 24.
13 Idem.

building…

title indicates, the *breathing house* is a house that breathes. This notion of breathing is a metaphor for the relationship that the house, which is situated in the park, has with the art center. This relationship presupposes a division, a separation, an interval between the two spaces. It also links back to a temporal relationship that has formed between the two spaces: time spent in the one or the other, the time needed to pass between the one and the other, the time of the exhibition and the time of the house (the exhibition ending in September 2012, while the house will continue to occupy its present location in the park for an as yet undetermined length of time). The house is a work, constitutes itself as a work by means of the complexity of its internal organization (its structure with its moveable walls, its furniture, its openings), as well as how the gestures, actions, events, and conversations that are set to take place in the house unfold within it. This fact, the fact that the house is a work, immediately places it in a paradoxical position in relation to the exhibition; that is to say, if the house which is physically outside of the exhibition can be said to be part of the exhibition. In the end, there no longer is a clear separation between these two distinct entities, i.e. "the exhibition" and "the house." Flavien also says: "the exhibition is the extension of the house." Instead, one can distinguish a series of moments that continually displace and reposition the house in relation to the exhibition. The artist, or one of his guests, could have decided that "sleeping" or "dreaming" does not belong to the exhibition but rather to the house. The sequence of activities normally seen as belonging to the exhibition rather than to the house could be reversed or shuffled. The interval that separates the house from the exhibition is essential to the act of breathing, offering up the exterior space as a line of flight, a decompression chamber, a space that is outside the frame, outside the text.

Stein and Flavien show us that continuity is simply inconceivable. Logical articulation is an artifice. Things, situations, and moments exist alongside one another. They are contiguous and not continuous or discontinuous. This contiguity can be imagined in many different ways, such as the circular form of Stein's "Rose is a rose is a rose is a rose."[14] or that of the line which Flavien often employs, as can be seen in a photograph of a line of pieces of furniture: "a cube, a day-bed, a chair, a ladder, a house." The list is also an exemplary form of a paratactic construction.

> "… if lists were inevitable if series were inevitable and the whole of it was inevitable beginning again and again could not trouble me …"[15]

respire». Cette notion de respiration est la métaphore de la relation entre la maison, située dans le parc, et l'espace d'exposition du centre d'art adjacent. Cette relation suppose une division, une séparation, un intervalle entre les deux espaces. Elle renvoie également à une relation au temps qui se déploie entre ces deux espaces, le temps passé dans l'un ou dans l'autre, le temps de circuler de l'un à l'autre, le temps de l'exposition, et le temps de la maison, l'exposition se terminant en septembre 2012 alors que la maison continuera d'occuper cet endroit du parc pour une durée encore indeterminée. La maison est une œuvre, elle fait œuvre dans toute la complexité de son organisation matérielle interne (sa structure dont les murs sont déplaçables, ses meubles, ses ouvertures) et dans le déploiement des gestes, des actions, des événements et des conversations dont la maison aura été le lieu pendant tout le temps de son existence. Ce fait là, que la maison soit une œuvre, la positionne d'emblée dans une relation paradoxale avec l'exposition. Si la maison qui est physiquement hors de l'espace d'exposition fait cependant partie intégrante de l'exposition, il n'y a finalement plus de séparation clairement établie entre deux entités distinctes «exposition» et «maison». Flavien dit aussi: «l'exposition est l'extension de la maison». On distinguera plutôt une série de moments qui sans cesse déplacent et repositionnent la maison par rapport à l'exposition. L'artiste, ou l'un de ses invités, aura pu décider que «dormir» ou «rêver» est un moment faisant partie de l'exposition, et non de la maison. La séquence des activités normalement considérée comme appartenant au domaine de l'exposition plutôt qu'à celui de la maison, pourra être inversée, réarrangée. L'intervalle qui sépare la maison de l'exposition est un espace essentiel à la respiration, offrant l'espace extérieur comme ligne de fuite, sas de décompression, espace hors-champ ou hors-texte.

Stein et Flavien nous révèlent que la continuité n'est simplement pas concevable. L'articulation logique est artificielle; les choses, les situations et les moments existent les uns à coté des autres; ils sont contigus, et pas continus, ou discontinus. Cette contiguïté peut s'imaginer sous des formes bien différentes, celle, circulaire, de «Rose is a rose is a rose is a rose»[14] de Stein, celle de la ligne, à laquelle Flavien a souvent fait appel comme le montre la photographie d'une ligne de meubles: «un cube, un lit de jour, une chaise, une échelle, une maison». La liste est aussi une forme exemplaire de construction parataxique

> «(…) si les listes étaient inévitables si les séries étaient inévitables et le tout était inévitable recommencer et recommencer encore ne pouvait pas me troubler (…)»[15]

14 Gertrude Stein, *Sacred Emily*, op. cit.
15 Gertrude Stein, *Composition et explication*, op. cit., p. 27.

---

14 Gertrude Stein, *Sacred Emily*, op. cit., p. 21–22.
15 Gertrude Stein, *Composition as Explanation*, op. cit., p. 27.

In 1923, Stein writes *List*, a play that seems to be nothing more than a list of the characters of the play itself. *PLAy* is an event imagined by Flavien as an extension of the *no drama house* and which consists in the activation of possible configurations of the material and immaterial elements of the house. In *PLAy*, a series of texts like lists are read out loud by the artist at different moments in the performance. Every iteration is titled *PLAy*, followed by the word "after" and the name of an author set as a point of reference. The words, which constitute each fragment of the cited text by said author, are placed in a column to constitute a sort of dialogue in which the words are reorganized so as to become characters. The text is placed as the exact mirror of the activity of the house. The house decomposes phrases and paragraphs so as to allow the words themselves to articulate new situations, and produce other moments.

En 1923, Stein écrit *List*, une pièce de théâtre qui semble n'être qu'une liste des personnages de la pièce elle-même. *PLAy* est un événement imaginé par Flavien comme une extension de la *no drama house* et consiste en une activation des agencements possibles des éléments matériels et immatériels de la maison. Dans *PLAy*, une série de textes sous la forme de listes sont lus à haute voix par l'artiste à différents moments de la performance. Chaque itération s'intitule *PLAy* suivi du terme anglais «after» (d'après) et du nom d'un auteur posé comme point de référence. Les mots, qui constituent chaque fragment de texte de l'auteur cité, sont placés en colonne pour donner forme à une sorte de dialogue dans lequel les mots sont réorganisés pour devenir des personnages. Le texte est placé en exact miroir de l'activité de la maison ; la maison décompose les phrases et les paragraphes afin que les mots énoncent eux-mêmes de nouvelles situations, produisent à leur tour d'autres moments.

building...

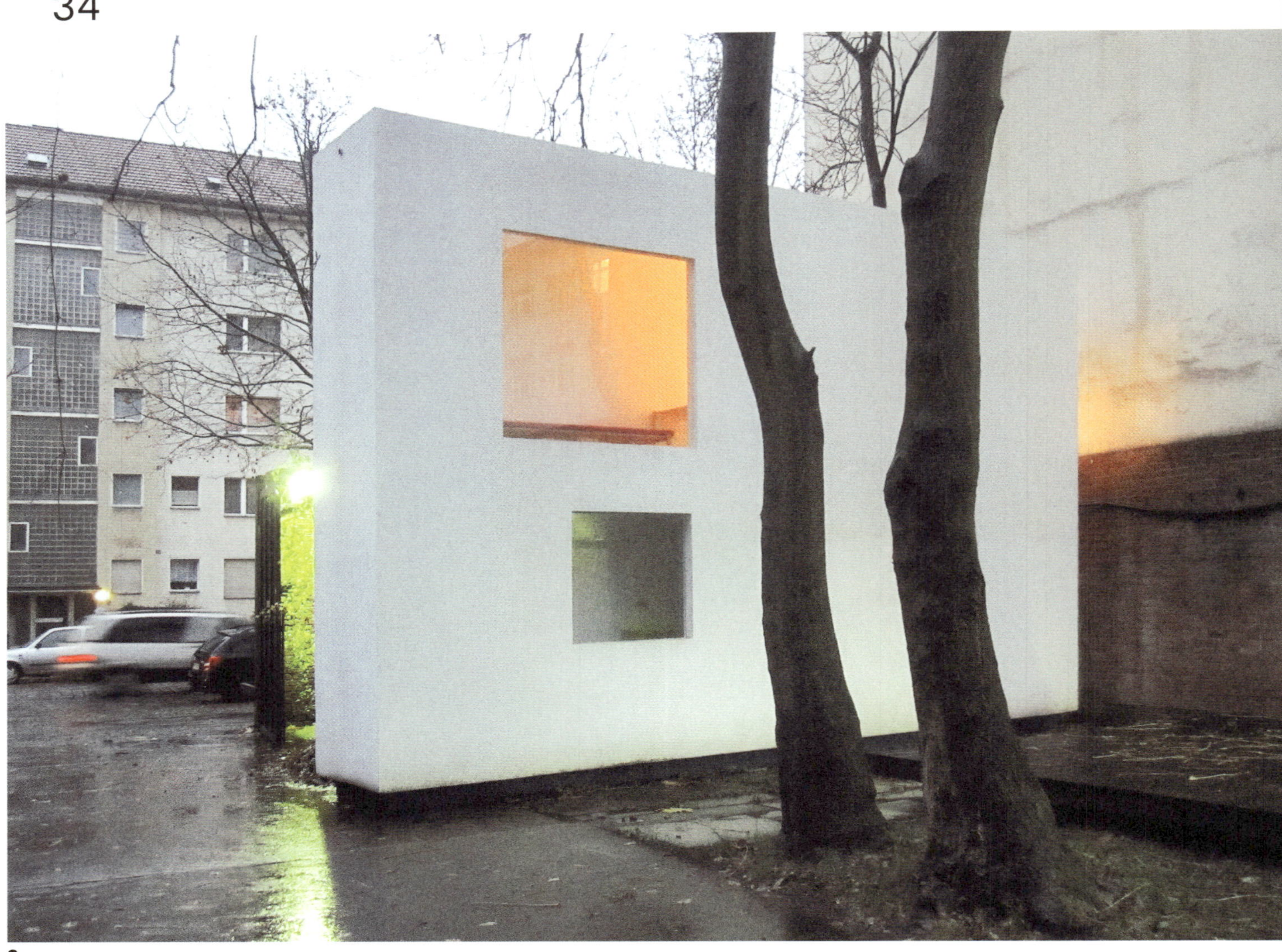

jean-pascal
flavien jean-pascal
flavien
no drama
no drama
architect
architect
jpflavien@gmail.com   49 (0) 176 24 38 10 17

no drama house

2009–2012
Kurfürstenstraße 12, Berlin

The *no drama house* was built in Berlin in the garden of the Galerie Giti Nourbakhsch. I designed and fabricated furniture specifically for this house. Two Devonian Press publications were produced for this project. A performative event, titled *PLAy*, was held at the house and then restaged at the Jan van Eyck Academie in 2011. A series of seventy microfilms was also made to document activities and gestures performed in and around the house. These films were shown first on the walls of the house, then at the South London Gallery as part of an event titled *Cinonema* in 2012. Arrangements of the furniture in various sequences were exhibited at the Kunstverein Langenhagen the same year.

I made a house with problems, not because I was attracted to problems, but because I was doubtful of their nature within the bothersome context of a spatial design whose function is defined as the resolution of these problems. To resolve nothing. To not find solutions and leave things in an open state, and then multiply. And then to let many problems, a suite of problems, problems of space, time, and means design a house and circumscribe an activity. The *no drama house* has as its plan the addition of one problem onto another, or their alignment. It is one meter wide, the electrical layout is uneven, it is too close to the wall, it spills onto the path. The house becomes a game and the life that takes place within it is the articulation of these states of affairs. Then, with time, these problems no longer hold. They efface themselves to become what they were dissimulating: situations. These function in a sequence, they condition and describe an activity that always leads to another. There are no stairs so I bring a ladder. I lose the ladder so I work downstairs instead. What at first seems like a spatial constraint is in fact only the nature of another space that we have ceased to neglect. The rooms are too narrow, there is too much furniture upstairs, none of the pieces of furniture can be moved without moving another piece, they form a line of which I am a part. That line is a sequence or a phrase that articulates what I am doing.

I sit, I work, I sleep, I sit.
The house introduces several equations:
living = writing, living = playing.

La *no drama house* a été construite à Berlin dans le jardin de la galerie Giti Nourbakhsch. J'ai dessiné et fabriqué son mobilier spécifiquement pour son espace. Deux publications Devonian Press ont été produites pour ce projet. Un évènement performatif intitulé *PLAy* s'est tenu à la maison ainsi qu'à la Jan van Eyck Academie en 2011. Un ensemble de 70 microfilms (séquences vidéos très brèves) documente les gestes des activités dans et autour de la maison. Ces films furent projetés d'abord sur les murs de la maison puis à la South London Gallery, comme faisant partie d'un événement intitulé *Cinonema* en 2012. Divers arrangements de meubles mis en séquence furent présentés à la Kunstverein Langenhagen cette même année.

J'ai fait une maison avec des problèmes, non pas par disposition pour les problèmes, mais parce je doutais de leur nature dans le contexte contrariant d'un design d'espace dont la fonction se définit comme la résolution de ces problèmes. Ne rien résoudre. Ne pas trouver de solution et laisser un état des choses ouvert, puis multiplier. Alors, plusieurs problèmes, une suite de problèmes, des problèmes d'espace, de temps, et de moyens ont dessiné une maison et circonscrit une activité. La *no drama house* a pour plan l'ajout d'un problème sur un autre, ou leur alignement. Elle a un mètre de large, la distribution électrique est inégale, elle est trop proche du mur, elle déborde sur la voie d'accès. La maison devient un jeu et la vie qui y prend place est l'articulation de ces états de fait. Puis avec le temps, les problèmes ne tiennent plus, ils s'effacent pour être ce qu'ils ont dissimulé: des situations. Celles-ci fonctionnent en chaîne, elles conditionnent et décrivent une activité qui mène chaque fois à une autre. Il n'y a pas d'escalier, j'amène une échelle, je perds l'échelle, je travaille en bas… Ce qui à première vue paraît être une contrainte spatiale n'est en fait que la nature d'un autre espace que l'on aurait cessé de négliger. Les salles sont trop étroites, il y a trop de meubles à l'étage, aucun ne bouge sans décaler l'autre, ils forment une ligne dans laquelle je m'inscris, cette ligne est une séquence ou une phrase qui énonce ce que je fais.

Je m'assois, je travaille, je dors, je m'assois.
La maison introduit plusieurs équations:
vivre = écrire, vivre = jouer.

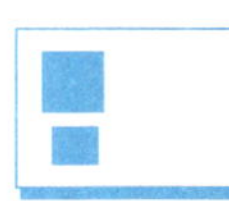

● *no drama house* on Kurfürstenstraße 20, Berlin, various materials, 5,5 × 7,75 × 1,2 m, 2009
●● *no drama architect* business card, inkjet print, 5,5 × 8,8 cm, 2009
●●● *no drama house* scenarios in *no drama house*, Devonian Press, 48 pages, 29,7 × 21,5 cm, 2005 (next spread)

Everything starts with a series of unsolvable problems. Too many things in the life of this house will happily get in the way.

a series of problems...

The bathroom, or what looks like a bathroom is partially open to the outside (missing one wall)

Some windows are too low

The entrance is located on the second floor, there are no stairs leading up to it, no access

There are too many places to shower at, and no proper bathrooms

Too many living rooms, not enough bedrooms

Beds or couches, pseudo-beds spread out everywhere. People end up sleeping anywhere, anytime...

Nothing looks like a kitchen, although all the appliances are there

Too many fire exits on the ground floor. People keep leaving the building.

A problem:

This new house, No Drama house, is very narrow. Almost too narrow to organize (arrange) your life comfortably. It is now a long corridor. It is also very high. A possibility for moving within the space is to walk sideways, like a crab.

Another problem:

The entrance door is on the second floor. And by mistake, or lack of attention, the opening for the staircase leading to the first floor happens to be located just behind the threshold of this entrance door. One must be careful not to fall. Maybe one could put a board to cover the staircase opening.

A problem again (narrowly):

A house with five corridors. The second floor consists of a series of parallel corridors. The name corridor is chosen for lack of better word for these are long rooms, running alongside next to each other, very narrow sometimes, all ending up in the same place (or not) unless they stop firmly in a sort of cul de sac. Each of them receives its content of natural light, sometimes even from the same source.

Another plan for living

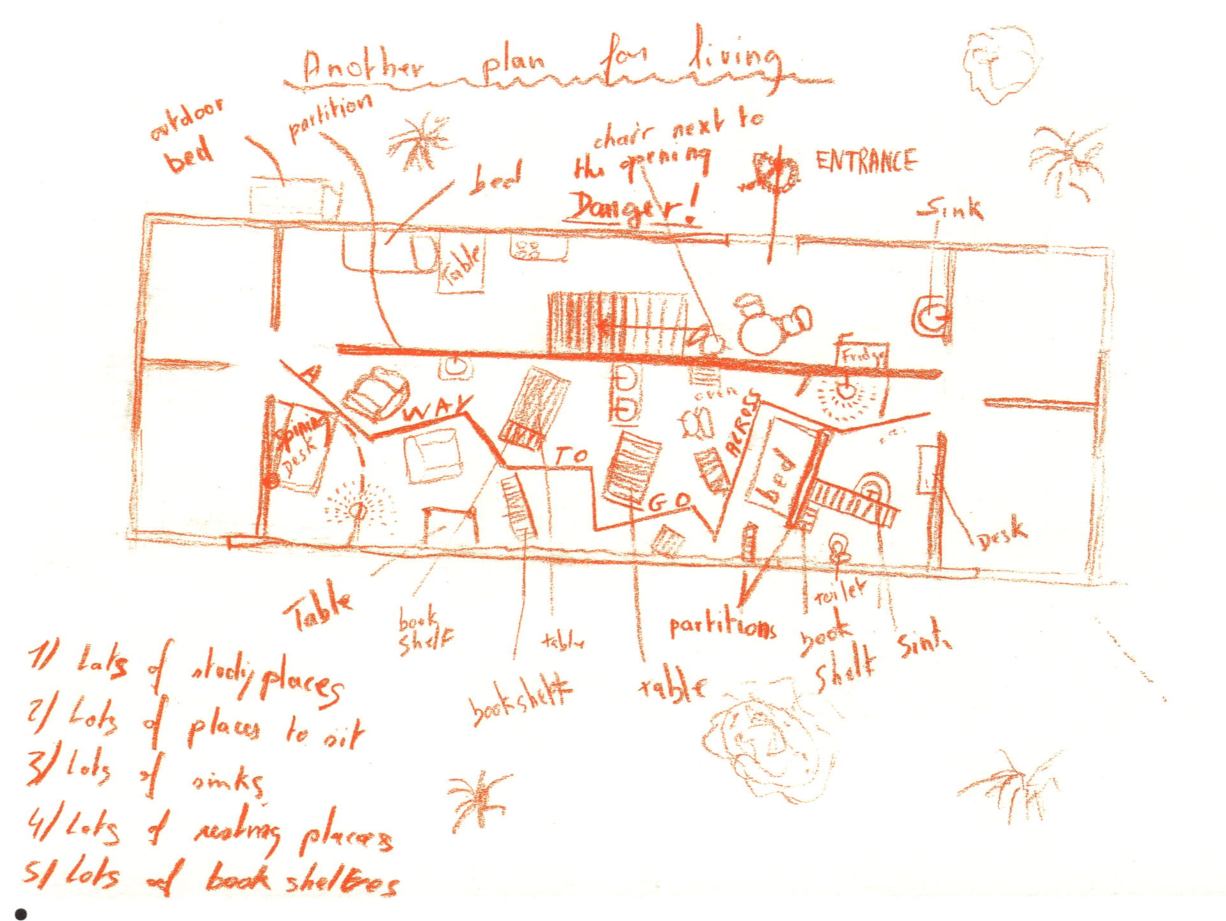

1) Lots of study places
2) Lots of places to sit
3) Lots of sinks
4) Lots of resting places
5) Lots of book shelves

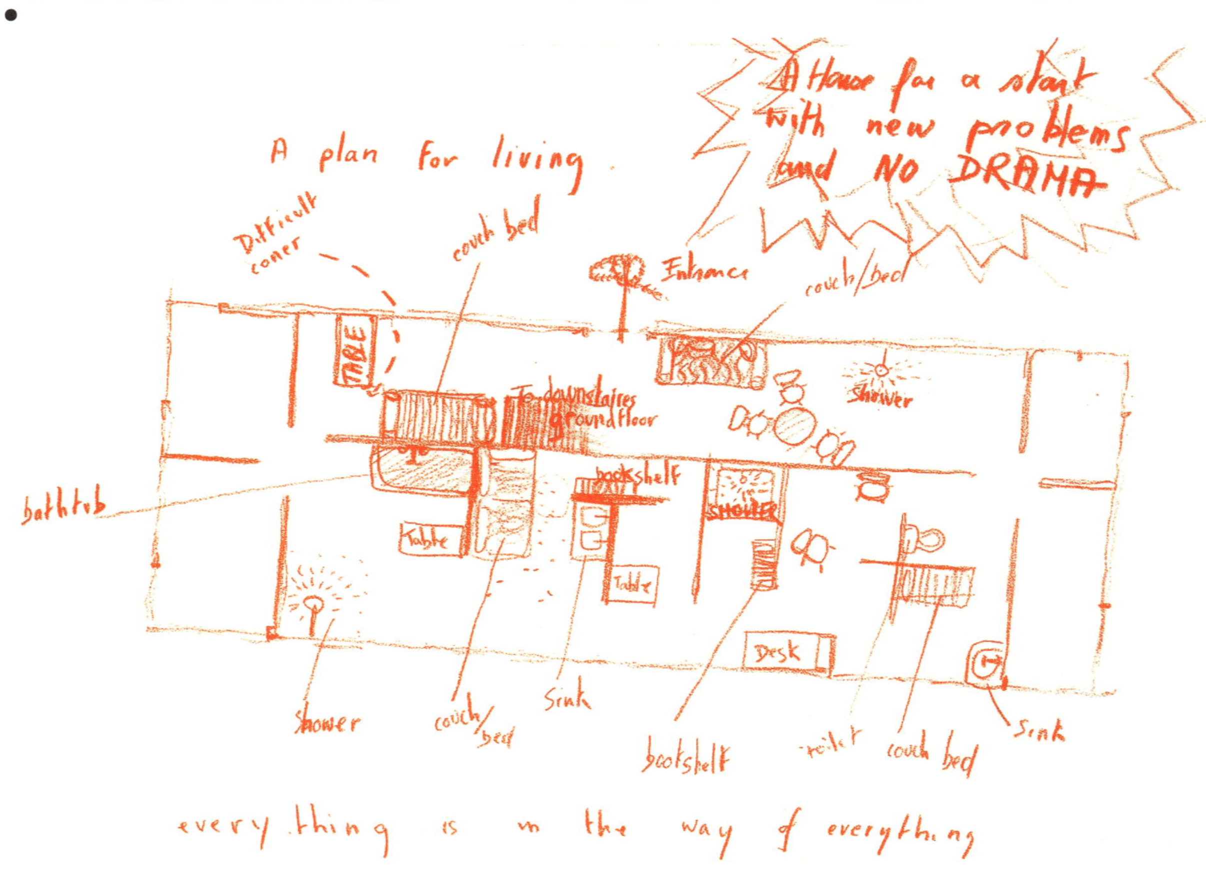

everything is in the way of everything

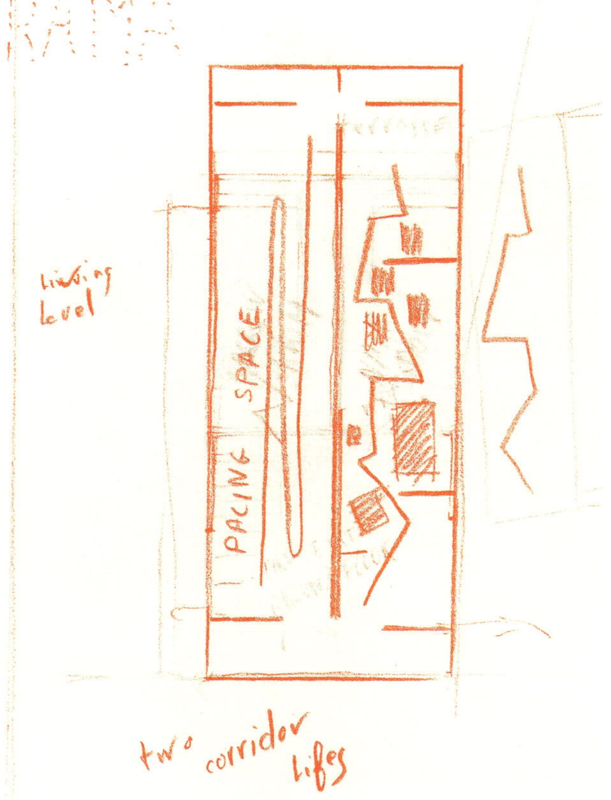

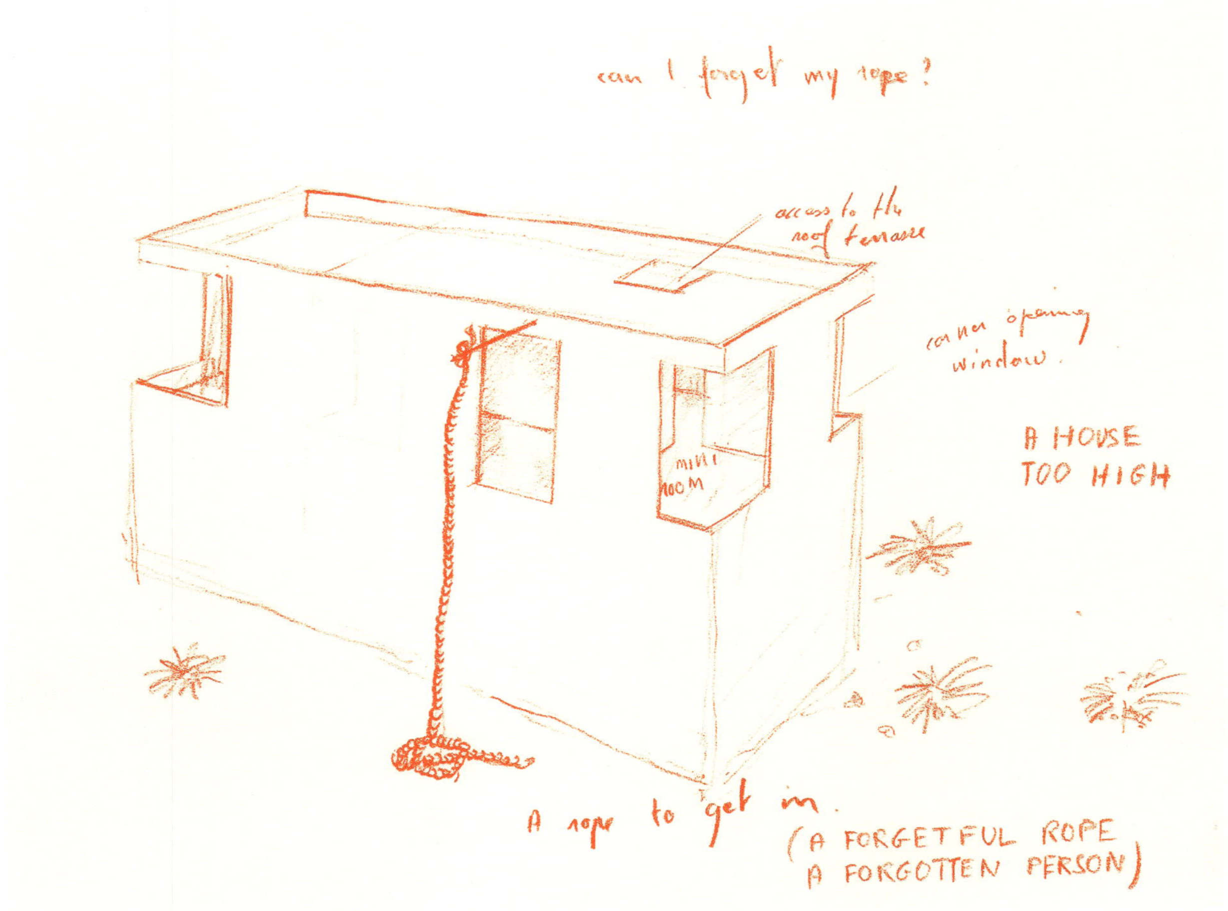

- Drawings of scenarios for the *no drama house* publication,
  red pencil on paper, 25×32 cm each, 2005
- ●● View of the ground floor of the *no drama house* (next spread)

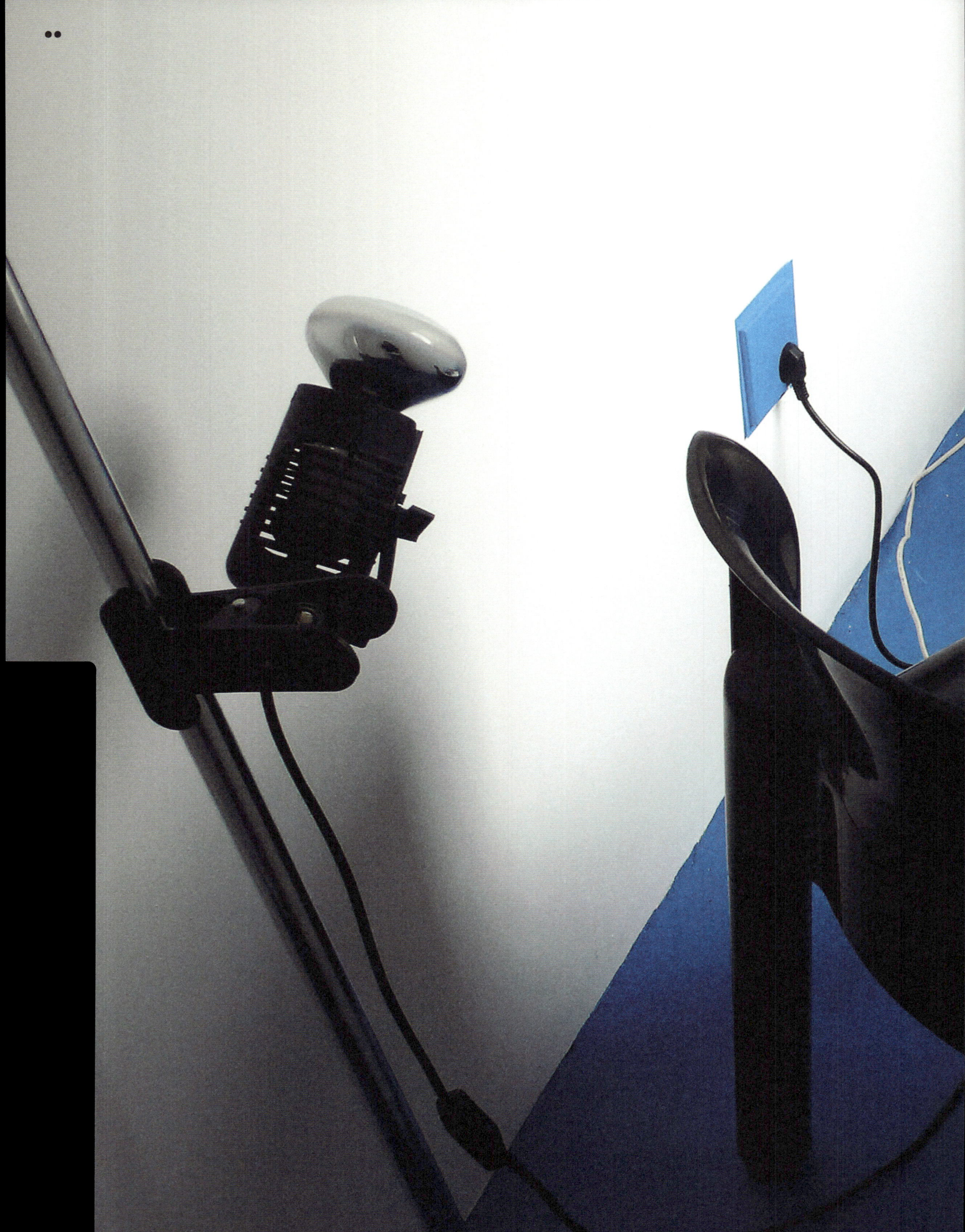

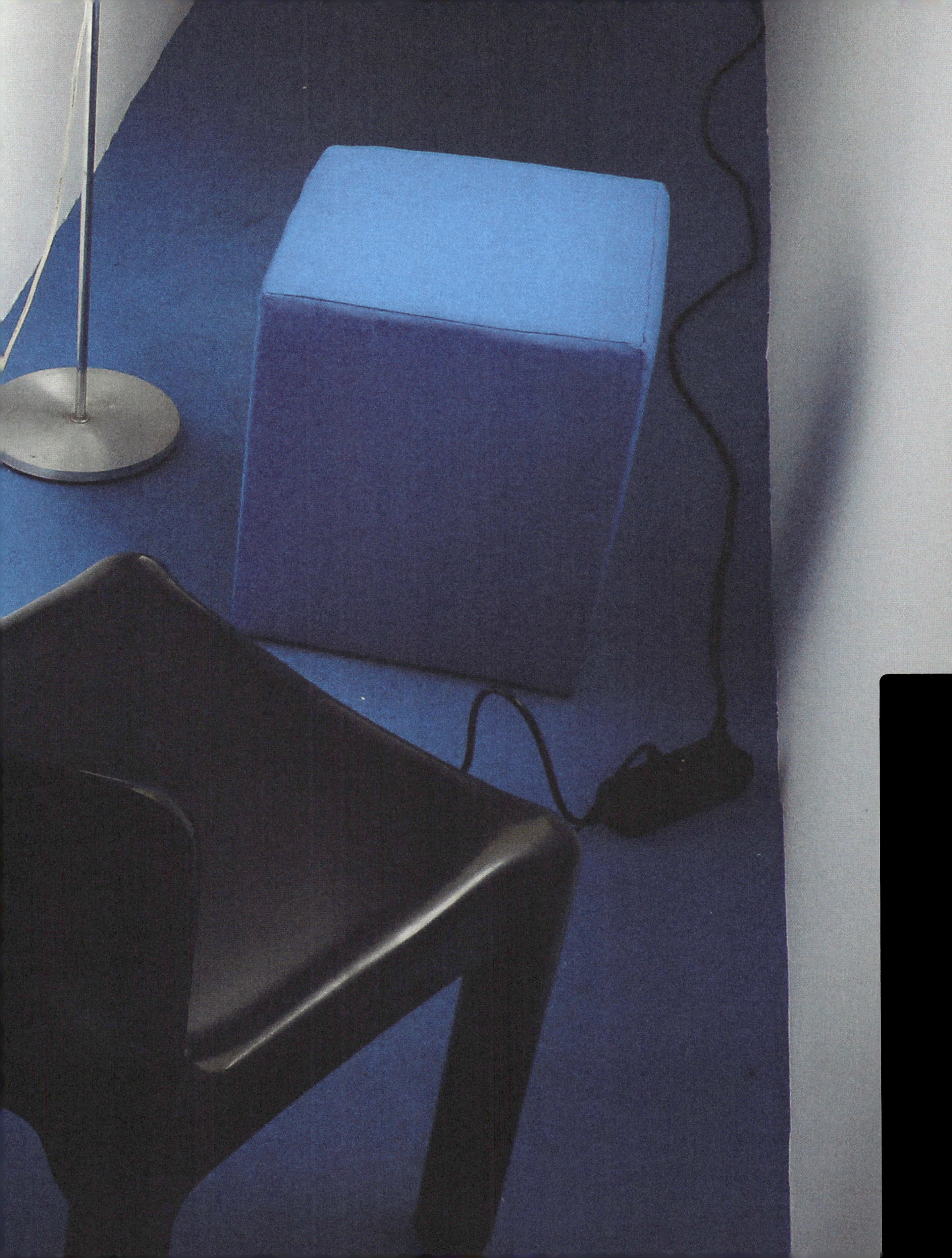

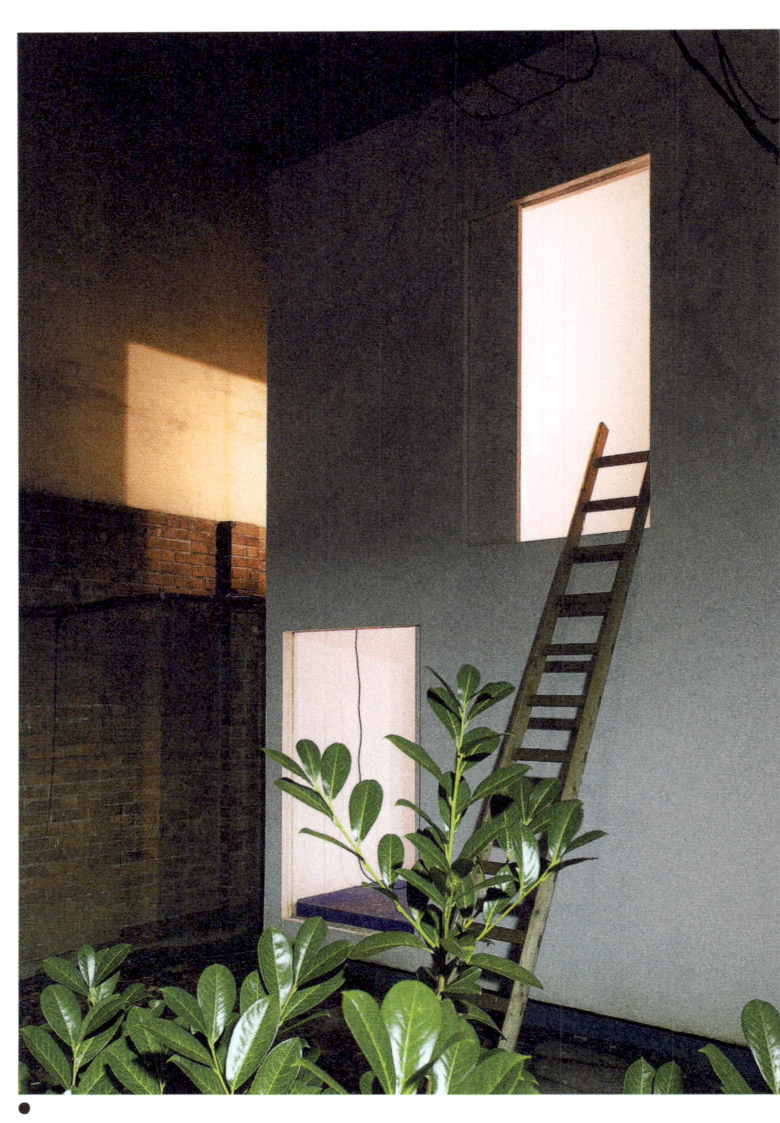

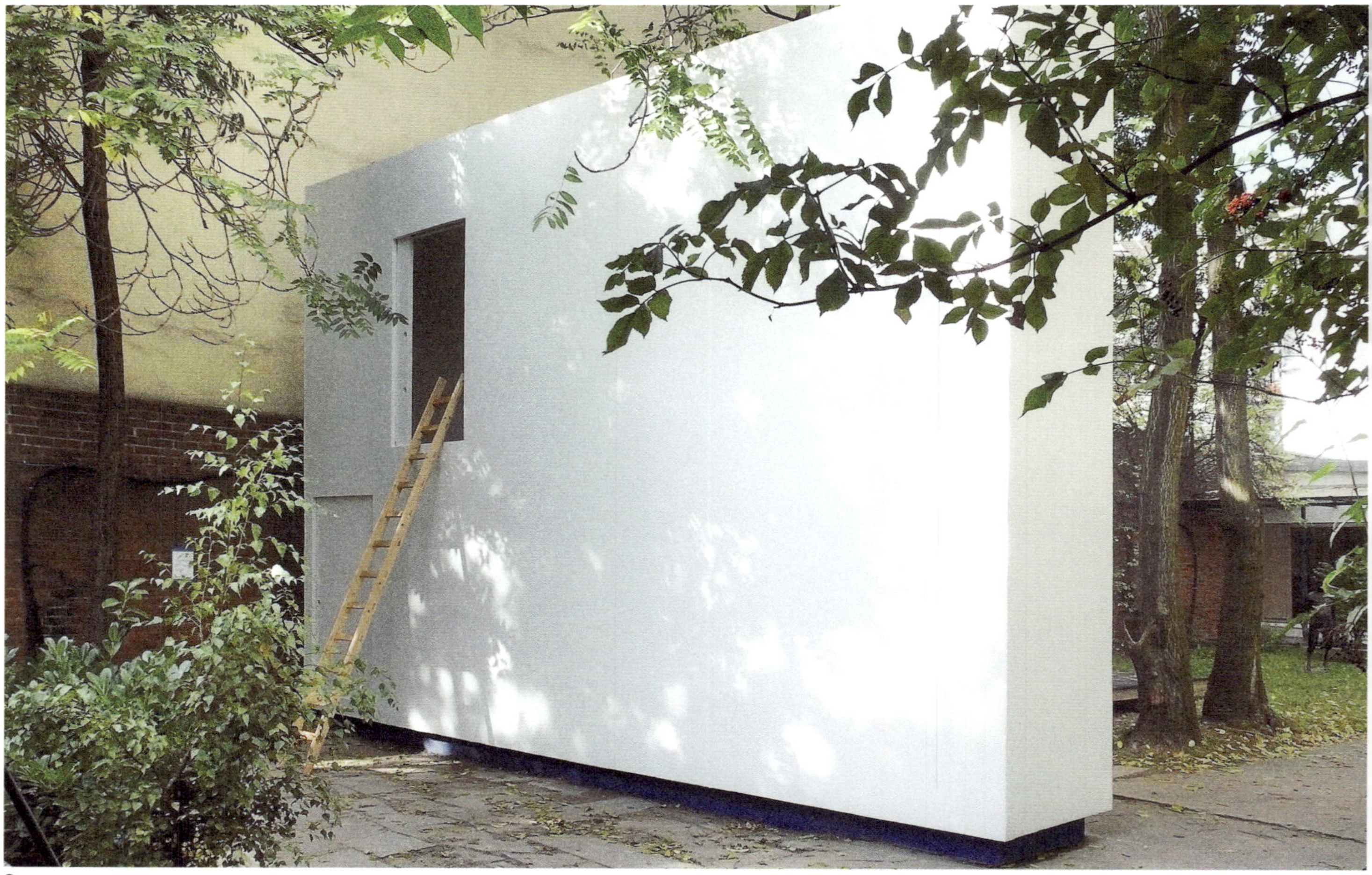

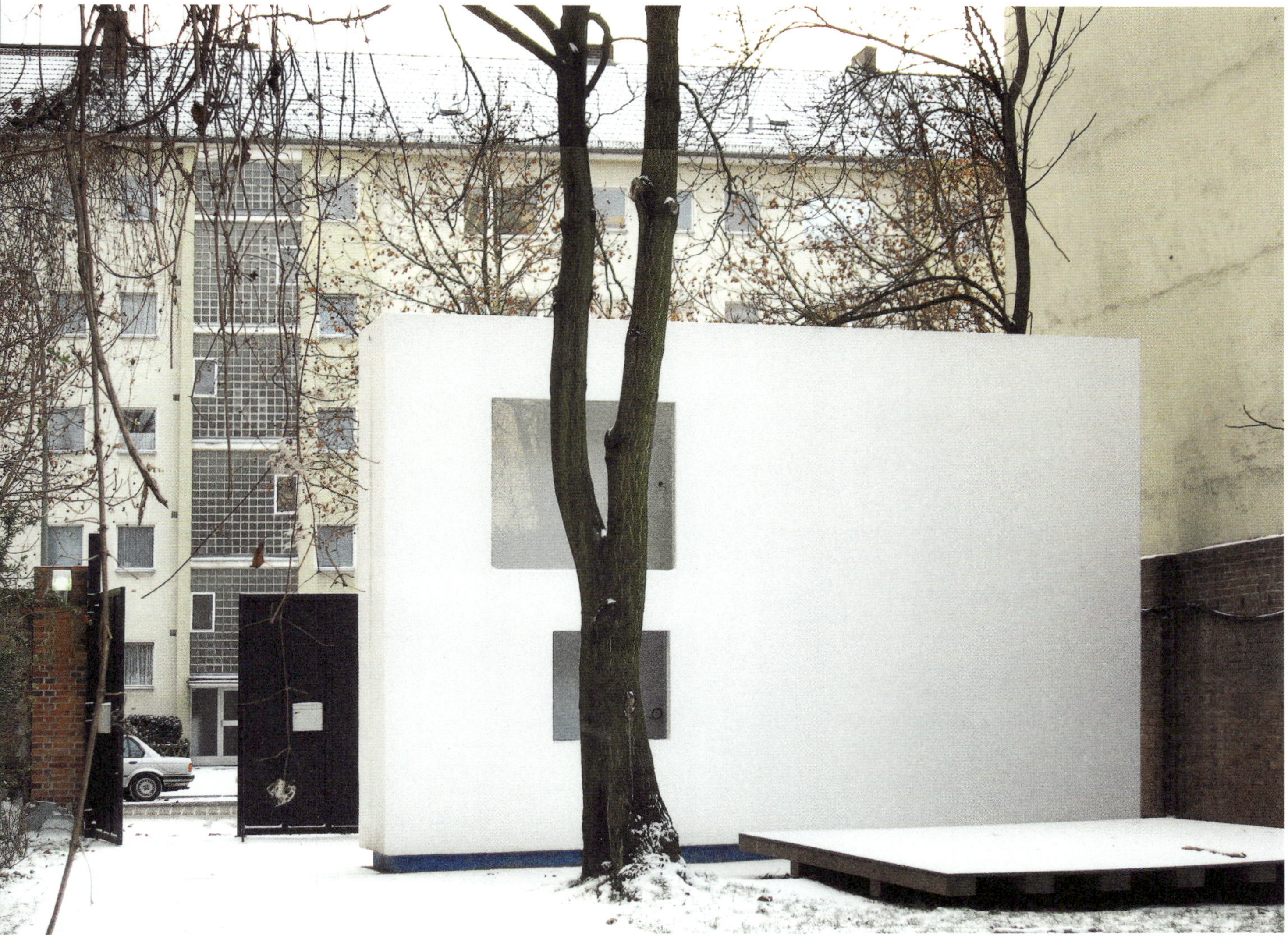

no drama house, 2009

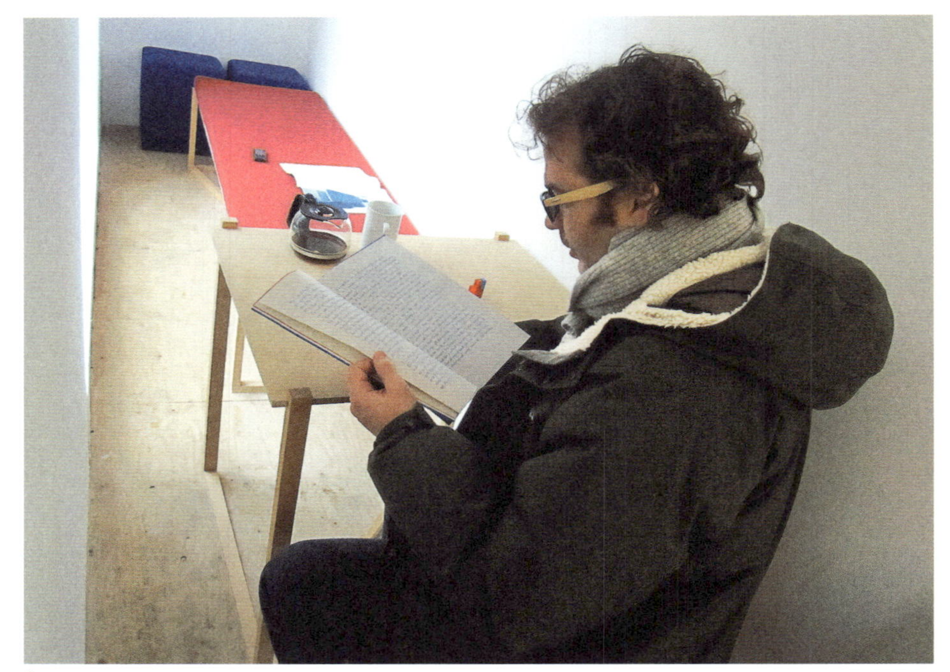

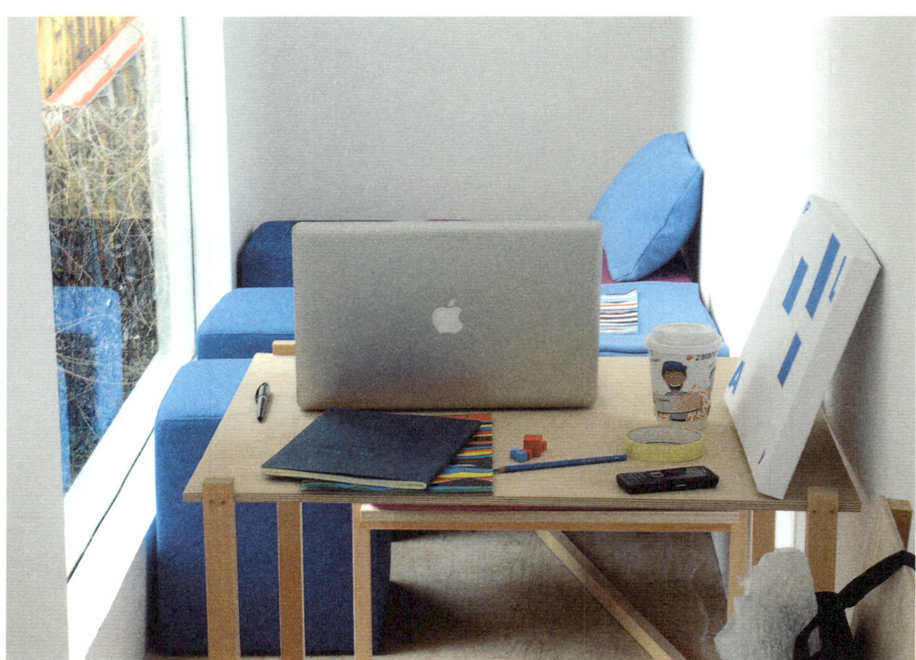

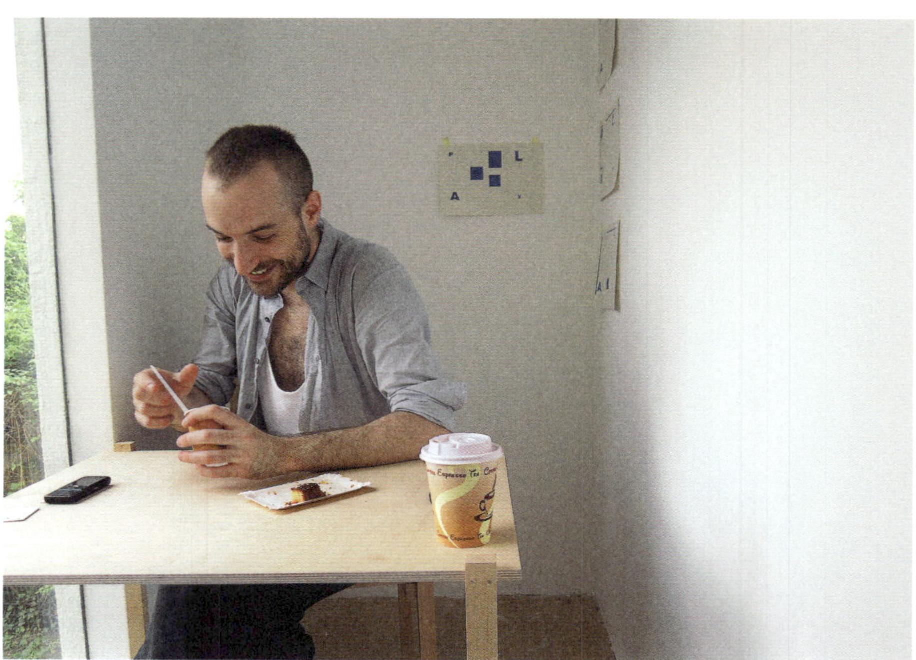

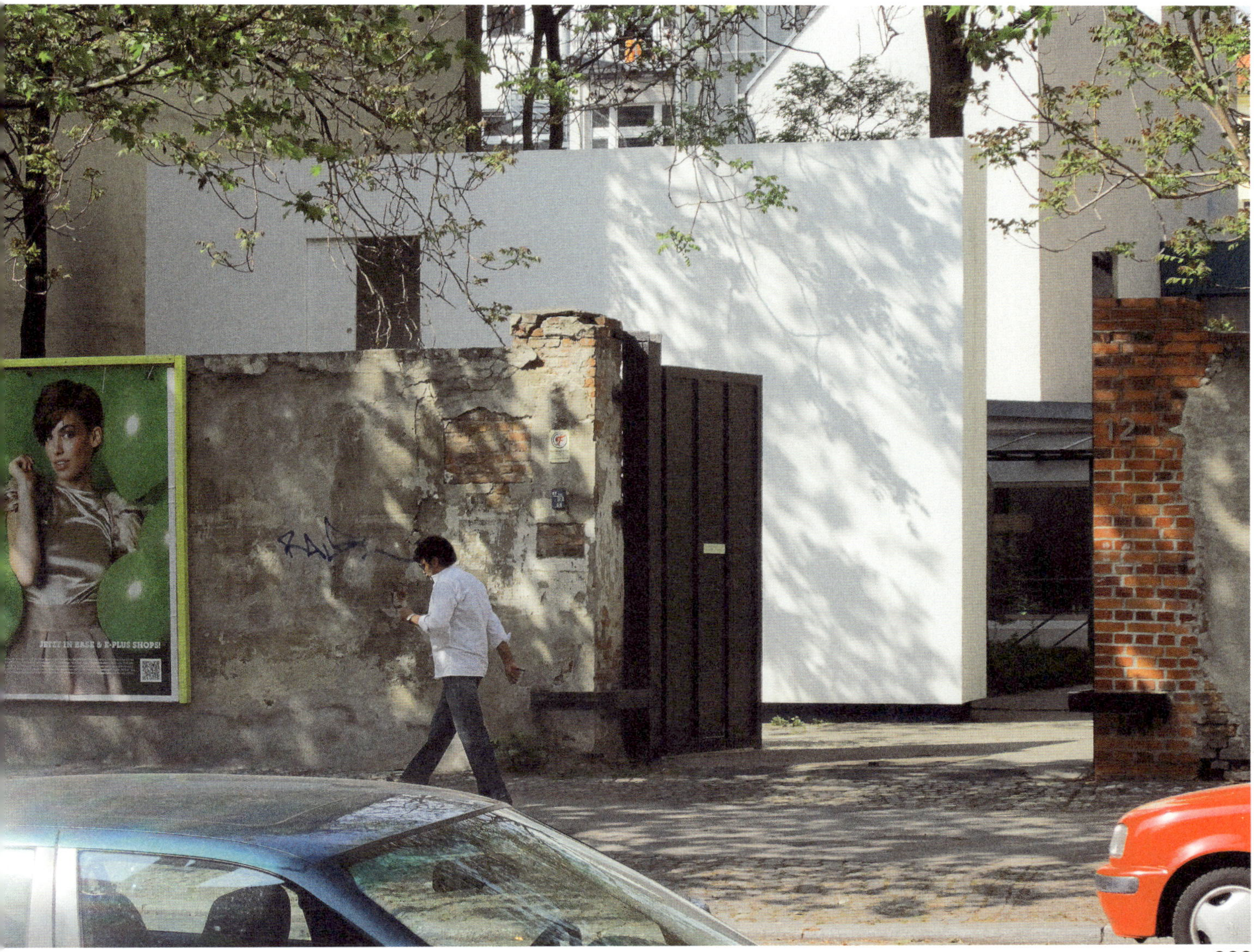

● Guests in the *no drama house*
●● Working upstairs in the *no drama house*
●●● *no drama house*, view from Kurfürstenstraße

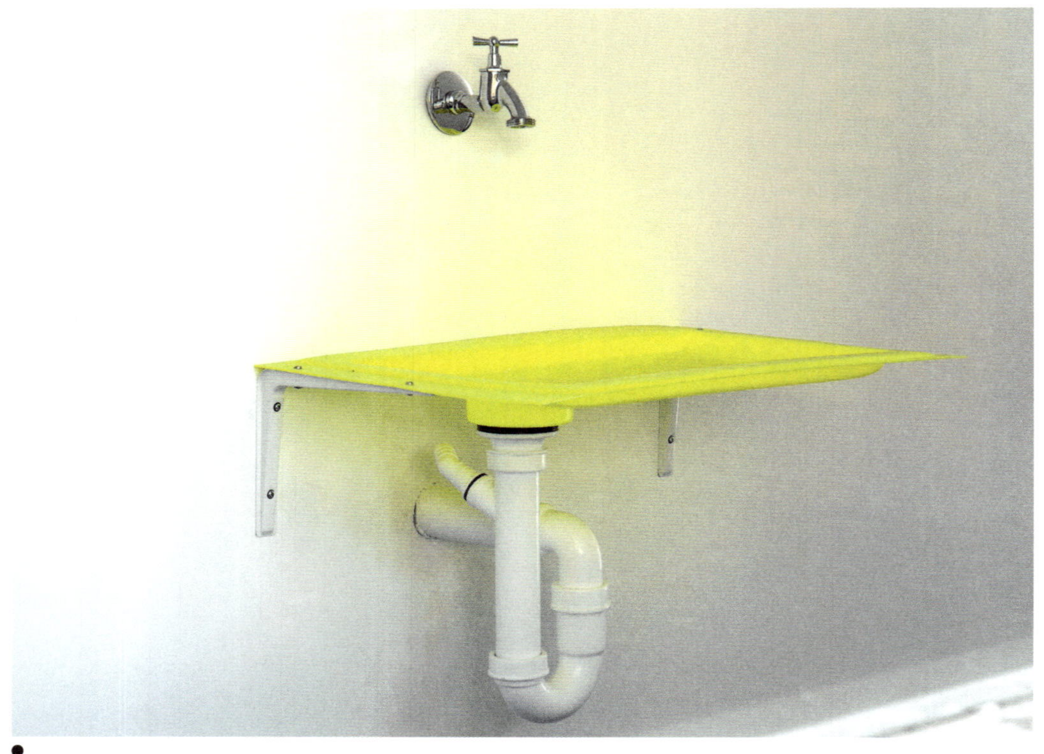

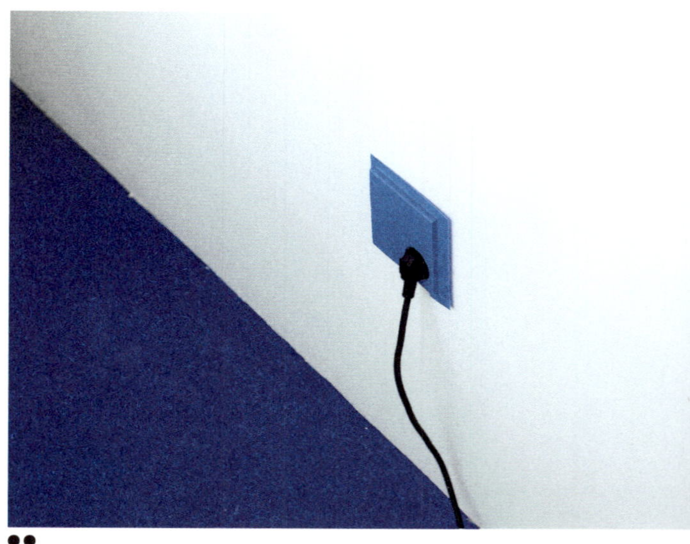

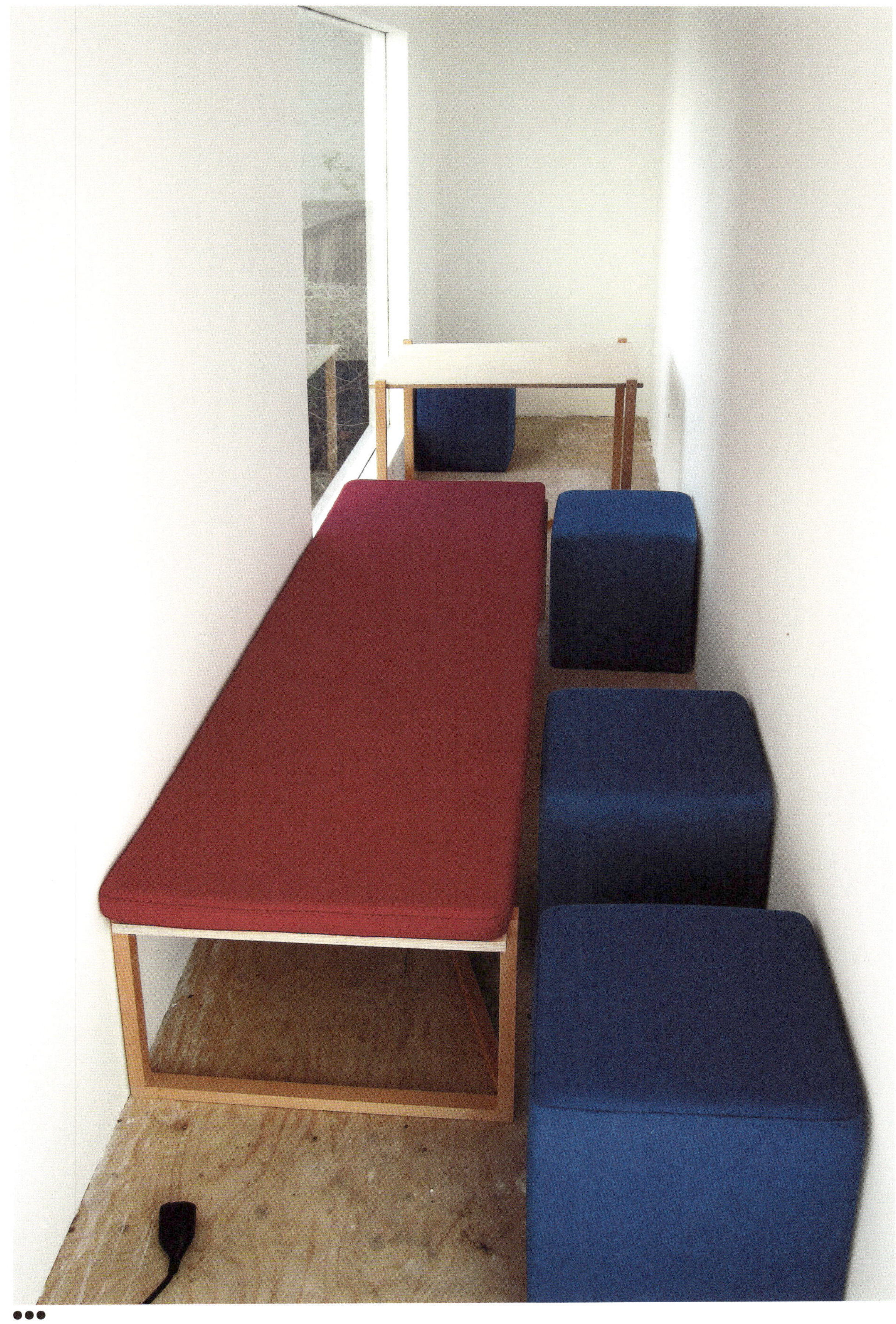

● *no drama house*, custom PVC sink (downstairs)
●● *no drama house*, custom plastic blue electrical outlet (downstairs)
●●● *no drama house*, custom furniture for the house (upstairs)

play — after a phrase

"Some words are separating the things."

Each word is coming as a character of sorts.

Some: the chair goes to the right
words: the other chair, the bed goes to this end of the room
are: yes, yes, yes
separating: the book is placed on the floor by the window
the: the ladder is put away, in another part of the garden
things: the stools stay put together, outside

play — after Robert Grenier

« that's little house too for the day »

Each word comes out as a character of sorts and plays a part.

that: the pressure of the ladder against the wall
's: light's cast on the façade
little: occupation of the width, and of the chair
house: it does it now
too: this piece from before
for: you too, you begin the placing
the: or not yet, I settle at the border of the door
day: Wednesday

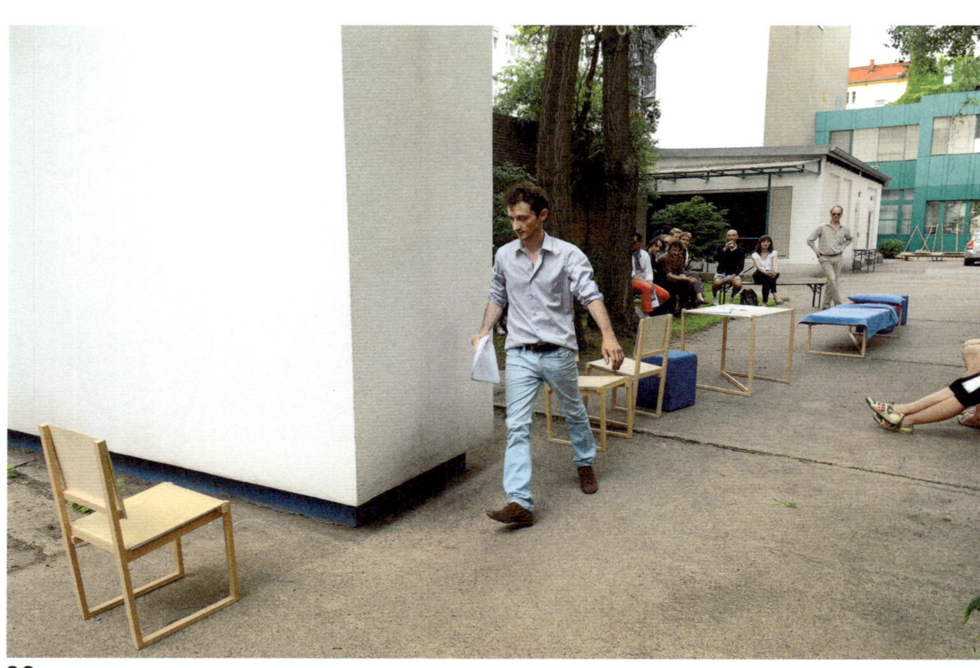

2012

While living in the house, I rearrange other people's phrases or my own, I reorganize the sequence of furniture in relation to my activity. *PLAy* is an event where such lines, such sequences or phrases, are deployed in front of a public, in the house's shadow, and like texts, they are read silently, they are whispered, they are read out loud, or they are given to be read by someone else. They are then unfolded, arranged over time.

These sequences were rearranged and read another time with Vanessa Desclaux on the occasion of a brief move of the furniture to the Jan van Eyck Academie in Maastricht.

En habitant, je réarrange des phrases d'autres personnes, ou les miennes, je ré-agence les séquences des meubles suivant mon activité. *PLAy* est un évènement où ces lignes, ces séquences ou ces phrases sont déployées devant un public, dans l'ombre portée de la maison, et comme les textes, sont lues silencieusement, à voix basse, à voix haute, ou données à lire. Elles sont alors dépliées, arrangées dans le temps.

Ces séquences ont été réarrangées et lues une autre fois avec Vanessa Desclaux à l'occasion d'un court déménagement des meubles à la Jan van Eyck Academie à Maastricht.

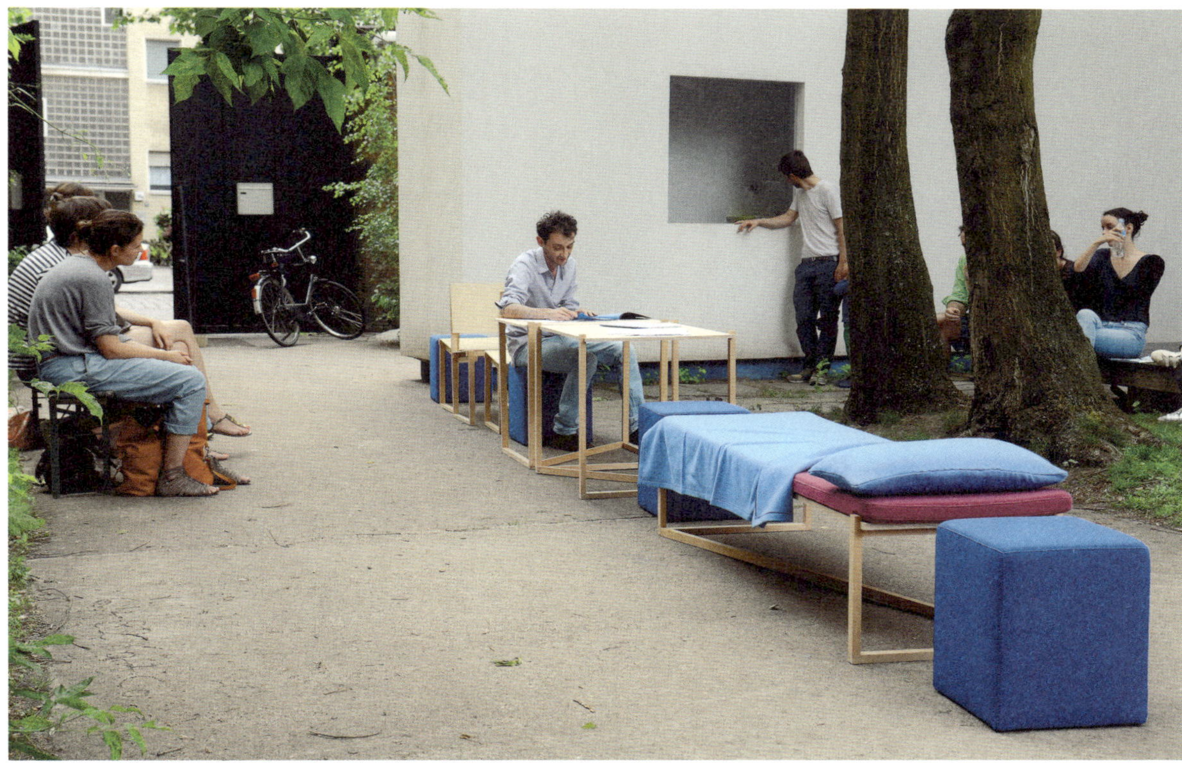

•

• *Play after…* two of eleven texts written in the house, all A4-size, that were read in various ways and combinations during *PLAy*

•• *PLAy*, making a sequence or phrase: *a chair, a house, a chair, a chair, a blue stool, a table, a daybed, …*, May 22, 2010

••• *PLAy*, reading in a low voice while sitting in sequence or phrase: *a chair, a chair, a chair . a table, a table . a daybed*, May 22, 2010

Cinonema

n o drama cine ma

May 09
South London
Gallery

65-67 Peckham Road,

London SE5 8UH

I imagine the thirties as a cinematic era. Through cinema, the cities and their edifices projected and extended themselves into countless film narratives which conversely were projected onto the walls of these same buildings, like punctuation marks scattered within the city grid. The walls were screens, the spaces projecting, projected. Urban spaces, along with their inhabitants, were the emitters, as well as the protagonists and the receivers of their own projections.

no drama house projecting onto another space, into another house, a house projected. Berlin projected on London, London replacing

some films on the left

a no dra-

ma house

with a cine-
ma of and
on its own

some films on the right

**by
jean-
pas-
cal
fla-
vien**

some words to look at to form yet another layout

this sheet of paper; an action captured in a film; an interruption between the spaces;

houses as projecting projected screens

i move the chair from be-hind the table

one action = one film

situation = micro film = projection

houses as projecting projected screens

shortcut

other films in the back

**Cinonema
an event
of play-
ing living
moving
displacing
reading**

a geo-graphy of plays

Cinonema is the contracted sequence of the no drama house and its cinematic offshoots, the micro-films, projecting the house onto the house or onto some other houses, spaces or interiors. The no drama house produces its own cinema by means of its constellation of unedited micro-films. Each action produced in relation to the no drama house gives rise to its own micro-film.

**March
02**
**no drama
house**

Kurfürstenstrasse 12,

10785 Berlin

(placing and placing or placing...)

n o drama cine ma

Cinonema

Without drama, that is to say without gravity or seriousness, only acts and actions. And for many of them, a film, a laconic microfilm curtailed by the end of the action it documents. The films are not edited, they appear and disappear, not necessarily in the same place each time. These projections (one in the house, three onto its exterior walls) produce a form of cinema that condenses itself: *Cinonema* for *no drama cinema*. These projections fold the house into itself, turning it into a screen, a projector, and into the protagonist of its own film. Meanwhile, the public unconsciously mimics gestures that appear in the films.

Cinonema was conceived as a dual event, which took place both at the house and at the South London Gallery. By being linked to an institution, the Berlin house projects itself onto another space, on its interior, its exterior, and its furniture.

Sans drame, c'est à dire sans gravité, sans sérieux, seulement des actes et des actions. Et pour beaucoup d'entre eux, un film, un microfilm laconique abrégé par le terme de l'action qu'il décrit. Les films ne sont pas montés, ils apparaissent et disparaissent, pas forcément au même emplacement. Ces projections, une dans la maison, trois sur les façades produisent une forme de cinéma qui se condense: *Cinonema* pour *no drama cinema*. Ces projections enchevêtrent la maison devenue écran, la maison projetant et la maison protagoniste. Pendant ce temps, le public répète inconsciemment des gestes apparaissant dans les films.

Cinonema fut conçu comme un double évènement qui eut lieu à la fois à la maison et à la South London Gallery. En se liant à une institution, la maison de Berlin se projette sur un autre espace, sur son intérieur, son extérieur et sur son mobilier.

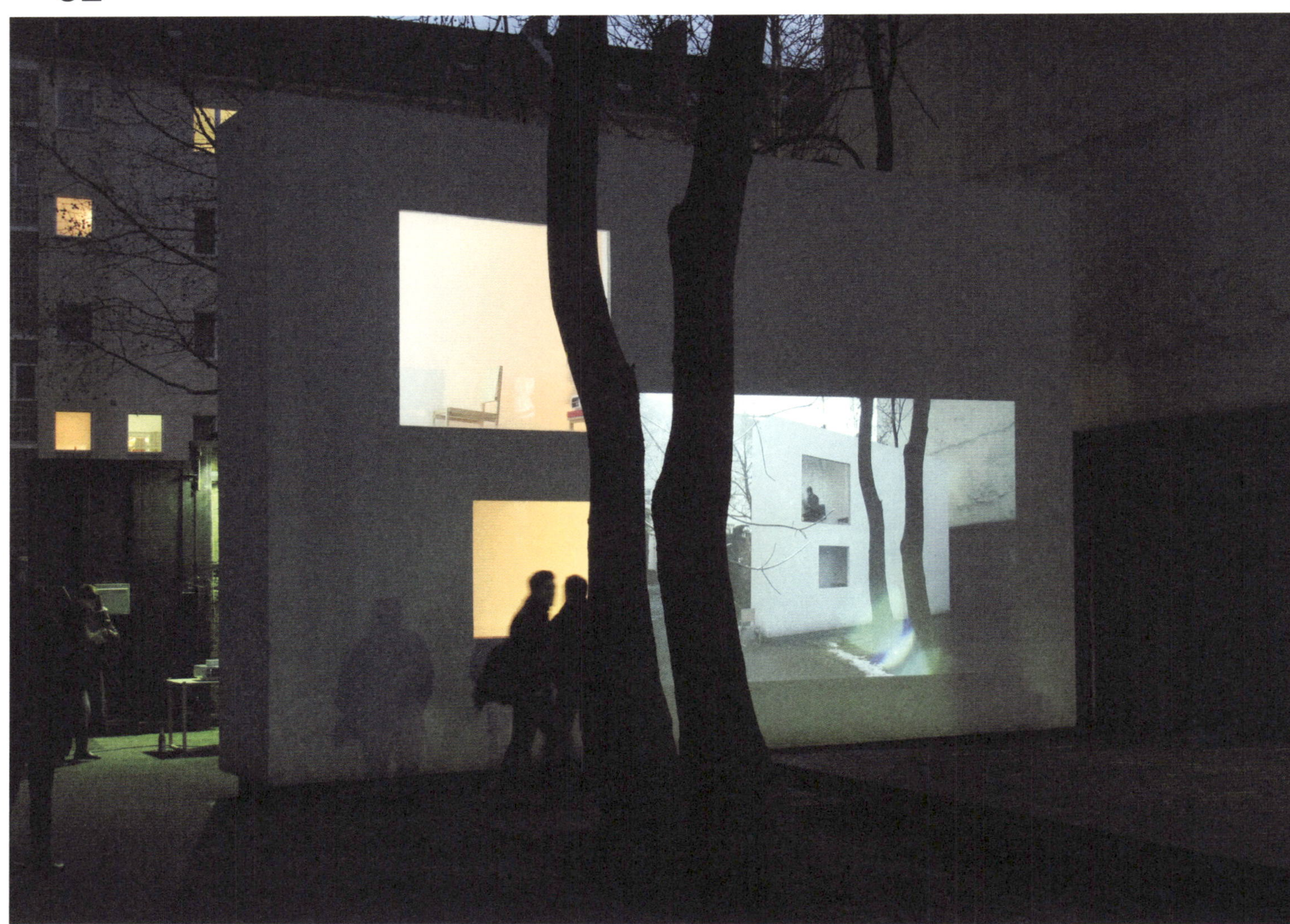

Documentation of the *Cinonema* event in Berlin,
microfilms projected on the house, March 2, 2012
Video stills from *nd microfilm 37*, 6 sec., 2011
Video stills from *nd microfilm 11*, 6 sec., 2011

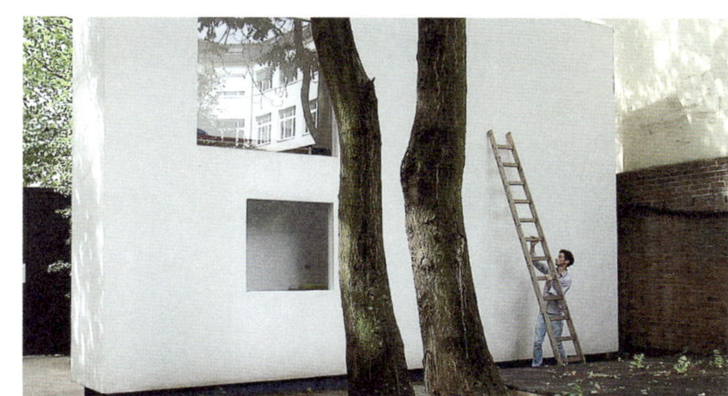

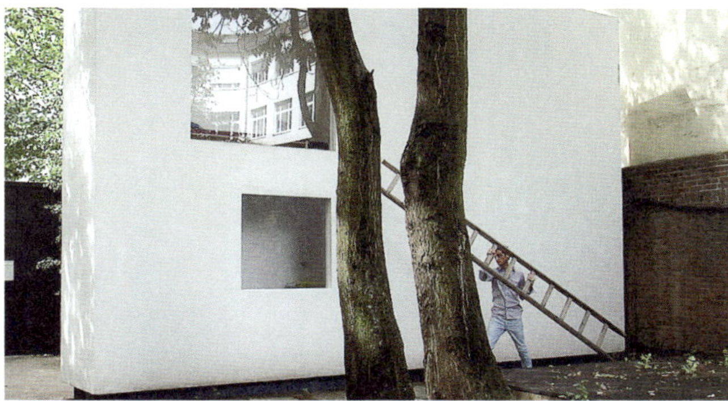

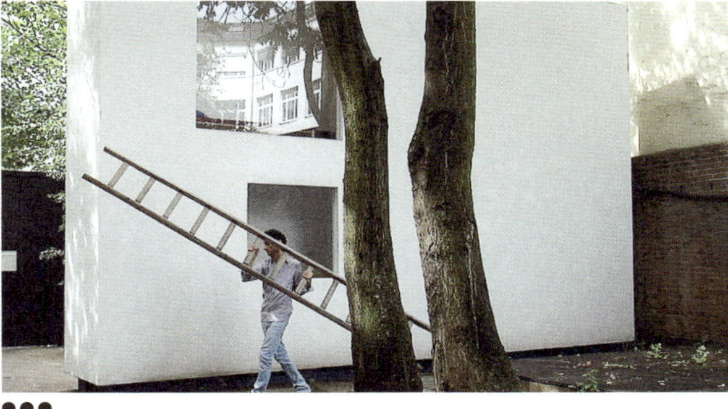

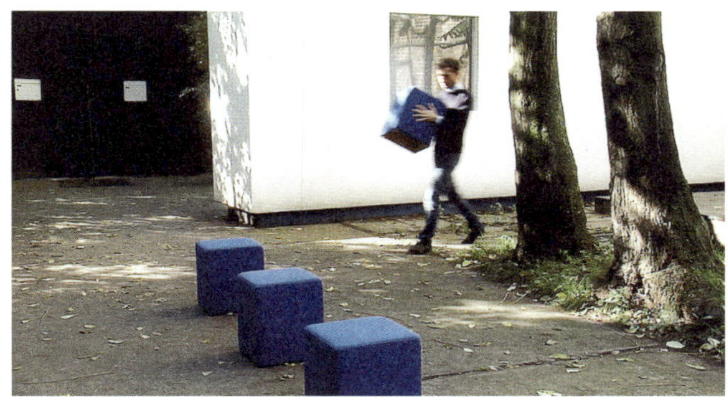

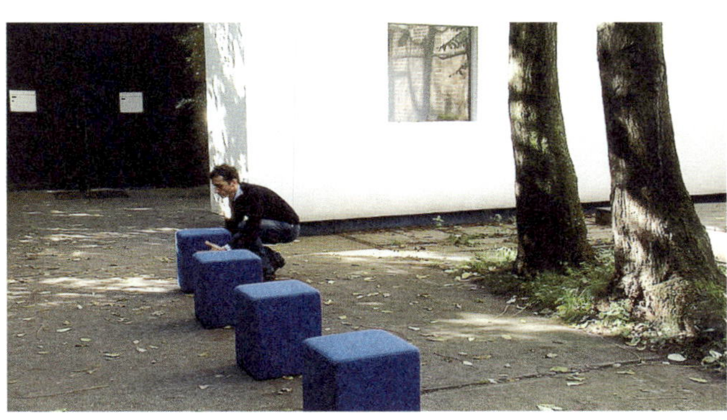

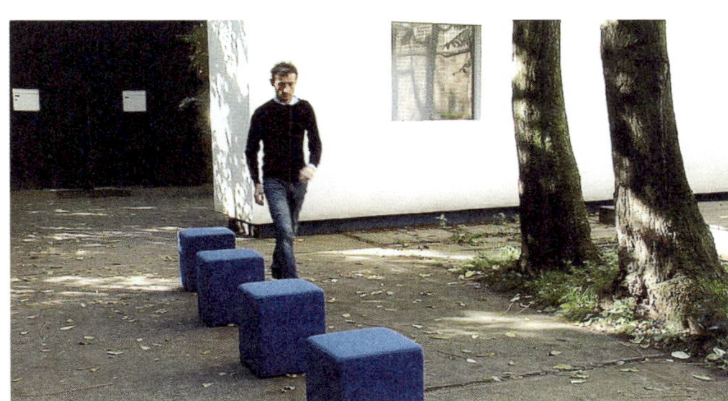

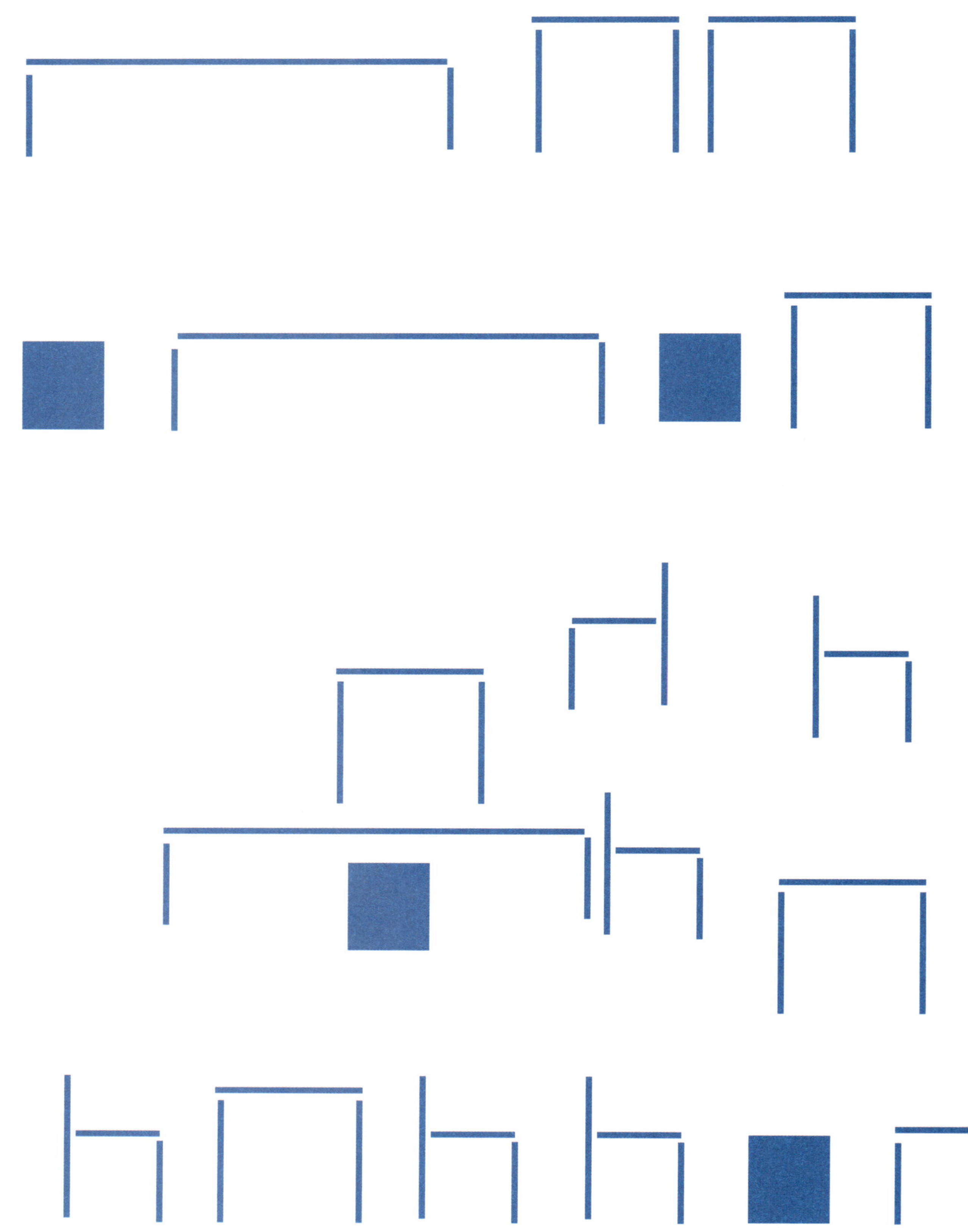

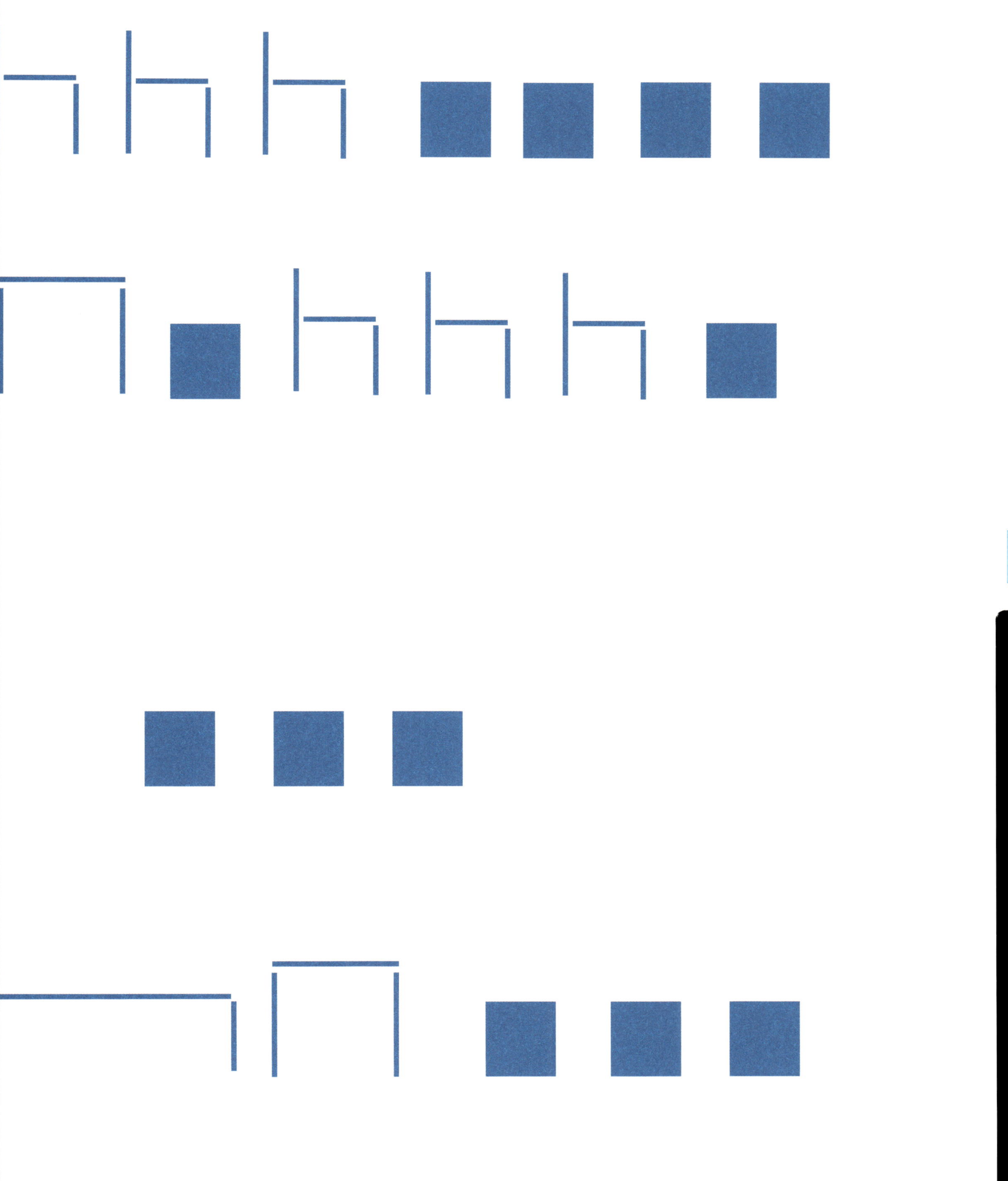

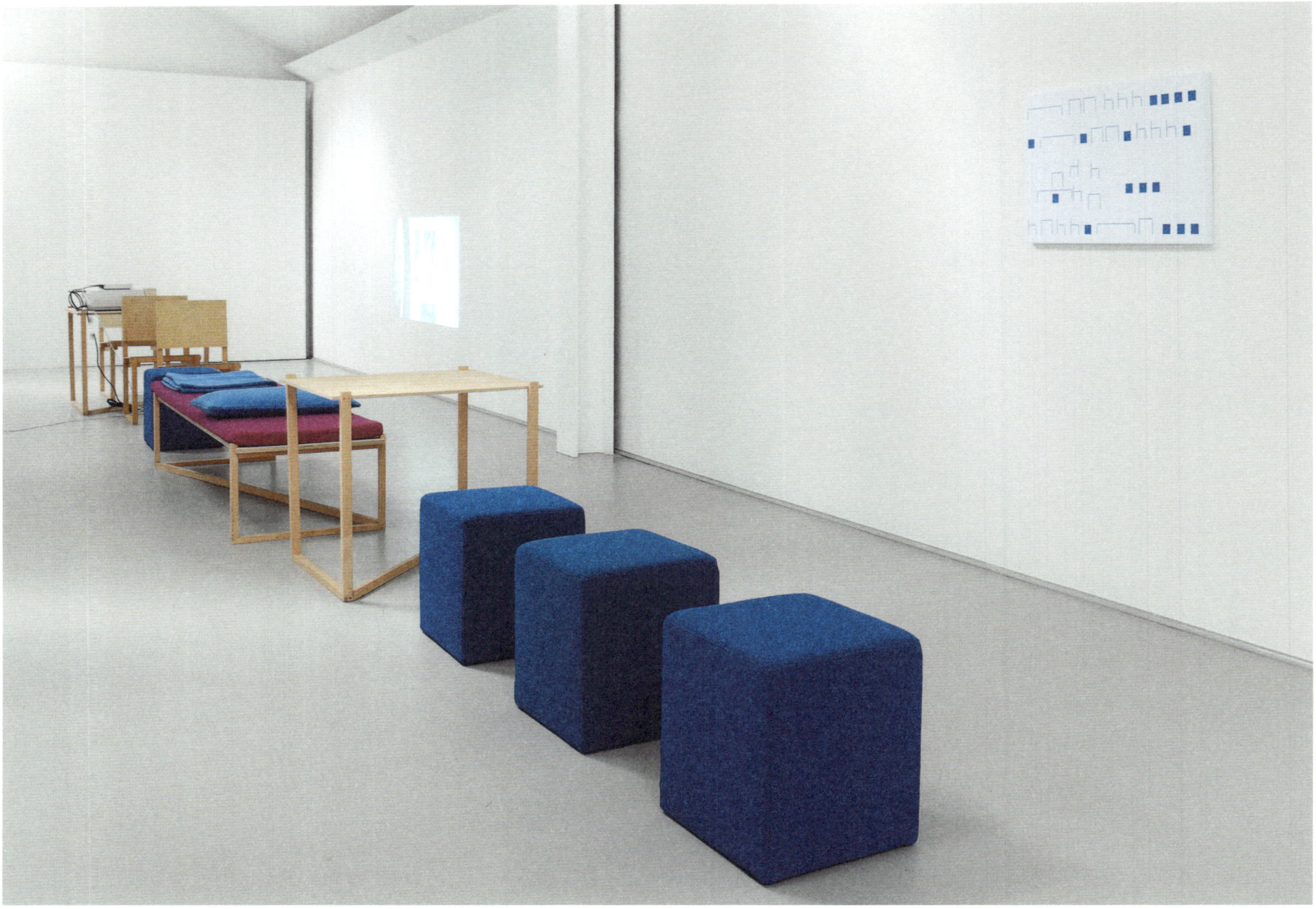

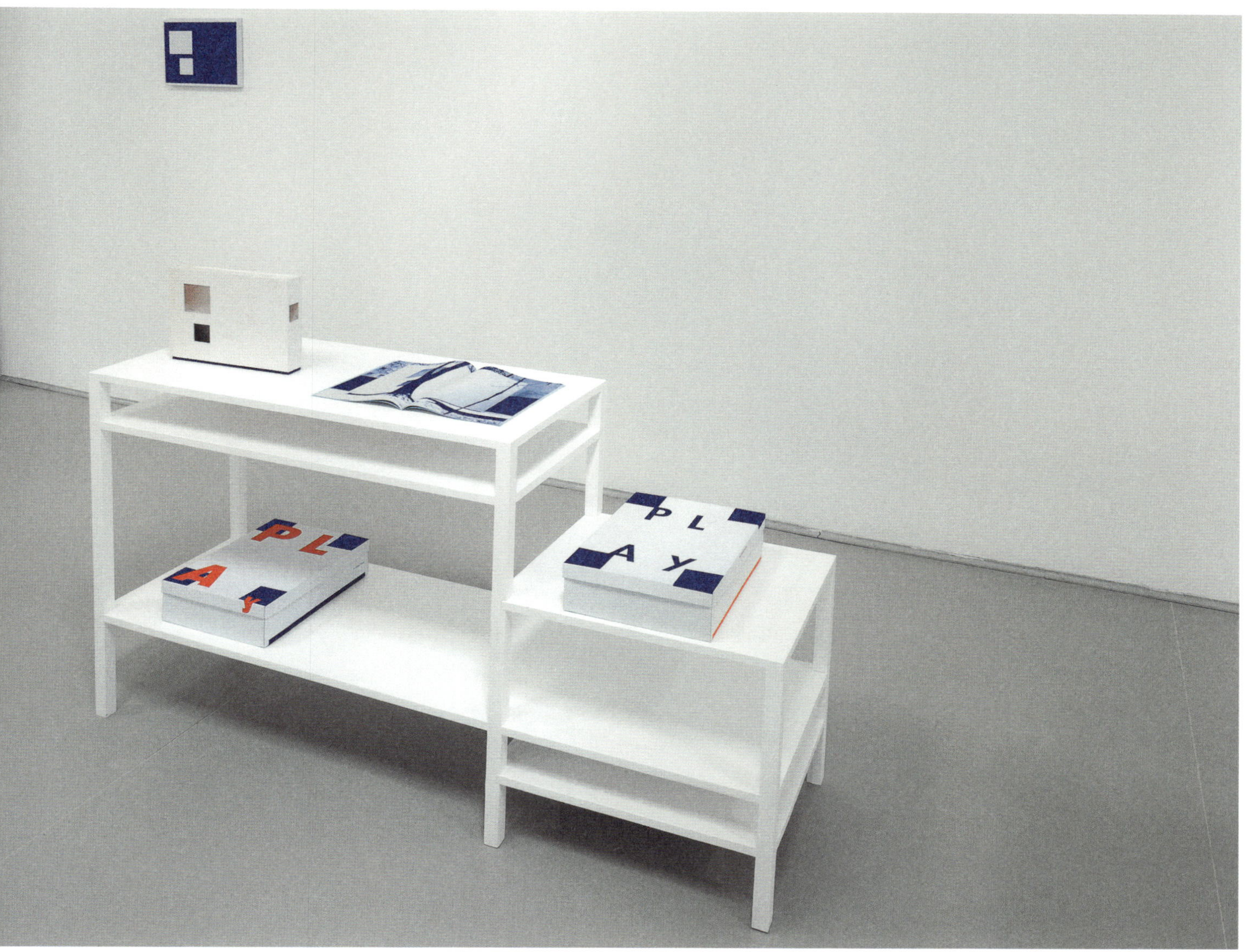

● Poster of the exhibition at Kunstverein Langenhagen, offset print,
28×42 cm, 2012 (previous spread)
●● Exhibition view, Kunstverein Langenhagen, 2012
●●● *book furniture*, Kunstverein Langenhagen, 40 pages, 21,6×30 cm, 2012
●●●● Exhibition view, Kunstverein Langenhagen, 2012

there are…

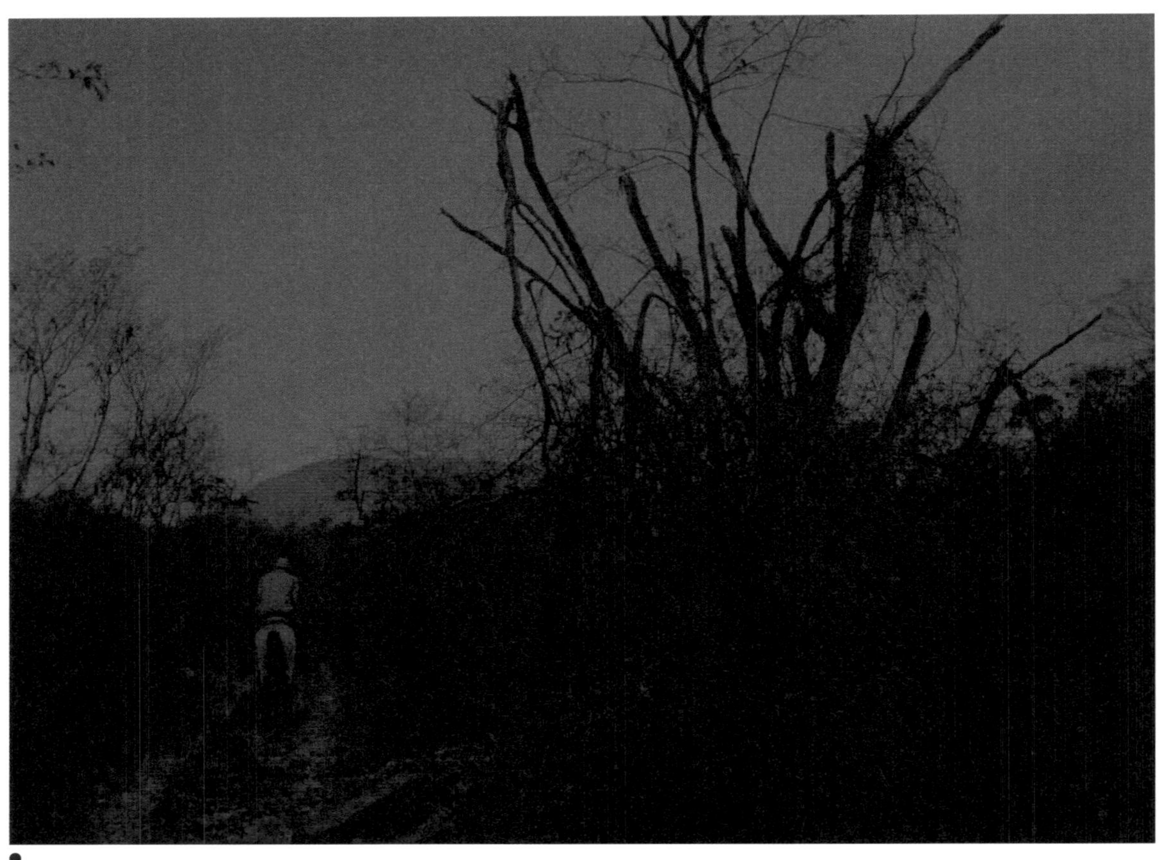

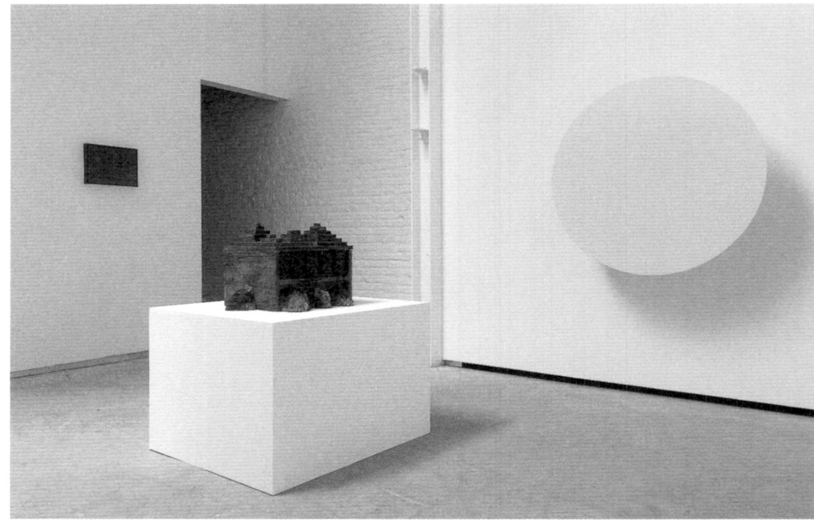

●   *Cowboy photo (05)*, C-print mounted behind tinted acrylic glass, 60×80 cm, 2011
●●   Exhibition view *night house at daytime*, Galerie Catherine Bastide, 2011:
     Le Bagne (Jean Genet), book mounted behind tinted acrylic glass, 30,5×40,5 cm, 2011
     Model of *night house at daytime*, tinted concrete and wood, tinted acrylic glass, 40×58×47 cm, 2011
     White sun, painted aluminum, 115×115×33 cm, 2011

"There are two mountains on which it is bright and clear,
the mountain of beasts and the mountain of gods.
But between them lies the dusky valley of men.
When once someone looks upwards,
an unquenchable longing seizes him forebodingly,
him who knows that he doesn't know
after them who don't know that they don't know
and after them who know that they know."[1]

We should not consider the power of abstraction that Gertrude Stein and Jean-Pascal Flavien share in their approach to language—an approach that Flavien has pertinently understood to shift into the field of architecture—as being disincarnate, detached from the exterior world and from all reference to the material and emotional realities of the social and political context. On the contrary, as Jane Bowers says with regards to Stein, "she discovered that language could do other things besides name, describe and report. It could, for instance, embody rhythms—the rhythm of personality, of conversation, of human action and interaction."[2] Flavien's houses deploy a visual and sculptural language wherein ways of living and thinking materialize that are as poetic as they are political. Flavien's houses produce setups at the heart of which habitual relationships to architectural space, objects, and human beings are called into question. With them, an ensemble of behaviors, ways of saying, doing, and acting are also unsettled, marginalized, and dissolved so as to make room for other possibilities.

Flavien presented the *night house at daytime* in the form of an exhibition in 2011. This house, which existed only as a model, has spawned a constellation of works which can be seen as its extensions, but which have also built an intensive space for it. The house was designed to be plunged into a permanent night, letting very little daylight in, as it was constantly illuminated by artificial light. The grammar of this is constructed by means of different variations around the opposition of shadow and light, natural and artificial light, as well as the extremities of the color spectrum. The house produces an allegory, by means of which the exterior landscape echoes the sepulchral interiority of artistic and literary creation.

One house, two models, a series of photographs, a series of texts, and two sculptures. Different figures and characters haunt this essentially private universe, stripped of daylight. Two aluminum discs, one painted off-white, the other

«Il est deux montagnes / où il fait lumineux et clair / La montagne des bêtes / et la montagne des dieux / Mais entre elles s'étend / La sombre vallée des hommes / Lorsqu'une fois l'un d'eux / regarde vers le haut, / Le saisit en présage / une nostalgie inextinguible / Lui qui sait / qu'il ne sait pas / De ceux qui savent / qu'ils ne savaient pas / Et de ceux / qui savent qu'ils savent.»[1]

Il ne faut pas considérer la puissance d'abstraction de l'approche de la langue que Gertrude Stein et Jean-Pascal Flavien partagent – une approche que Flavien a pertinemment su faire basculer dans le champ de l'architecture – comme étant désincarnée, détachée du monde extérieur et de toute référence à la réalité matérielle et émotionnelle du contexte social et politique. Bien au contraire car, comme l'écrit Jane Bowers à propos de Stein, «elle avait découvert que le langage pouvait faire autre chose que de nommer, décrire et rapporter. Il pouvait, par exemple, matérialiser des rythmes – le rythme d'une personnalité, d'une conversation de l'action et de l'interaction humaines».[2] Les maisons de Flavien déploient un langage plastique à travers lequel se matérialisent des modes de vie et de pensée dont la portée est aussi poétique que politique. Les maisons de Flavien produisent des emplacements au sein desquels les relations habituelles à l'espace architectural, aux objets ou aux êtres humains sont mis en question, et avec elles, ce sont alors un ensemble de comportements, de manières de dire, de faire, d'agir qui sont alors déréglés, marginalisés et dissous pour faire *place* à d'autres possibles.

Flavien a présenté la *night house at daytime* sous forme d'exposition en 2011. Cette maison, existant sous forme de maquette, a donné le jour à une constellation d'œuvres qui n'en sont pas seulement l'extension, mais en ont bâti l'intense espace. La maison a été pensée pour être plongée dans une nuit permanente, ne laissant que peu rentrer la lumière extérieure, constamment éclairée de manière artificielle. La grammaire de cette maison est construite à partir de différentes variations autour de l'opposition entre l'ombre et la lumière, la lumière naturelle et la lumière artificielle, ainsi que les extrémités du spectre coloré. La maison produit une allégorie, par le biais de laquelle un paysage extérieur fait écho à l'intériorité sépulcrale de la création artistique ou littéraire.

Une maison, deux maquettes, une série de photographies, une série de textes et deux sculptures. Différentes figures, personnages, hantent cet univers pratiquement privé de lumière naturelle: deux disques en aluminium, l'un peint en blanc cassé, l'autre en couleur sombre, matérialisent deux «soleils»; un cowboy

1   Paul Klee, 1903, cité par Roman Jakobson, *L'art verbal des poètes-peintres*, in: *Huit questions de poétiques* (Paris: Points Essais, Seuil, 1977), p. 153.
2   Jane Palatini Bowers, *Gertrude Stein* (New York: St. Martin's Press, 1993), p. 35, traduit par l'auteur.

1   Paul Klee, 1903, quoted from Roman Jakobson, *On the Verbal Art of William Blake and Other Poet-Painters*, in: *Language in Literature*, ed. Krystyna Pomorska and Stephen Rudy (Boston: Harvard University Press, 1987), p. 498.
2   Jane Palatini Bowers, *Gertrude Stein* (New York: St. Martin's Press, 1993), p. 35.

60

a dark hue, materialize two "suns." A cowboy travels on horseback in a series of photographs. Fragments of texts unite several authors whose writing is installed in a night of their own. The photographs, like the texts, are placed behind tinted glass. This last element immerses the arid landscape through which the cowboy travels in an eternal twilight, and alters the visibility of the texts. The evocation of artificial lighting, whose blinding effect we sense, is linked to the multiple representations of this crepuscular universe, in which the sun has definitely been sacrificed.

"Ah! See! Look over there!"
"See what? ... Yes, a night rainbow!"
"It's formed by the light of the moon. It's a rare and extraordinary phenomenon! Few people have ever seen such a thing. It's double, see, there's a paler one above it ... And, a small boat is moving just underneath ..."[3]

In *Huzo Lumnst* (1973), Guy de Cointet, fascinated as he was by the dense materiality of language that he ceaselessly explored in his work, invited us to imagine "a night rainbow." In this performance by Cointet, the words pronounced by the actress resonate like an undecipherable suite of letters and numbers written in red ink on large white sheets hung on the wall. With the *night house at daytime*, Flavien once more makes us spectators of a landscape both material and mental, pictorial and poetic, materializing his perception of an exterior reality by means of the decomposition of its different elements. This house, plunged into the night, incarnates the solitude of an artistic practice, or the experience of insomnia. Upon encountering the house, its viewers are simultaneously immersed in different literary experiences multiplying the visual possibilities that this decor delineates.

Stein described her plays as landscapes. This reference can seem somewhat disorienting, unless one contextualizes it within the author's historical environment, so as to immediately establish a link between the notion of landscape and the pictorial tradition—Renaissance painting—which forged its understanding. Landscape is undeniably a composition whose esthetic dimensions play an essential role in the construction of our gaze. When Stein was writing, painting was going through a great upheaval at the hands of Cubism, whose visual rebellion called into question the ways in which the laws of perspective and geometry dictated the composition of a painting. Stein's landscapes are thus intimately tied to cubist pictorial composition, reducing the unstable frontier between abstraction and representation to a marginal divide. If the stakes of this distinction between abstraction and figuration have been radically displaced

se déplace à cheval dans une série de photographies ; des fragments de textes rassemblent plusieurs auteurs dont l'écriture s'est installée dans une nuit. Les photographies comme les textes sont placés derrière le verre teinté. Ce dernier plonge le paysage aride chevauché par le cowboy dans un éternel crépuscule et altère la visibilité des textes. L'évocation de la lumière artificielle, dont on pressent l'aveuglement, rejoint les multiples représentations d'un univers crépusculaire, dans lequel le soleil a été définitivement sacrifié.

« Ah ! Voyez ! Regardez là-bas ! Ne voyez-vous rien ? »
« Quoi donc ? ... Oui, un arc-en-ciel de nuit ! »
« C'est la lumière de la lune qui le forme. C'est un phénomène rare et extraordinaire ! Bien des gens n'ont jamais vu cela. Il est double, vous voyez, il y en a un plus pâle au-dessus ... Et, une barque s'avance juste au-dessous ... »[3]

Dans *Huzo Lumnst* (1973), Guy de Cointet, lui-même fasciné par la dense matérialité du langage qu'il n'a cessé d'explorer dans son travail, nous invitait à imaginer un « arc-en-ciel de nuit ». Dans cette performance conçue par Cointet, les mots prononcés par l'actrice résonnaient contre des suites indéchiffrables de lettres et de chiffres inscrits à l'encre rouge sur de larges feuilles blanches accrochées au mur. Avec la *night house at daytime* Flavien nous rend à son tour spectateurs d'un paysage à la fois plastique et mental, pictural et poétique, matérialisant sa perception d'une réalité extérieure par l'intermédiaire d'une décomposition de ses différents éléments. Cette maison, plongée dans la nuit, incarnerait la solitude de la pratique artistique ou l'expérience de l'insomnie. Au contact de la maison, les spectateurs sont parallèlement immergés dans différentes expériences littéraires qui multiplient alors les possibilités de visions qu'esquisse ce décor.

Stein décrivait ses pièces de théâtre comme des paysages. Cette référence peut paraître quelque peu déroutante, à moins qu'on la repositionne dans le contexte historique de l'auteur et qu'on établisse immédiatement le lien entre la notion de paysage et la tradition picturale – la peinture de la Renaissance – qui en a forgé la compréhension. Le paysage est indéniablement une composition dont les dimensions esthétiques jouent un rôle essentiel dans la construction de notre regard. Lorsque Stein écrit, la peinture connaît cependant un grand bouleversement à travers le mouvement cubiste, dont la révolte plastique remit en cause la manière dont les règles de la géométrie et de la perspective dictaient la composition du tableau. Les paysages de Stein sont ainsi intimement liés à la mise en espace cubiste du tableau, réduisant à un écart marginal la frontière instable entre

3   Guy de Cointet, *Huzo Lumnst*, tapuscrit original de 1973 reproduit dans le livret consacré à la performance, édité à l'occasion de la re-création de *Huzo Lumnst* le 31 mars 2012 chez Air de Paris, Paris, p. 1.

3   Guy de Cointet, *Huzo Lumnst*, original manuscript from 1973, reproduced in the booklet edited on the occasion of its re-enactment at Air de Paris, Paris, on March 31, 2012, p. 1.

today, Flavien manipulates this back and forth between these different modes of representation and different degrees of realism far more intuitively, and his works continue to highlight the importance of questioning the ways in which we articulate the links between architecture, landscape, language, and signification. He brings us back to the essential question of the meaning that we invest into our actions, and reminds us that all of the forms which we surround ourselves with, as well as all the architectural and grammatical constructions that we manipulate daily, reveal modes of thought, and allow for or block our action, imagination, and faculty of invention.

> "Let action be the exception, not the rule. Action is in the aorist tense; it must be contrasted with a static situation. If I want to act light, the static situation must be laid on a dark basis. If I want to act dark, we need a light base for our static situation. The effectiveness of the action is greater when its intensity is strong and the quantity of space occupied by it is small, but with slight situational intensity and great situational extension. … On a medium-toned static ground, however, a double action is possible, depending on whether one considers it from the point of view of lightness or that of darkness."[4]

With the *night house at daytime*, Flavien chooses to plunge us into obscurity in full light. Night invades all aspects of the composition of the work under the well-adjusted lights of the white-walled space in which his works are installed. The house is the scenario of a fiction to which no particular narrative or drama is attached. It solicits our gaze, addresses another scenographic volume, an interior scene whose depth can no longer be measured in metrical dimensions. "Three hundred and sixty-five massive nights without the days, this is what I wish upon the haters of the night."[5]

figuration et abstraction. Si les enjeux de cette distinction entre figuration et abstraction se sont radicalement déplacés aujourd'hui, si Flavien manipule de manière beaucoup plus intuitive ces va-et-vient entre de multiples registres de représentation et des degrés différents de réalisme, les productions de l'artiste continuent de mettre en lumière l'importance de questionner les manières dont nous articulons les liens entre architecture, paysage, langage et signification. Il nous ramène à la question essentielle du sens que l'on investit dans nos actions, et nous rappelle que toutes les formes dont nous nous entourons, toutes les constructions architecturales, grammaticales que nous manipulons au quotidien, révèlent des modes de pensée, rendent possible, ou au contraire entravent, notre action, notre imagination et notre faculté d'invention.

> « Que l'action se déroule d'une manière extraordinaire et non selon la règle. L'action est aoristique, elle doit se détacher sur fond de permanence. Si je veux agir en sombre, cela présuppose un fond clair. L'effet de l'action augmente selon que l'intensité est plus forte et l'étendue plus restreinte, mais étant donné que le fond présente une intensité plus faible et une plus vaste étendue … Sur fond moyen de permanence une double action serait possible, vers le clair ainsi que vers le sombre. »[4]

Avec la *night house at daytime* Flavien choisit en pleine lumière de nous immerger dans l'obscurité. La nuit envahit tous les aspects de la composition de l'œuvre sous les lumières bien réglées de l'espace aux murs blancs où se distribuent les pièces. La maison est le scénario d'une fiction à laquelle ne se rattache aucun récit particulier, aucun drame. Elle sollicite autrement notre regard, adresse un autre volume scénographique, une scène intérieure dont la profondeur ne se mesure plus en dimensions métriques. « Trois cent soixante-cinq nuits sans les jours, bien massives, c'est ce que je souhaite aux haïsseurs de la nuit. »[5]

there are…

4 *Journal de Paul Klee de 1908*, n° 832, cité par Roman Jakobson, *L'art verbal des poètes-peintres*, op. cit., p. 160.
5 René Char, *Le nu perdu*, (Paris: Gallimard, 1971), p. 121.

4 Paul Klee quoted from Roman Jakobson, *On the Verbal Art of William Blake and Other Poet-Painters*, op. cit., p. 503.
5 René Char, *Le nu perdu* (Paris: Gallimard, 1971), p. 121, transl. by the author.

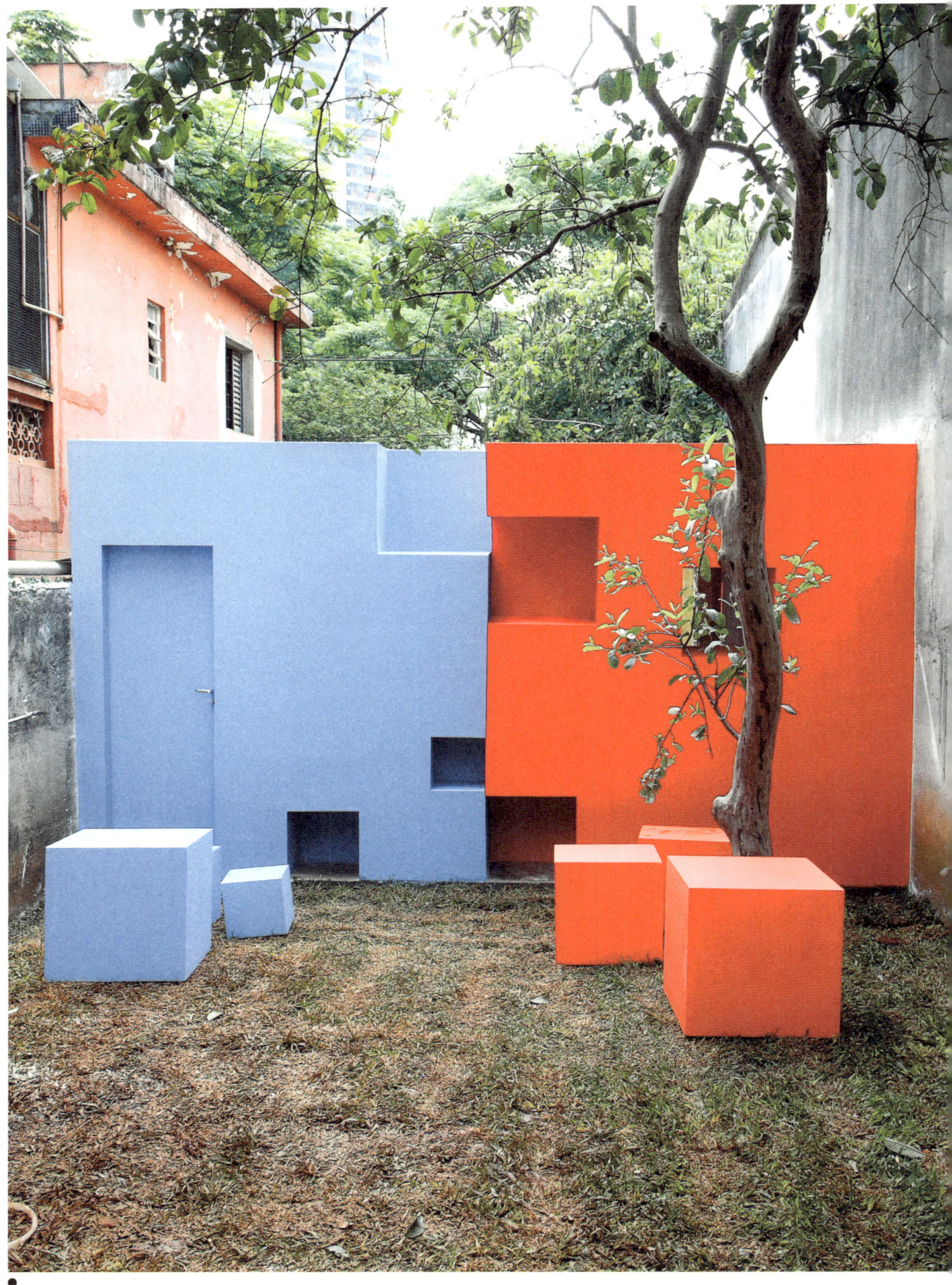

two persons house, south side, various materials, 2,4×4,65×4,55 m, 2010
"the house is in my hand"

63   two persons house

2010–2011
332–   –342 Rua Dr. Francisco Figueiredo Barreto,
05027-020 São Paulo

The *two persons house* was produced upon invitation by Capacete for the São Paulo Art Biennial in 2010. It was built in Carla Zaccagnini's garden. Two Devonian Press books were produced to accompany this project, as well as a set of written dialogues, filmed dialogues, and installations of objects and furniture that were exhibited independently. For one week in 2011, I lived in the house with Helmut Batista. We invited guests for dinner every night.

The *two persons house* is a house for two persons: person A and person B. The space between the two persons, which is also the space of their dialogue, constructs the space of the house. Each space more or less covers the other. As a result, the space fragments itself into a multitude of cubes and mobile objects. These cubes shape the living space and insert themselves between the two persons. Each color—A's color and B's color—marks a chain of elements that includes the building, the seats, the beds, the bigger cubes as well as the smaller ones that fit into a pocket and are then lost. When the cubes are in my pocket, "I have my house in my pocket." If I lose the cubes, "I've lost the house." A and B modify one another's spaces by speech, by conversation, by dialogue, and materially by displacing the cubes: displacing a word in a phrase or a cube in the house, replying to the other or obstructing a red window with a blue cube.

The house has two facades. Each gives out onto the part of the garden that it occupies and cuts it in half. The address of the house is the interval between two street numbers: 332 and 342.

La *two persons house* a été conçu à la suite d'une invitation de Capacete dans le cadre de la Biennale de São Paulo en 2010. Elle fut bâtie sur le jardin privé de la maison de Carla Zaccagnini. Deux livres de Devonian Press ont été produits à sa suite, ainsi qu'une série de dialogues écrits, de dialogues filmés et d'arrangements d'objets, lesquels ont été exposés indépendamment. Pendant une semaine en 2011, j'y ai habité avec Helmut Batista. Chaque soirée était l'occasion d'un diner avec plusieurs invités.

La *two persons house* est une maison pour deux personnes: personne A et personne B. L'espace entre deux personnes, qui est aussi l'espace du dialogue, construit l'espace de la maison. Chaque espace recouvre plus ou moins l'autre. Pour se faire, cet espace se fragmente en une multitude de cubes et d'objets mobiles, ces cubes façonnent l'espace habitable et s'immiscent entre les deux personnes. Chaque couleur, la couleur de A et la couleur de B, marque une chaine d'éléments comprenant aussi bien le bâtiment, que les sièges, les lits, les grands cubes et ceux petits qui entrent dans la poche et sont perdus ensuite. Quand les cubes sont dans ma poche «j'ai la maison dans ma poche», si je perds les cubes «j'ai perdu la maison». Chacun modifie l'espace de l'autre par la parole, la conversation, le dialogue, et matériellement en déplaçant les cubes; déplacer un mot dans une phrase, ou un cube dans la maison, répliquer à l'autre ou obstruer la fenêtre rouge par un cube bleu.

La maison a deux façades, chacune donnant sur une partie du jardin qu'elle occupe et coupe par le milieu. L'adresse de la maison est l'intervalle entre deux numéros de rue, le 332 et le 342.

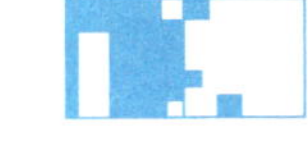

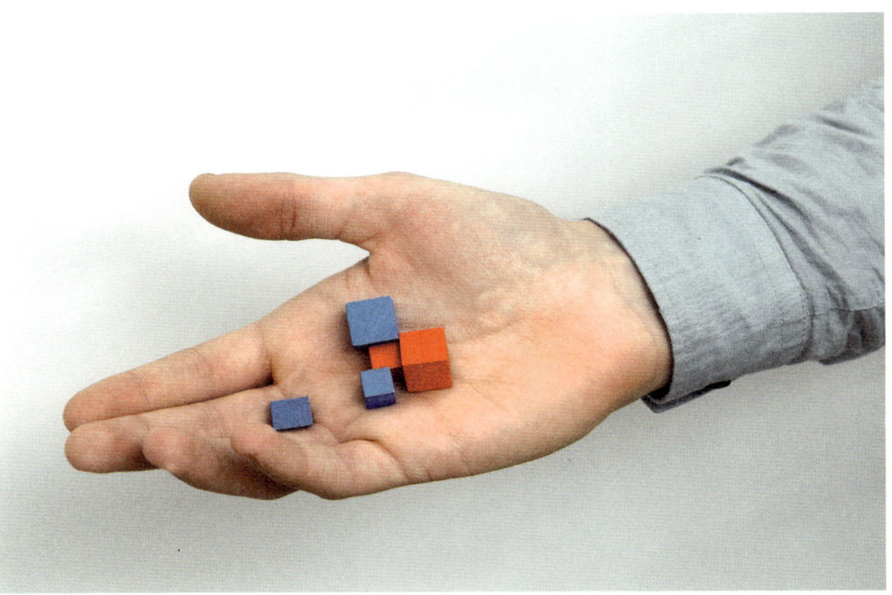

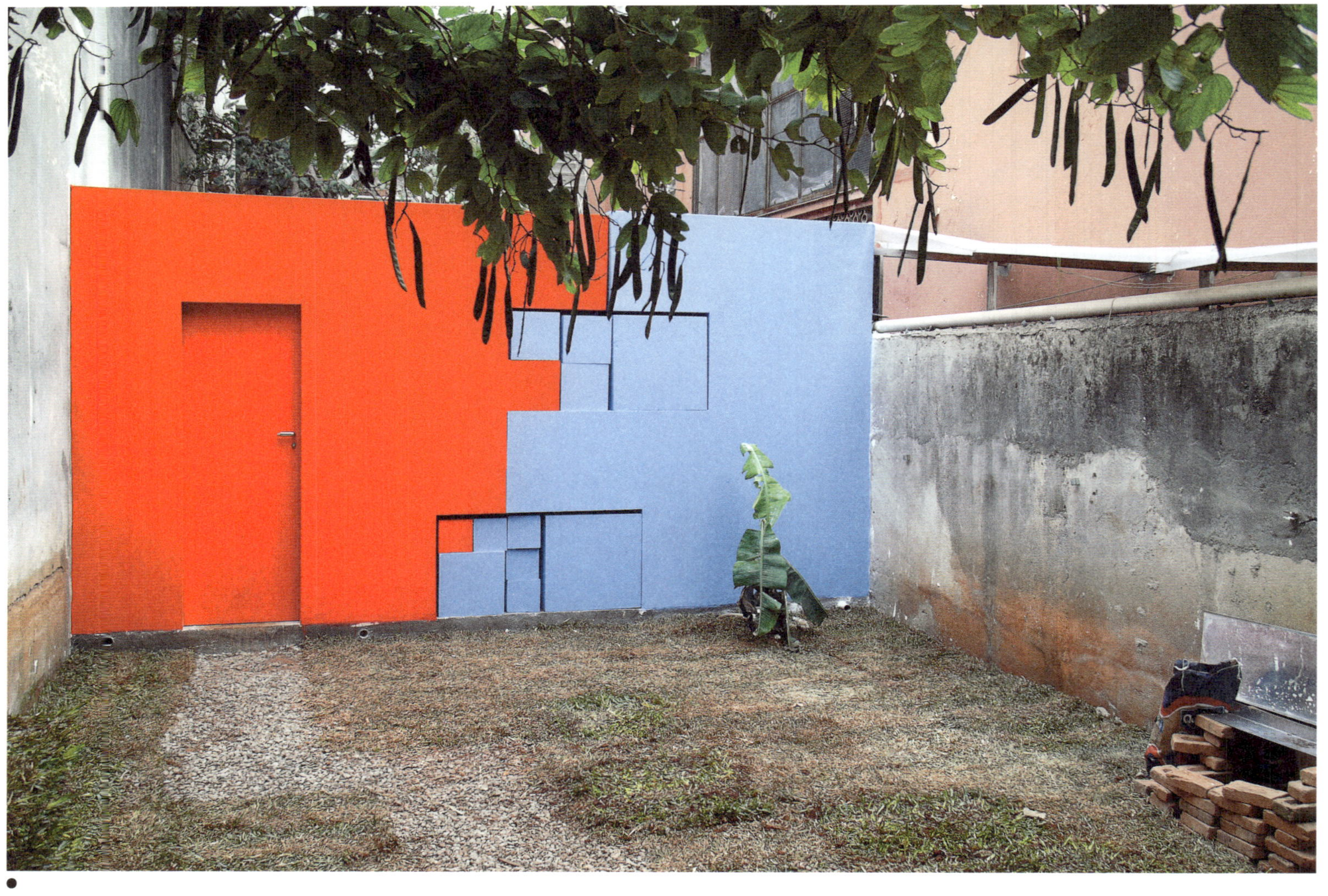

two persons house, north side

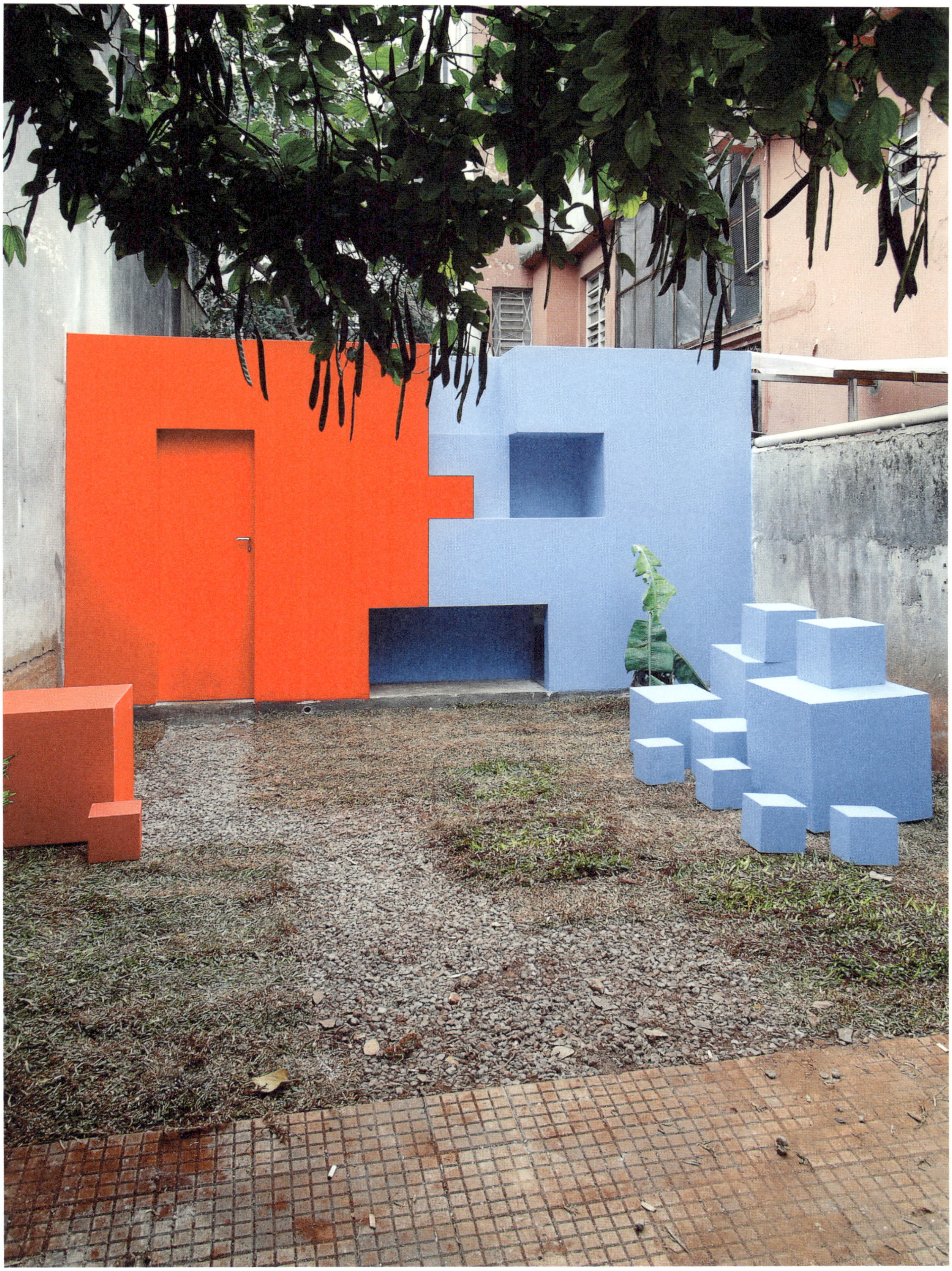

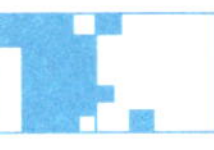

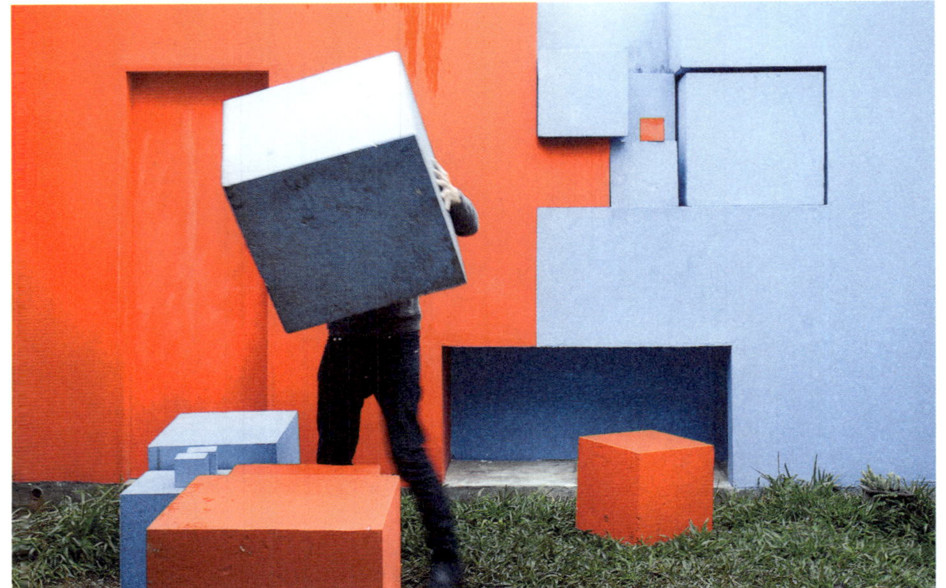

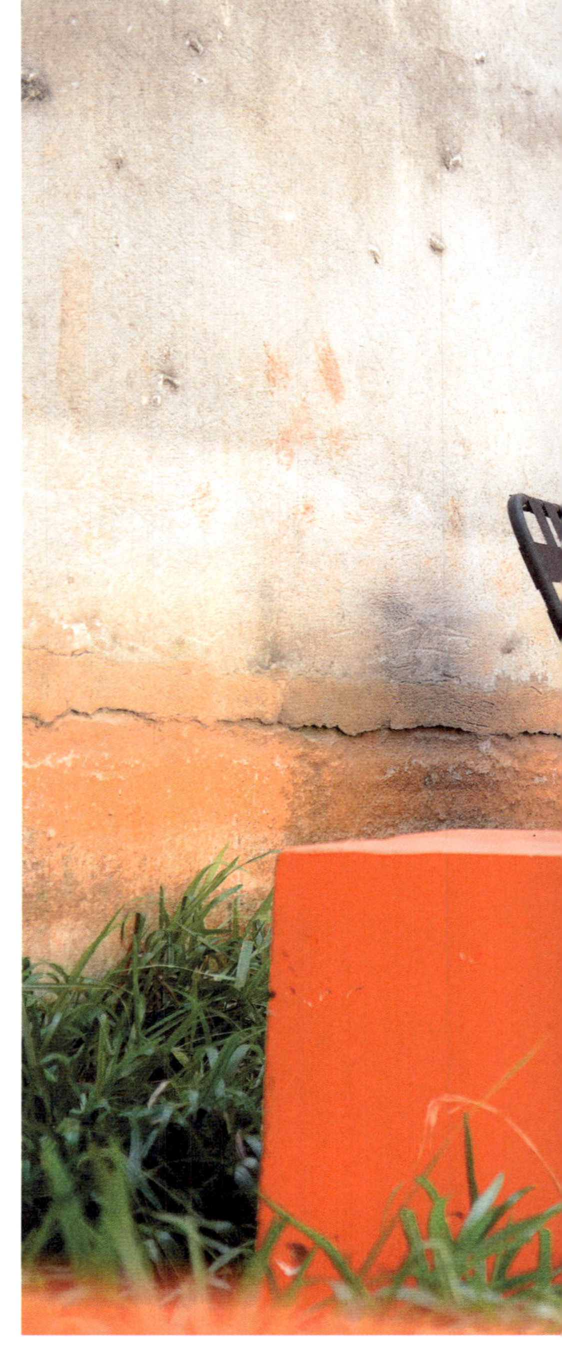

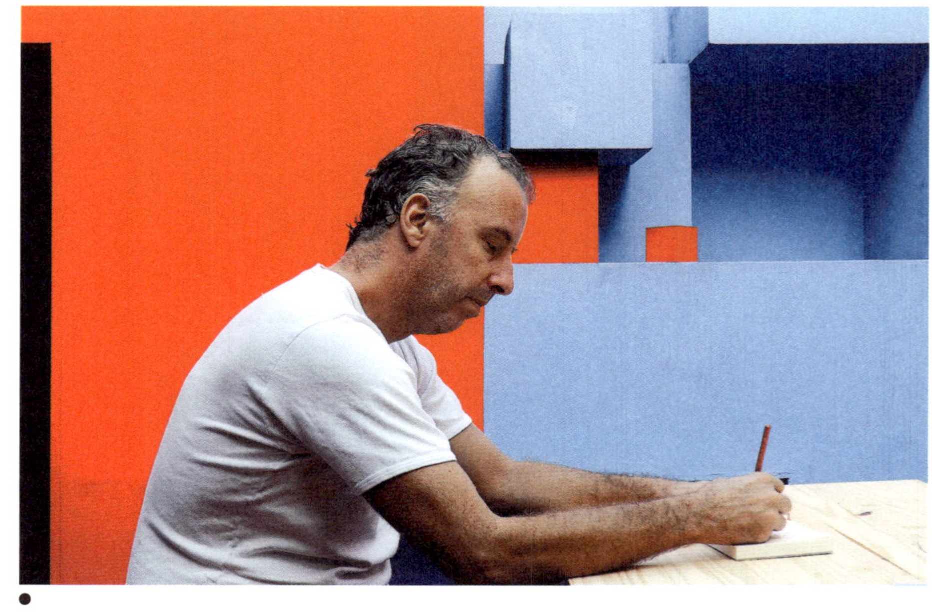

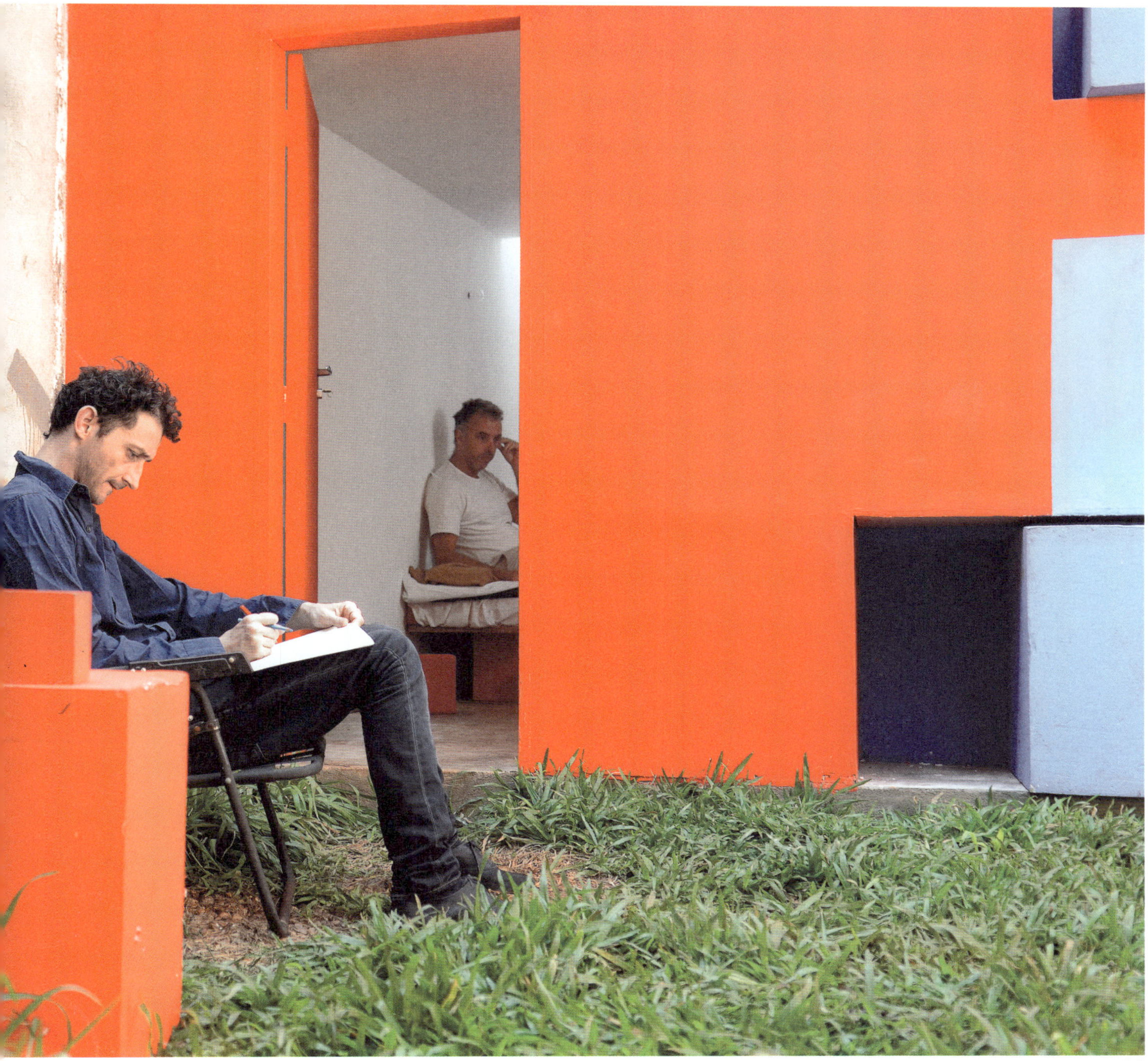

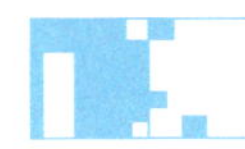

● Helmut Batista (person A) writing for the *two persons house*, 2011
●● Jean-Pascal Flavien (person B) writing for the *two persons house*, 2011
●●● *re- two persons house*, Devonian Press, 40 pages, 29,7 × 21,5 cm, 2013 (next spread)

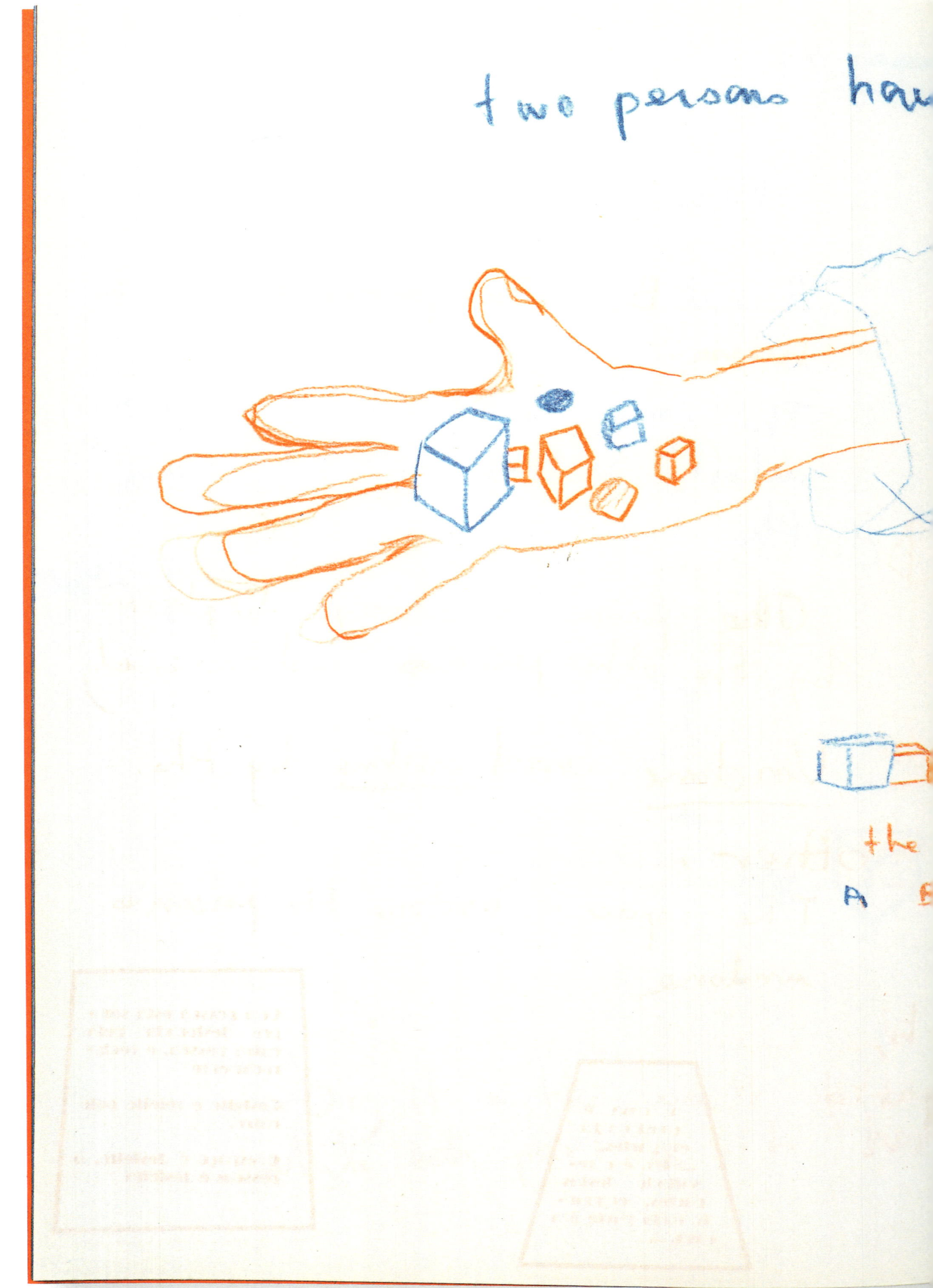

two persons hau
the
A B

principle

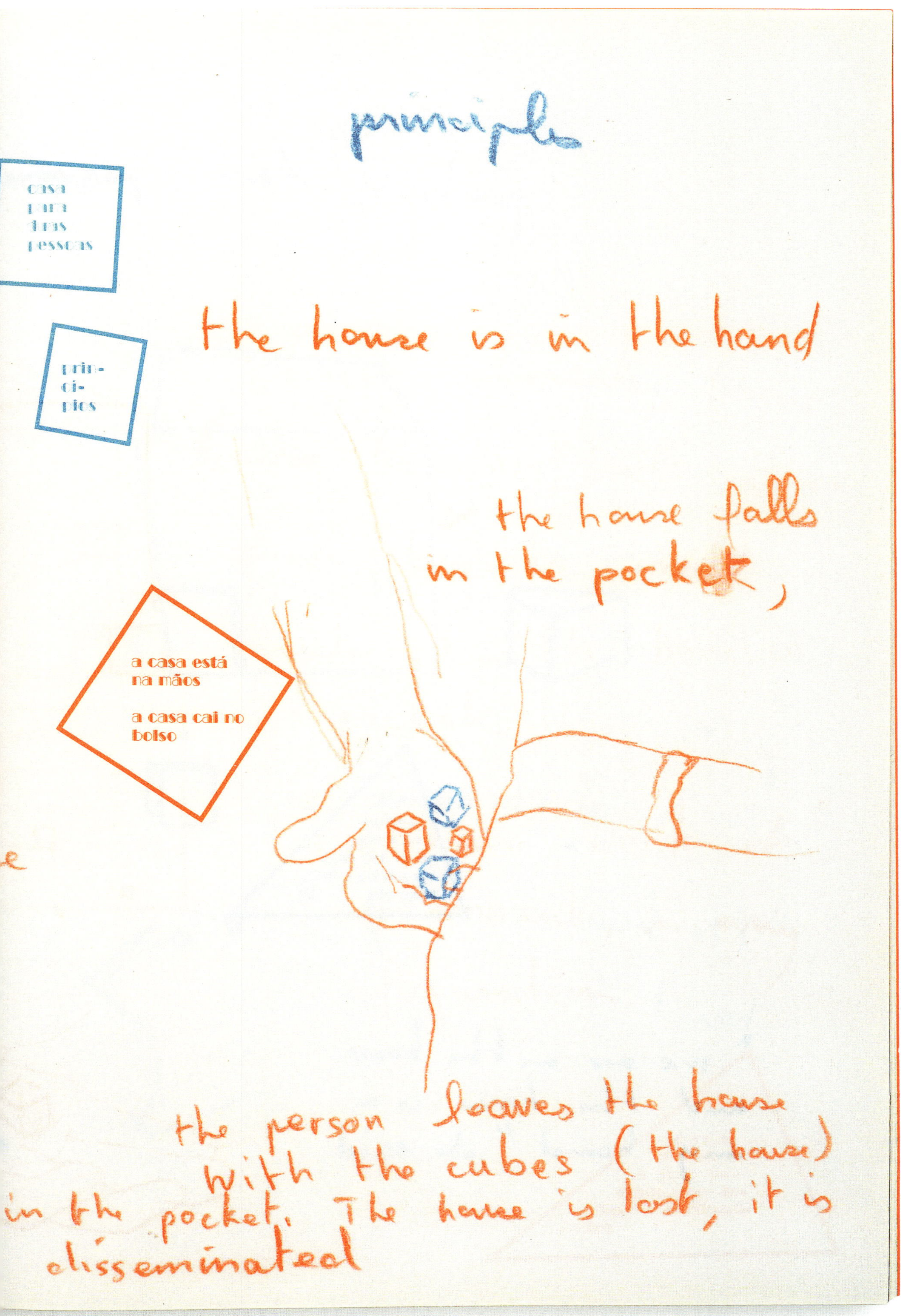

the house is in the hand

the house falls
in the pocket,

the person leaves the house
with the cubes (the house)
in the pocket. The house is lost, it is
disseminated

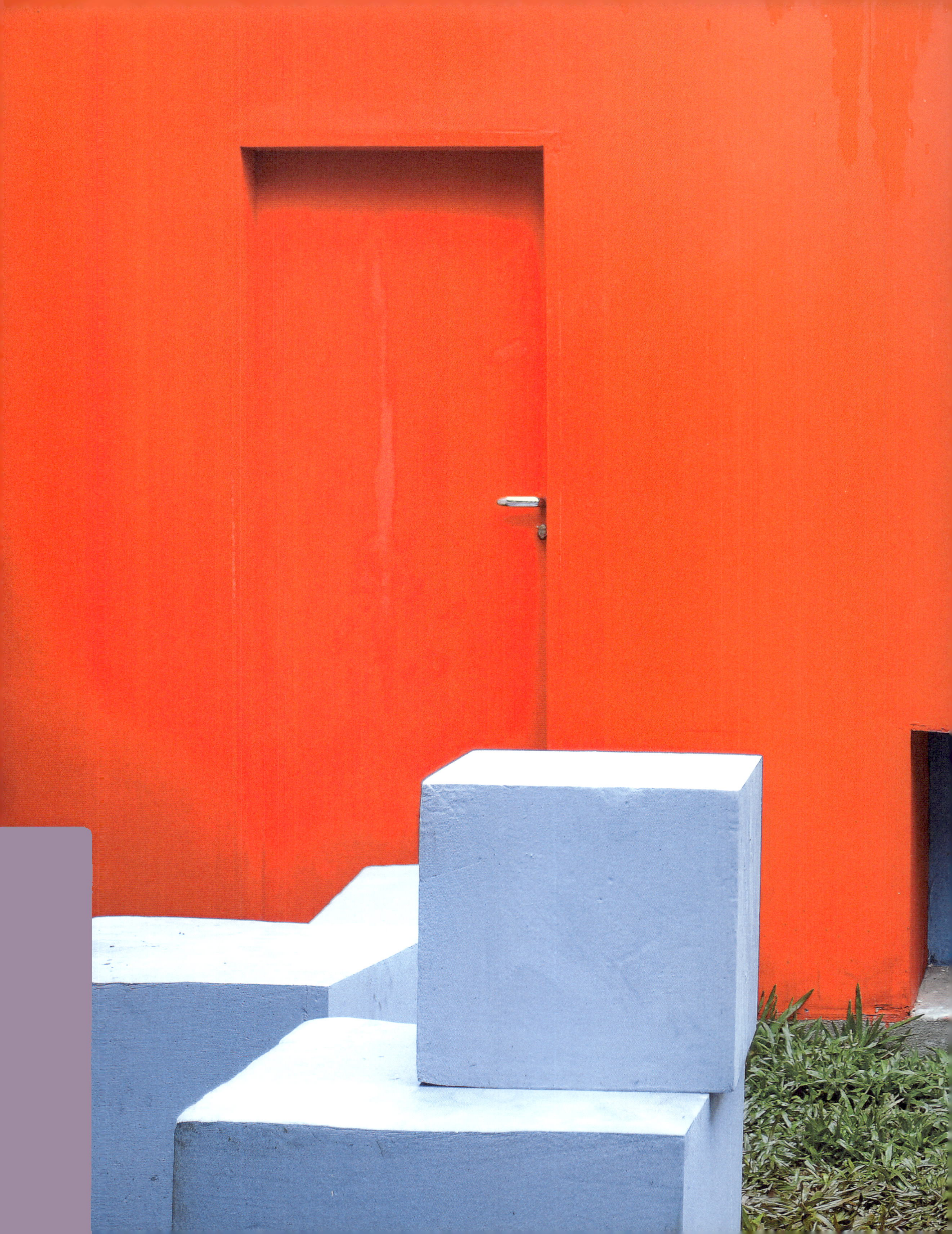

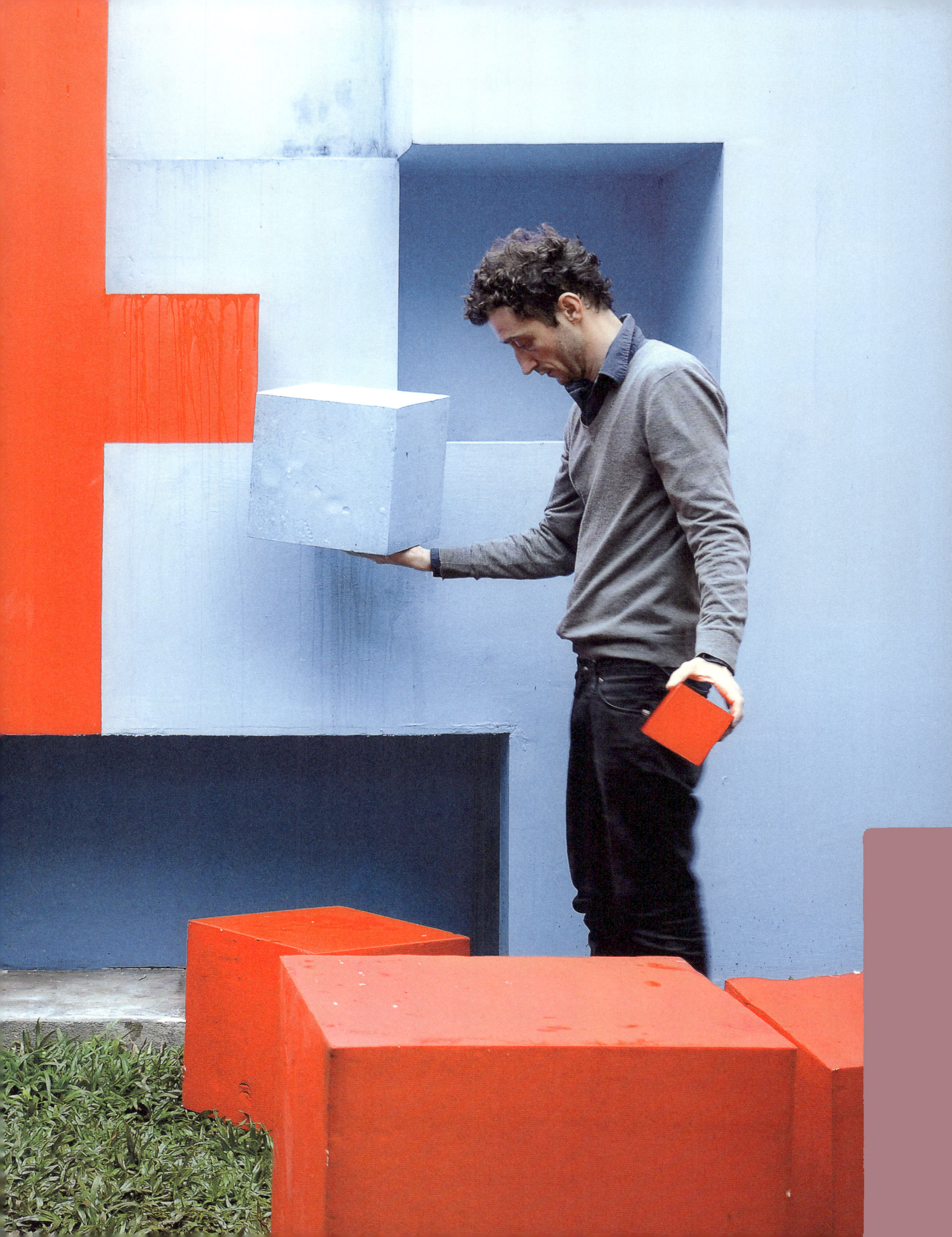

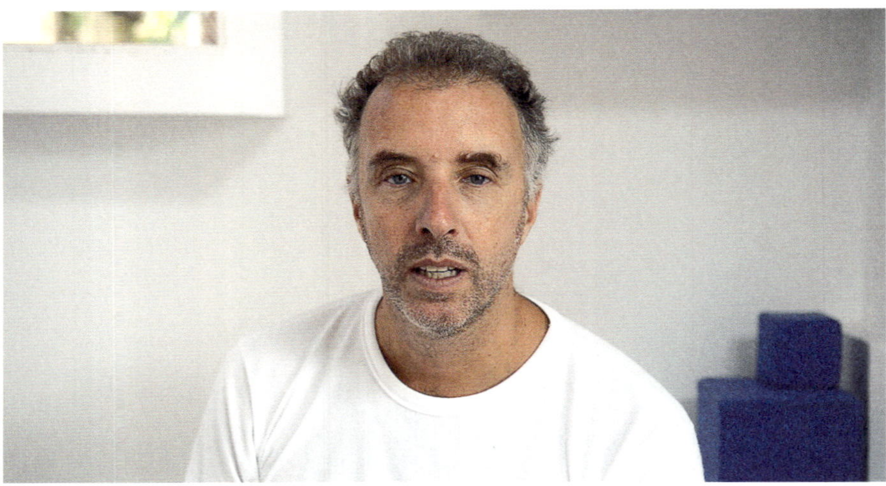

"I go get the newspaper"

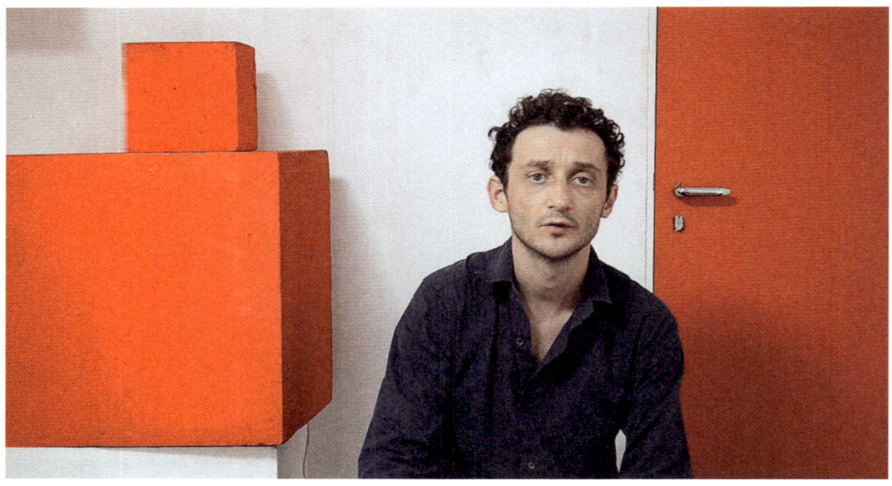

"I wait"

● Video stills from *new dialogue (05)*, 29 sec., 2011
●● Interior view of *two persons house*

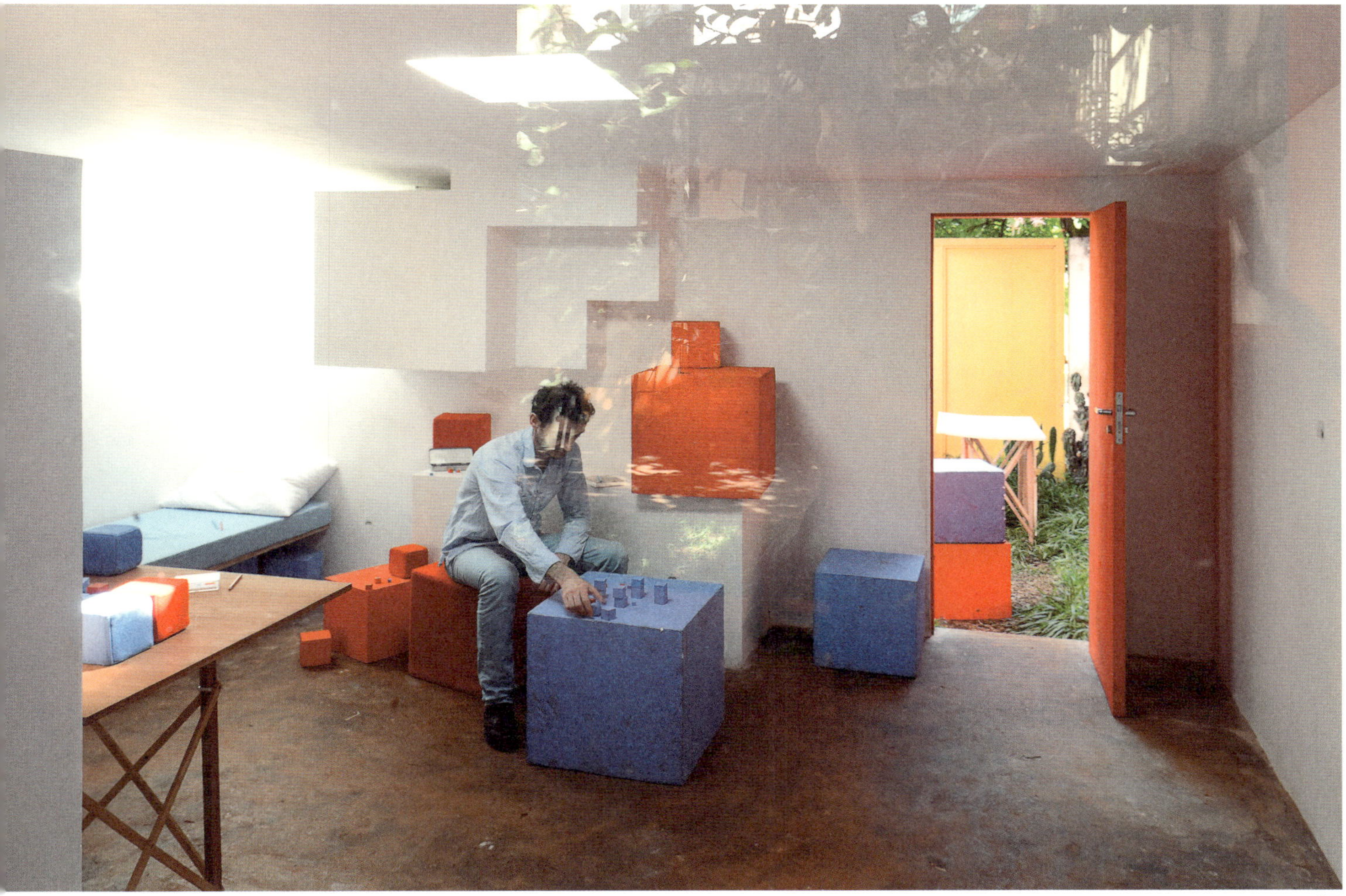

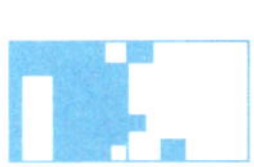

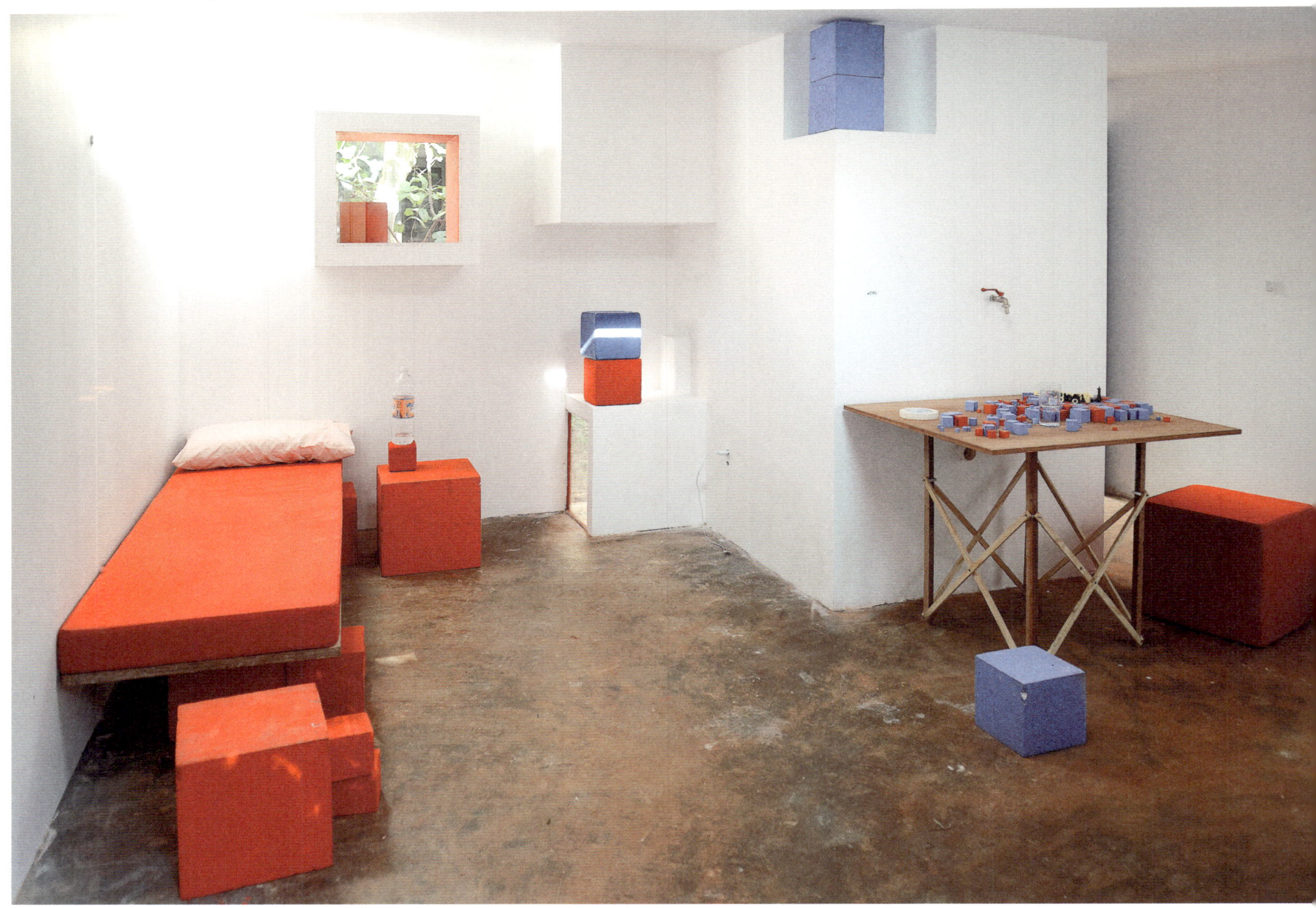

●   Interior view of *two persons house*
●● Exhibition view from *two persons house*, Galerie Michel Rein, 2010:
arrangement (cube, model, chair), painted wood, fabric, foam, various dimensions, 2010

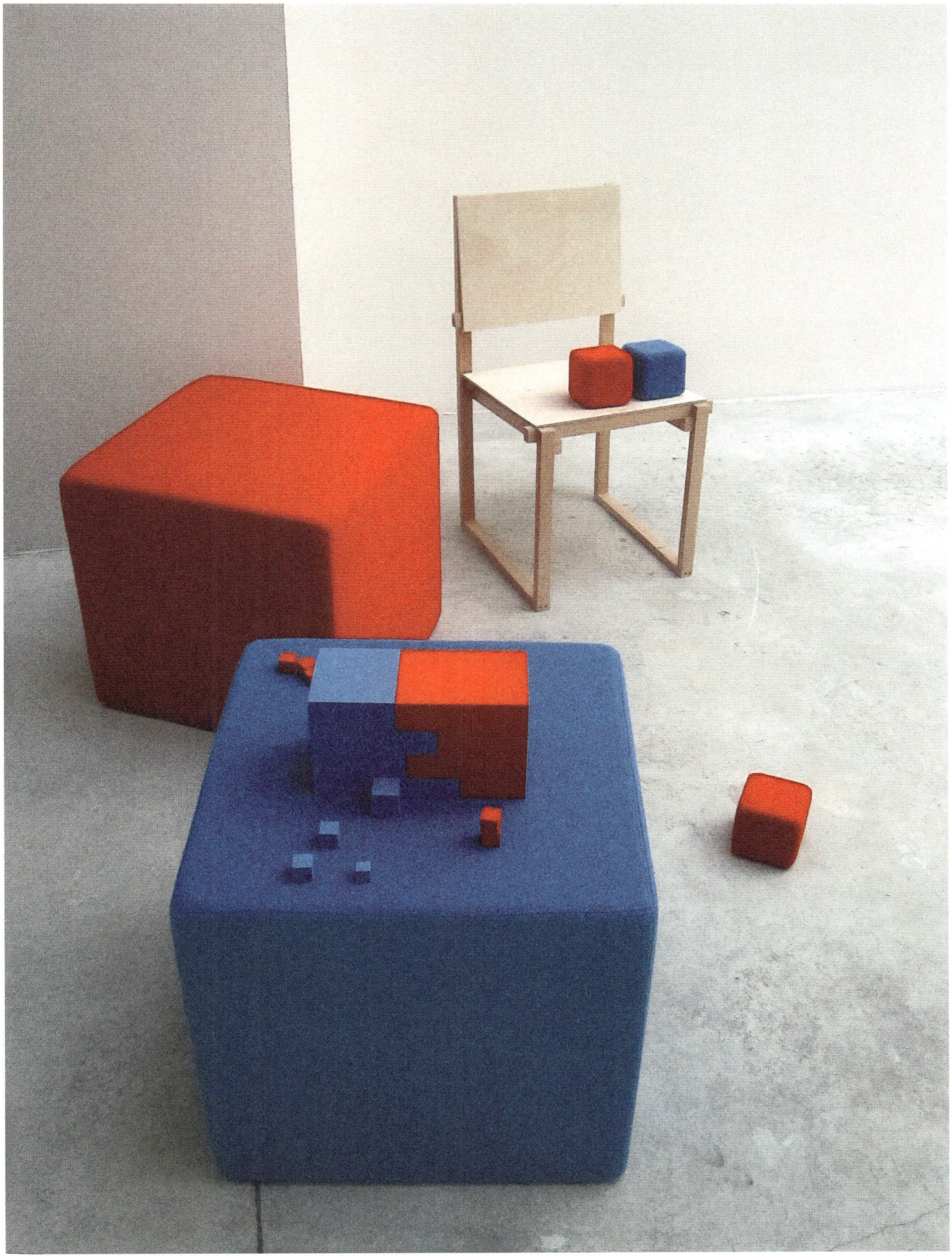

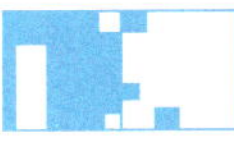

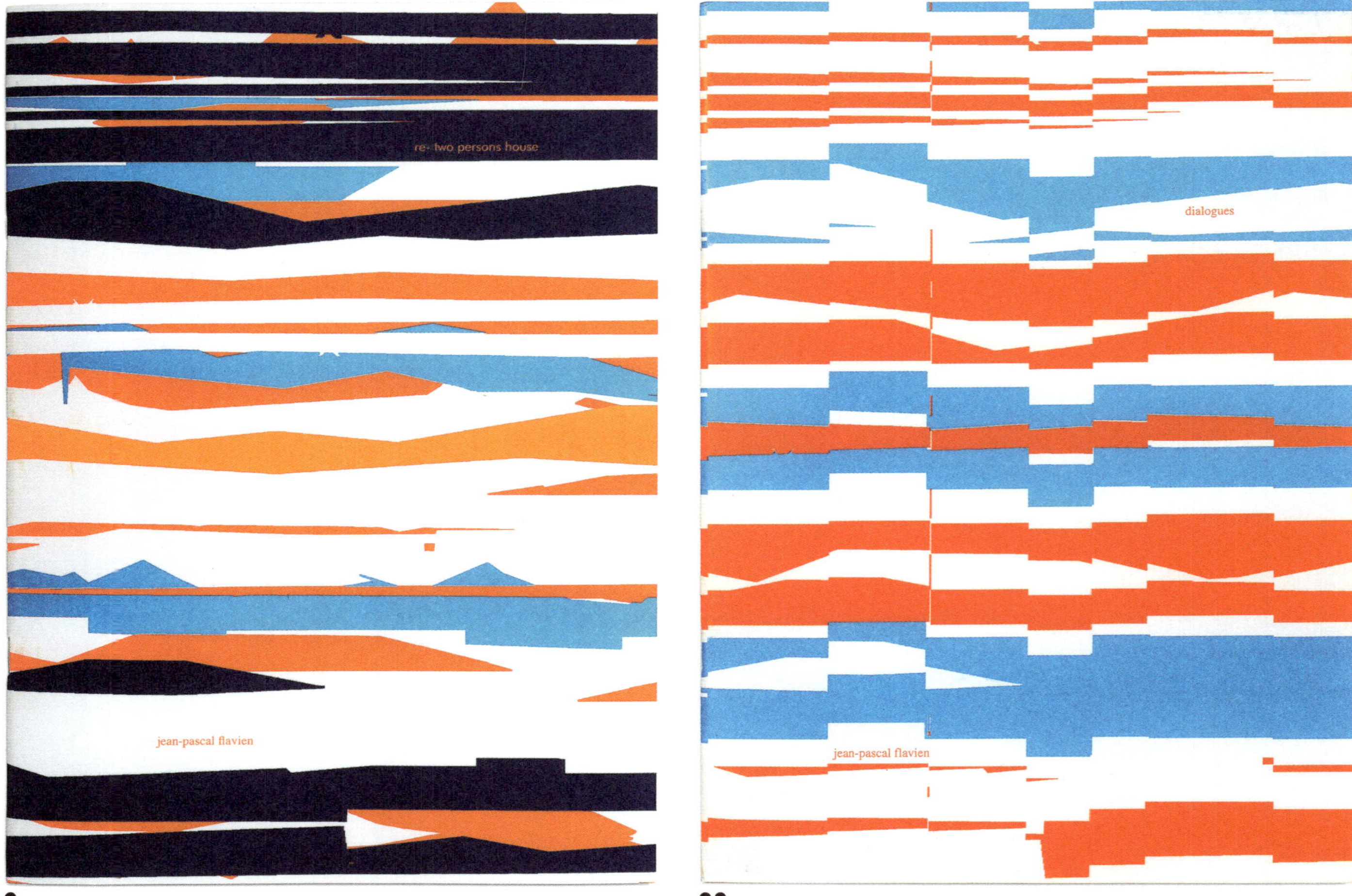

person

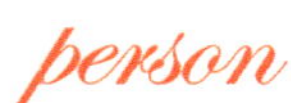

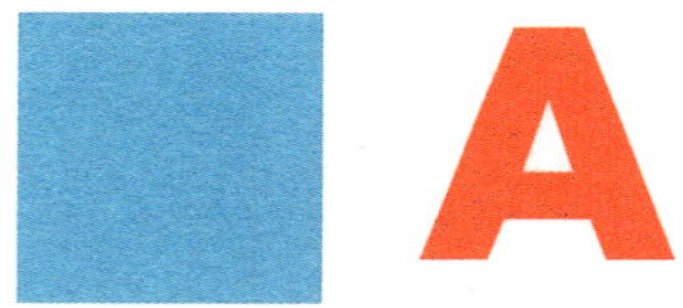

person

dialogue

- who would you prefer to be ? you or
  me ? I'd go for me if I were you
- the trouble about you is...
- don't worry yourself about me
- that's exactly...
- you see !

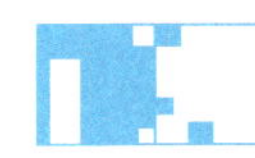

••••

• Cover of *re- two persons house*, Devonian Press, 40 pages, 29,7×21,5 cm, 2013
•• Cover of *dialogues*, Devonian Press, 48 pages, 29,7×21,5 cm, 2013
••• Business cards, *person A* and *person B*, inkjet print, each 5,5×8,8 cm, 2010
•••• *Dialogue 04*, A4-size, 2010

ein haus...

a house...

A house as an exhibit in which one can live and that breathes through its sliding walls. Such a house, independent of its material form, is always also a metaphor. Not in the sense of a constructed utopia or an idea that has become form, but as an expression of space and being in terms of the mode of its presentation. If breathing means that oxygen diffuses through the inner surface of the lungs and is delivered to tissues and cells, and carbon dioxide is duly removed from cells and ultimately exhaled, then we are talking about a complex process of transformation. The *breathing house* is based on the exchange between inside and outside, the revocation of certain juxtaposed opposites still accepted as realities (such as the opposition between private and public spaces, cultural and utilitarian spaces, leisure and the work spaces[1]), as well as upon processes of activation and latency within a precisely engineered form. It provides a scenario that changes situationally, recontextualizing itself and reacting to the viewer, whom we should think of as the occupant: the person who responds to the house. In this regard, the *breathing house* proposes a spatially realized conception of migrating ideas, such as the transparency between a collective notion of public and private (private understood here to mean a temporary refuge from the public), between what is exhibited and what is exposed.

It evokes associations with various artistic experiments involving constructed living. It calls to mind different typologies of houses, as well as of other types of both public and private spaces. However, it also eludes easy categorization of any kind. It is certainly not a sculpture, because you can and are supposed to work, live and sleep in the *breathing house*. External similarities with Gerrit Rietveld's buildings and the De Stijl circle do indeed exist, but they are by no means decisive factors. On the other hand, the fact that the sliding walls recall El Lissitzky's *Abstract Cabinet* is more obvious. This artwork, designed in 1927 for the Landesmuseum Hannover, provided a physical, conceptual dwelling for abstract art which was not only a vehicle for its exhibition, but also activated it via the museum visitor, thereby creating a direct link to life in modernity. Lamella-like walls that changed from grey to white to black when spectators passed in front of them and sliding panels that partially concealed the artworks on display transformed the *Abstract Cabinet* into a demonstrative space for dealing with contemporary art, thus placing the viewer, who had

1   Michel Foucault commences his argument with juxtapositions and pairings of opposites in his article *Of Other Spaces: Utopias and Heterotopias*. In: Neil Leach, ed., *Rethinking Architecture: A Reader in Cultural Theory* (New York: Routledge, 1997), pp. 330–36. Foucault speaks of a "veiled sacredness" of these opposites, which we still take for granted despite the fact that a theoretical desanctification of space has occurred.

Ein Haus, das ein Exponat ist, in dem man wohnen kann und das über seine verschiebbaren Wände atmet – ein solches Haus ist unabhängig von seiner materiellen Manifestation stets auch eine Metapher. Nicht im Sinne einer gebauten Utopie oder einer Form gewordenen Idee, sondern in Bezug auf eine durch die Art und Weise, wie es sich präsentiert, zum Ausdruck gebrachte Vorstellung von Raum und Sein. Wenn Atmung bedeutet, dass Sauerstoff durch die innere Lungenoberfläche diffundiert, zum Gewebe und den Zellen weitergeleitet und dass Kohlenstoffdioxid aus diesen Zellen geleitet und schließlich ausgeatmet wird, sprechen wir von einem komplexen Prozess der Transformation. Auch das *breathing house* basiert auf dem Austausch von Innen und Außen, der Aufkündigung bestimmter Entgegensetzungen, die noch immer als Gegebenheiten akzeptiert sind (privater und gesellschaftlicher Raum, kultureller und nützlicher Raum, Raum der Freizeit und Raum der Arbeit[1]), sowie der Aktivierung und der Latenz innerhalb einer präzise konstruierten Form. Es liefert ein Szenario, das sich situativ verändert, neu kontextualisiert und auf den Betrachter, den wir uns als Bewohner denken sollten, reagiert, so wie dieser auf das Haus reagiert. Das *breathing house* ist insofern vor allem eine räumlich realisierte Vorstellung migrierender Ideen, der Transparenz zwischen einem als kollektiv gedachten Öffentlichen und dem sich temporär aus diesem zurückziehenden Privaten, dem Ausstellen und dem Exponiertsein.

Es ruft verschiedene Assoziationen an künstlerische Experimente mit gebautem (Wohn-) Raum hervor, entzieht sich zugleich jedoch jeder einfachen Kategorisierung. Es ist ganz gewiss keine Skulptur, denn man kann und soll im *breathing house* leben und arbeiten, wohnen und schlafen. Äußere Ähnlichkeiten mit Bauten Gerrit Rietvelds und des De Stijl Umkreises sind zwar vorhanden, aber nicht entscheidend. Dass die verschiebbaren Wände eine Erinnerung an El Lissitzkys *Kabinett der Abstrakten* für das Landesmuseum Hannover hervorrufen, jene 1927 konzipierte Behausung abstrakter Kunst, die diese nicht nur ausstellte, sondern über den Museumsbesucher aktivierte und damit einen unmittelbaren Bezug zum Leben in der Moderne selbst herstellte, ist hingegen intendiert. Lamellenartige Wände und verschiebbare Paneele verwandelten das *Kabinett der Abstrakten* in einen Demonstrationsraum für den Umgang mit zeitgenössischer Kunst ebenso wie für die Aktivierung des bislang vor allem als kontemplativ gedachten Betrachters. Das *Kabinett der Abstrakten* war ein intimer

1   Diese Entgegensetzung bildet den Auftakt von Michel Foucaults Argumentation in *Andere Räume*, in: *Aisthesis. Wahrnehmung heute oder Perspektiven einer anderen Ästhetik*, hg. von Karlheinz Barck, Peter Gente, Heidi Paris, Stefan Richter, (Leipzig: Reclam, 1990), S. 34–46. Foucault spricht von einer „stummen Sakralisierung" dieser Gegensätze, die noch immer akzeptiert sind, gleichwohl es eine theoretische Entsakralisierung des Raumes gegeben hat.

a house…

until then been prescribed a far more contemplative role, in a more active position. The *Abstract Cabinet* was an intimate space that created a context for the works on display, exposing their radical difference from other artworks in the collection of the Landesmuseum. The exhibited works were geared towards nothing less than the resolution of the strict separation between art and life, their interpenetration even, by means of the revolutionary energy, which was the very hallmark of Constructivist art, a revolutionary energy that had fled the sphere of purely esthetic innovation. For El Lissitzky, the *Abstract Cabinet* was a demonstration model for the potential of contemporary art.[2] The *breathing house* is in turn a space of demonstration for the potential of a new experience of the seemingly quotidian along the axis of working and sleeping, and thus those elemental categories in which our differentiated present still allows itself to be summarized. Like the *Abstract Cabinet*, Jean-Pascal Flavien's houses are responses to a given situation that can only develop their potential through spatial shifts on the part of the visitor or occupant.

The *breathing house* seems thus to be a design which has become real and in turn exemplifies something. The aspect of breathing might conjure up the idea of a house which expands and then contracts, deriving its transformative potential from this temporary expansion. One might call it a kind of *Alice in Wonderland* house, but it could also be a house which is itself a breathing body, adjusting itself to the rhythm of its respective occupants, opening and closing and modifying its shape. It could be asleep or awake, working or dreaming, and might thus not embody a set of conditions so much as create situations that correspond to different activities—or perhaps we should even speak of conditions?—without simply conforming to different needs. Ultimately, the *breathing house* doesn't symbolize the doctrines of functionalism, but instead embodies latent activities and situations.

The furniture of the *breathing house* belongs to the house, and relates to its spatial shell as a word relates to a sentence. You can vary the syntax but the sense is preserved. The chair can sit by the side of the bed, the table can move towards the stool, or vice versa. However, if a different vocabulary is used with the same syntax, only the form itself

2 "With every movement of the spectator in the room the impression of the walls changes—what was white becomes black and vice versa. Thus an optical dynamic is generated as a consequence of the human stride. This makes the spectator active. ... He is physically compelled to come to terms with the exhibited objects." El Lissitzky, *Exhibition Rooms*. Typescript, in: *Die Zwanziger Jahre in Hannover* (Hannover: Kunstverein Hannover, 1962). Quoted from Céline Condorelli, ed., *Support Structures* (Berlin: Sternberg Press, 2009), p. 251.

Raum, der für die gezeigten Werke ein Umfeld schaffte, das ihre radikale Differenz zu den anderen Kunstwerken aus der Sammlung des Landesmuseums exponierte. Die präsentierten Werke intendierten selbst nichts weniger als die Auflösung der strikten Trennung von Kunst und Leben, die Durchdringung beider durch die den Bereich allein ästhetischer Innovation weit hinter sich lassende revolutionäre Energie, die vor allem den konstruktivistischen Arbeiten anhaftete. Das *Kabinett der Abstrakten* war für Lissitzky ein Demonstrationsraum für das Potenzial zeitgenössischer Kunst.[2] Das *breathing house* wiederum ist ein Demonstrationsraum für das Potenzial einer neuen Erfahrung des scheinbar Alltäglichen entlang von Leben, Arbeiten und Schlafen, und damit jener elementaren Kategorien, in denen sich selbst noch unsere ausdifferenzierte Gegenwart fassen lässt. Wie das *Kabinett der Abstrakten* sind die Häuser von Jean-Pascal Flavien Reaktionen auf eine gegebene Situation, die erst in der Aktivierung und der Geste räumlicher Verschiebungen durch den Besucher/Bewohner ihr Potenzial entfaltet.

Das *breathing house* erscheint damit wie ein real gewordener Entwurf, der etwas exemplifiziert. Die Vorstellung des Atmens ließe abstrakt betrachtet die Idee eines Hauses aufkommen, das sich ausdehnt und dann wieder zusammenzieht und aus dieser temporären Expansion sein transformatives Potenzial gewinnt. In gewisser Weise wäre das ein *Alice im Wunderland* Haus. Es könnte aber auch ein Haus sein, das selbst ein atmender Körper ist und sich dem Rhythmus seines jeweiligen Bewohners anpasst, sich öffnet und schließt und seine Form modifiziert. Es könnte schlafen oder wach sein, arbeiten oder träumen und verkörperte insofern weniger Zustände als es Situationen schaffte, die mit unterschiedlichen Aktivitäten – oder sollten wir vielleicht sogar von Zuständen sprechen? – korrespondieren, ohne sich einfach nur unterschiedlichen Bedürfnissen anzupassen. Das *breathing house* versinnbildlicht schließlich keine Doktrinen des Funktionalismus, sondern verkörpert Aktivitäten und Situationen in Latenz.

Es ist ein Haus mit einem Mobiliar, das sich zu seiner Raumhülle verhält wie ein Wort zu einem Satz. Man kann die Syntax variieren und die Bedeutung bleibt erhalten. Der Stuhl kann stehen wo das Bett steht, der Tisch zu dem Hocker rücken oder umgekehrt. Wenn man jedoch bei gleicher Syntax ein anderes Vokabular wählte, bliebe nur die Form erhalten, so wie jedes Haus ein Bett, einen Tisch und

2 „With every movement of the spectator in the room the impression of the walls changes—what was white becomes black and vice versa. Thus an optical dynamic is generated as a consequence of the human stride. This makes the spectator active. ... He is physically compelled to come to terms with the exhibited objects." El Lissitzky, *Exhibition Rooms*, Typoskript in: *Die Zwanziger Jahre in Hannover* (Hannover: Kunstverein Hannover, 1962). Zitiert nach: Céline Condorelli (Hg.), *Support Structures* (Berlin: Sternberg Press, 2009). S. 251.

remains, in the same way that every house can be said to have a bed, a table and chairs, regardless of how they are arranged. The *breathing house* is thus based on an inherent systematization, a parataxis, which develops its own grammar of living, whereby living isn't meant as a form of furnishing, but rather as a form of temporary presence in a particular place. This home is therefore not a solitary structure which could be built anywhere. Rather, it is part of an exhibition concept, in which an exchange of ideas, options, and proposals takes place for dealing with what is given, what is on hand. The night-time furniture of the house—the bed, the bedside stool—was on view during the day in the exhibition space, thus highlighting what had been put at rest in the house. Meanwhile, the house was also able to expand into the institution when one of the invited houseguests moved her table there in order to work.

Although the *breathing house* appears at first sight to be a dwelling for individual use, it is in essence a constructed manifestation that showcases the social aspect as an elementary function of our society. It is defined as a private space in order to enable another form of being-in-public for the potential inhabitant. Theoretically, in the *breathing house*, one could cut oneself off from the outside world, but it would then be more like a meteorite in the park, alien and inaccessible. By being there, the *breathing house* actually invites us to relate to its environment, and establish a connection with the models of other potential houses exhibited in the museum, in order to reflect back onto these scenarios of social and intellectual interaction. Seen in this way, the adjustable rooms of the *breathing house* are paths and trails that lead back from the public sphere and exhibition space to the house itself. As a result, both the exhibition and the house change into semi-public, in-between spheres that, interrupted by different thresholds, constitute a space which refuses to be either an exterior or a finite interior.

If there is one spatial concept which has emphatically influenced thinking in terms of space as a sphere of the social, it is the concept of heterotopia introduced by Michel Foucault. We live in a complex set of relationships "that define positions which cannot be equated or in any way superimposed." However, within these relationships there are arrangements "that are endowed with the curious property of being in relation with all the others, but in such a way as to suspend, neutralize, or invert the set of relationships designed, reflected, or mirrored by themselves."[3]

Spaces that distinguish themselves in this way are those "real and effective spaces which are outlined in the very institution of society, but which constitute a sort of counter arrangement, of effectively realized utopia, in which all

Stühle besitzt. Das *breathing house* basiert insofern auf einer inhärenten Systematisierung, einer Parataxe, die ihre eigene Grammatik des Wohnens entwickelt, wobei Wohnen nicht eine Form des sich Einrichtens meint, sondern eine Form temporärer Präsenz an einem bestimmten Ort. Dieses Haus ist deshalb auch kein Solitär, der überall errichtet werden könnte. Es ist vielmehr Teil eines Ausstellungskonzeptes, bei dem ein Austausch von Ideen, von Optionen, von Vorschlägen des Umgangs mit dem Gegebenen stattfand. Das nächtliche Mobiliar des Hauses – das Bett, der Hocker, ein Stuhl – war tagsüber im Innenraum der Institution zu sehen und brachte zur Anschauung, was im Haus deaktiviert war. Gleichzeitig konnte das Haus in den institutionellen Innenraum expandieren, wenn der Bewohner dort seinen Tisch aufstellte, um zu arbeiten.

Auch wenn es sich auf den ersten Blick um eine Behausung für den individuellen Gebrauch handelt, ist das *breathing house* im Kern eine gebaute Manifestation, die das Soziale als eine elementare Funktion unserer Gesellschaft zur Schau stellt. Sie lokalisiert sich im privaten Raum, um dem potentiellen Bewohner eine andere Form des In-der-Öffentlichkeit-Seins zu ermöglichen. Theoretisch könnte man sich im *breathing house* von der Außenwelt abschotten, aber dann ähnelte es einem Meteoriten im Park, fremd und unzugänglich. Tatsächlich lädt es bereits über sein bloßes Da-Sein zum Austausch mit seiner Umgebung ein. Es stellt eine Verbindung mit den im institutionellen Innenraum gezeigten Modellen anderer potentieller Häuser und anderem Mobiliar her, um seine reale Präsenz in diese Möglichkeitsszenarien sozialer wie intellektueller Interaktion zurückzuspielen. Die variablen Räume des *breathing house* sind so betrachtet Pfade und Spuren, die vom öffentlichen und Ausstellungsraum ausgehend zu ihm zurückführen. Dadurch verwandeln sich sowohl Ausstellung als auch Haus in Sphären des Halböffentlichen, des Dazwischen, die, von unterschiedlichen Schwellen unterbrochen, einen Raum konstituieren, der weder Außenraum noch finiter Innenraum sein will.

Wenn es ein räumliches Konzept gibt, welches das Denken in Bezug auf Raum als Sphäre des Sozialen nachdrücklich beeinflusst hat, dann ist dies der von Michel Foucault eingeführte Begriff der Heterotopie. Wir leben in einer Gemengelage von Beziehungen, „die Platzierungen definieren, die nicht aufeinander zurückzuführen und nicht miteinander zu vereinen sind." Innerhalb dieser gibt es jedoch Platzierungen, die „die sonderbare Eigenschaft haben, sich auf alle anderen Platzierungen zu beziehen, aber so, dass sie die von diesen bezeichneten oder reflektierten Verhältnisse suspendieren, neutralisieren oder umkehren."[3] Solcherart sich auszeichnende Orte sind „wirkliche Orte, wirksame Orte, die in die Einrichtung der Gesellschaft hineingezeichnet sind,

a house...

3 Michel Foucault, a.a.O., S. 38.

3 Michel Foucault, op. cit., p. 332.

the real arrangements, all the other real arrangements that can be found within society, are at one and the same time represented, challenged, and overturned: a sort of place that lies outside all places and yet is actually localizable."[4] The spatial spectrum of heterotopias is broad and includes youth clubs, nursing and rest homes, as well as psychiatric hospitals, prisons, barracks and cemeteries, but also theatres, cinemas, museums and libraries, gardens and colonies. These are spaces that are not readily accessible to everyone, some of which are even subject to strict regulations. However, some heterotopias also actuate reflection and critical engagement with given norms and expectations by virtue of their discernible alterity. Heterotopias also differ structurally from other spaces because they are able to combine several essentially incompatible spaces within a single location and place them in relation to one another. They are structured differently from ordinary spaces, they require a different kind of behavior, and widen, partially at least, the scope for imagining another world. In view of this, can't the *breathing house* be considered a heterotopic space? It is, after all, a building situated in a park, alongside an art institution. It can be visited as part of the exhibition, it can even be seen as an extension of the exhibition, while also remaining a functional living space, actuated as such only when someone lives inside of it, and activates and adapts its structure and furniture to their specific needs.

But how does this relate to the remark made at the outset that, like all of Jean-Pascal Flavien's houses, the *breathing house* is a metaphor? Indeed, the structure of each of these very different spatial configurations, sketched out in the models, follows a principle which assigns a quality to a given house, or suggests a specific relationship to be adopted by their inhabitants. With respect to the conceptual framework of the house as a sphere of social interaction between people and architecture, this may entail a delimitation, while nevertheless articulating existential traits in its endorsement of certain modalities of living, of behavior, and of movement within the defined environment of each of his houses.

If we assume that spaces create limitations that are made visible on a physical level by their occupants, then behaviors, perceptions, and physical sensations might prove to be determined by these spatial structures. In architecture, the interior structure of the building extrapolates the relationship between individuals as well as that of the individual to himself as is a possibility for development and as an instance of self-perception. On the other hand, the exterior of a building stages and affirms the ideas and functions which have produced these social and psychological spatializations

sozusagen Gegenplatzierungen oder Widerlager, tatsächlich realisierte Utopien, in denen die wirklichen Plätze innerhalb der Kultur gleichzeitig repräsentiert, bestritten und gewendet sind, gewissermaßen Orte außerhalb aller Orte, wiewohl sie tatsächlich geortet werden können."[4] Das räumliche Spektrum der Heterotopien ist breit und umfasst Jugend-, Alten- und Erholungsheime ebenso wie psychiatrische Kliniken, Gefängnisse, Kasernen und Friedhöfe, aber auch Theater und Kinos, Museen und Bibliotheken, Gärten und Kolonien. Es sind Orte, die nicht für jeden jederzeit zugänglich sind, die teilweise sogar strikten Reglementierungen unterworfen sind. Manche Heterotopien animieren jedoch durch ihre erkennbare Alterität auch zur Reflexion und Problematisierung gegebener Normen und Erwartungen. Auch in ihrer Struktur differieren Heterotopien von anderen Räumen, denn sie sind in der Lage, mehrere, eigentlich unvereinbare Räume an einem einzigen Ort zu vereinen und zueinander in Beziehung zu setzen. Sie sind anders strukturiert als die üblichen Orte, verlangen ein anderes Agieren, und eröffnen zumindest zum Teil Freiräume zur Imagination einer anderen Welt. Wäre das *breathing house*, das zum Centre d'art contemporain du Parc Saint Léger gehörende, in einem Park liegende Gebäude, in dem man auf Einladung wohnen, das man während der Öffnungszeiten des Centre d'art besichtigen kann, das mit diesem eine eigenwillige Symbiose bildet, und das sich durch eine Struktur auszeichnet, die erst in der Aktivierung durch den Bewohner und seine jeweilige funktionale Adaption des Mobiliars zur Artikulation findet, so betrachtet nicht durchaus ein heterotoper Ort?

Doch wie verhält sich diese Einordnung zu der anfangs gemachten Bemerkung, das *breathing house* – wie eigentlich alle Häuser Jean-Pascal Flaviens – sei eine Metapher? Tatsächlich folgt die Struktur der jeweils sehr unterschiedlichen, skizzenhaft im Modell visualisierten räumlichen Konfigurationen einem Prinzip, das einem Haus eine Eigenschaft zuweist oder den Bewohnern des Hauses eine ganz bestimmte Beziehung zu diesem nahe legt. Diese kann in Bezug auf die Vorstellung des Hauses als Sphäre sozialer Interaktion zwischen Mensch und Architektur durchaus etwas Limitierendes haben, bringt in ihrer Forcierung einer bestimmten Art des Verhaltens, der Bewegung, des Lebens in einer solchermaßen definierten Umgebung jedoch existenzielle Züge des Seins zum Ausdruck.

Wenn wir davon ausgehen, dass Räume Eingrenzungen mit sich bringen, die als Konstitution des Subjekts im Raum auf physischer Ebene weiter transportiert werden, erweisen sich Verhaltensweisen, Wahrnehmungen und körperliche Empfindungen entsprechend als von diesen räumlichen Strukturen determiniert. In Architekturen schreibt sich im

---

4 Ebd., S. 39.

---

on the inside, as a normative instance. In the *breathing house*, but also in the *no drama house* (an extremely narrow building whose furniture was designed to interact, sometimes awkwardly, with its confines), these normative instances have been deliberately suspended. They achieve this by starting from the fundamental difference between the interior or inside of the house, and its exterior or outside. This differentiation between inside and outside confirms and facilitates our orientation in both types of spaces. However, there are spaces, and this includes those designed by Flavien, that develop an interiority without completely becoming an interior, defining a kind of threshold to the outside without abandoning the idea of the outside as something collective and undifferentiated. Space and the place itself develop here via the subject's movements in space, and the activation of the space with the furniture, as well as through their associated activities. However, the paradigm of private space and internalization does not give way to an uncontrolled opening up to the outside, but rather affirms the idea of the collective exterior space through a form of exchange, which can be read as a mediation between different spheres, such as a permeable space and its surroundings, or a living space and an exhibition space. Ultimately, it is about spatial configurations that facilitate a multiplicity of interstitial and transitional spaces, irrespective of the constraints of architectural functional thinking. Although there are doors, there is no place that clearly defines the boundaries of the private. Instead, there is a repertoire of half-public and semi-private places, places for dwelling and working, sleeping and living that transform the house into a climatic envelope that appears to be both a subject and an object at the same time: both a breathing extension of the ego and its dwelling.

This also implies the question—itself containing existential overtones—of what it means to live in such a place, that is to say, how life differs in this place as opposed to another place. As is the case when conducting an experiment, possibilities for interaction arise in relation to the furniture, the ways in which it can be put to use, which do not exist when the house is uninhabited. The occupant adjusts the house according to his personal criteria, which does not mean, however, that the uninhabited house does not exist when it is uninhabited. It is then (and this is indeed a striking parallel to El Lissitzky's *Abstract Cabinet*, which points to a context that unites art and life as the origin of these houses) merely a shell for a number of objects contained within it that are simply waiting to be used and recharged semantically in the course of that use. Of course, there is a bed on which to sleep, but during the day it may become a couch. You could put the mattress on the floor and look at the room from a different perspective.

Interieur die bauliche Struktur als Beziehung zwischen den Individuen untereinander und zu sich selbst als Möglichkeit ihrer Entfaltung und als Selbstwahrnehmung fort. Im Exterieur inszeniert und affirmiert sie wiederum die Ideen und Funktionen, die diese sozialen und psychischen Verräumlichungen im Inneren hervorgebracht haben, als normative Instanz. Im *breathing house*, aber auch im *no drama house*, sind diese normativen Instanzen punktuell außer Kraft gesetzt. Das beginnt bereits mit einer fundamentalen Differenz, denn Raum und somit Haus werden üblicherweise als ein Innen definiert, das sich klar von einem Außen abgrenzt. Diese Differenzierung von Innen und Außen ermöglicht die Orientierung in Raum und Ort und bestätigt und vereinfacht die Positionierung derjenigen, die sich im Raum bewegen. Es gibt jedoch Räume, und dazu zählen die von Flavien entworfenen, die Innerlichkeit entwickeln, ohne vollständig zum Innenraum zu werden, und eine Schleuse zum Außenraum definieren, ohne die Vorstellung des Außen als etwas Kollektivem und Undifferenziertem aufzugeben. Raum und Ort entwickeln sich hier vielmehr anhand der Bewegung des Subjekts im Raum und der Aktivierung des Raumes durch das Mobiliar und die mit ihm verbundenen Aktivitäten. Dabei weicht das Paradigma des privaten Raumes und der Verinnerlichung jedoch nicht der unkontrollierten Öffnung nach Außen, sondern affirmiert vielmehr die Idee des kollektiven Außenraums durch eine Form von Austausch, die sich als Mediation zwischen verschiedenen Sphären lesen lässt – dem durchlässigen Raum und seiner Umgebung, dem Lebens- und Ausstellungsraum. Letztlich handelt es sich um räumliche Konfigurationen, die eine Vielzahl von Zwischenräumen und Übergängen unabhängig von den Zwängen architektonischen Funktionsdenkens ermöglichen. Obschon es Türen gibt, existiert kein Ort, der die Grenze des Privaten klar definiert. Stattdessen bildet sich ein Repertoire halböffentlicher wie halbprivater Orte, von Orten des Wohnens und des Arbeitens, des Schlafens und Lebens, die das Haus zu einer klimatischen Hülle erheben, die Subjekt und Objekt zugleich zu sein scheint: eine atmende Extension des Ich und seine Behausung zugleich.

Das impliziert auch die durchaus existenzialistisch zu verstehende Frage, was es bedeutet, an einem solchen Ort zu leben, das heißt, wie das Leben an diesem Ort von dem an einem möglichen anderen differiert. Wie in einer experimentellen Anordnung ergeben sich Möglichkeiten der Interaktion mit dem Mobiliar, den Funktionen, die es bietet, und des Austauschs zwischen den verschiedenen Sphären des Ausstellens und Ausgestellt-Seins. Der Bewohner aktiviert das Haus gewissermaßen nach seinen Maßstäben, was aber nicht heißt, dass das Haus im unbewohnten Zustand nicht existierte. Es ist dann nur (und das ist in der Tat eine auffällige Parallele zu Lissitzkys *Kabinett der Abs-*

a house...

And that brings us once more to the question of the metaphorical quality of the *breathing house*, which resists the atomism of purely conceptual language. Just as the furniture produces its own syntax, the walls generate their own rhythms, so too does the house as a whole elude unequivocal determination. It would seem best described by something like a modulation of sounds rather than by the syntactical differentiations of a sentence, in the same way that the forms of living, working and sleeping within such a house will repeatedly produce new narratives and modulations that will then resonate with its occupants or visitors, the seasons or the weather. Interestingly, in his thesis on the *other spaces* in our contemporary world, Foucault's structuralist way of thinking opens itself up towards Gaston Bachelard's seemingly antithetical topoanalysis in *The Poetics of Space*. This (implicit) connection is indeed significant, despite the consideration of Foucault's ideas in general as an alternative to more phenomenological interpretations of space. However, in an earlier version of his thesis on heterotopias, conceived as a radio broadcast, Foucault specifically highlighted the imaginative potential of "counter arrangements," further stressing their scope as the "greatest reserve of imagination:" "We do not live in a homogeneous and empty space, but in a space that is saturated with qualities, and that may even be pervaded by a spectral aura."[5] This verbalization of space as a space of the interior, as a space of the subject that responds to an external space, is perhaps the core of the *breathing house*: an intuitive charging of the manifestly given with qualities that can be described, but that also involve the experience and imagination of the viewer/occupants in ways that elude the teleology of language. As a vehicle for a non-self-reflexive and, productively speaking, incompatible "set of relations", the *breathing house* is endowed with a great and varied potential for articulation, not to be confused with that of an instruction manual. Rather, what it proposes are other possibilities of interaction with that which opens up to thought beyond architecture and space as realms of possibility for being and doing.

trakten, welche die Provenienz dieser Häuser aus einem Kunst und Leben verbindenden Kontext verrät) eine Hülle für eine Anzahl in ihm befindlicher Gegenstände, die darauf warten, benutzt zu werden und sich im Zuge dieser Benutzung mit einer jeweils neuen Semantik aufzuladen. Natürlich ist ein Bett zum Schlafen da, aber tagsüber ist es möglicherweise eine Couch. Man könnte die Matratze auch auf den Boden legen und den Raum aus einer anderen Perspektive betrachten.

Und damit wären wir erneut bei der Frage nach der metaphorischen Qualität des *breathing house*, das sich gegen den Atomismus einer rein begrifflichen Sprache wehrt. Wie die Möbel ihre eigene Syntax hervorbringen, die Wände ihre eigenen Rhythmen generieren, so entzieht sich auch das Haus als Ganzes einer eindeutigen Festschreibung. Es scheint durch verschiedene Modulationen des Klanges eher beschreibbar als durch ausdifferenzierte Satzstrukturen, so wie die Formen des Lebens, Arbeitens und Schlafens in ihm immer wieder neue Erzählungen und Modulationen hervorbringen werden in Resonanz auf die Bewohner, Besucher, die Jahreszeiten oder das Wetter. Interessanterweise öffnet sich die strukturalistische Denkweise Foucaults gerade in seinen Ausführungen zu den *anderen Räumen* unserer Gegenwart gegenüber einer eigentlich konträren Topo-Analyse, nämlich der von Gaston Bachelard in *Poetik des Raumes* beschriebenen. Diese (implizite) Anknüpfung ist durchaus bemerkenswert, gelten Foucaults Ausführungen im Allgemeinen doch als Gegenentwurf zu eher phänomenologischen Rauminterpretationen. Insbesondere in einer früheren, als Radiovortrag konzipierten Fassung des Textes zu den Heterotopien wird jedoch das imaginative Potenzial der *Gegenräume* hervorgehoben, ihr Potenzial als „Reservoir der Fantasie" betont: „Wir leben nicht in einem leeren oder homogenen Raum, sondern in einem Raum, der mit Qualitäten aufgeladen ist, der vielleicht auch von Phantasmen bevölkert ist."[5] Diese Versprachlichung des Raumes als ein Raum des Innen, als Raum des Subjets, der auf einen externen Raum reagiert, ist vielleicht der Kern des *breathing house*: eine intuitive Aufladung des manifest Gegebenen mit Qualitäten, die sich beschreiben lassen, aber auch Erfahrungen und Imaginationen der Betrachter wie der Bewohner involvieren, die sich der teleologischen Sprache entziehen. Als nicht aufeinander zurückzuführende und im produktiven Sinne inkompatible „Gemengelage von Platzierungen" verfügt das *breathing house* über ein Repertoire von Artikulationsmöglichkeiten, die nicht etwa als Handlungsanweisungen zu verstehen sind, sondern als Offerte eines anderen Umgangs mit dem, was sich jenseits von Architektur und Raum als Möglichkeitssphäre von Tun und Sein denken lässt.

5   Ebd., S. 37.

5   The texts and audio of the original radio broadcasts have now been published respectively in Michel Foucault, *Le corps utopique, Les hétérotopies* (Clamecy: Nouvelles Editions Lignes, 2009) and *Utopies et Hétérotopies* (Paris: INA Mémoire Vive, IMV056, 2004).

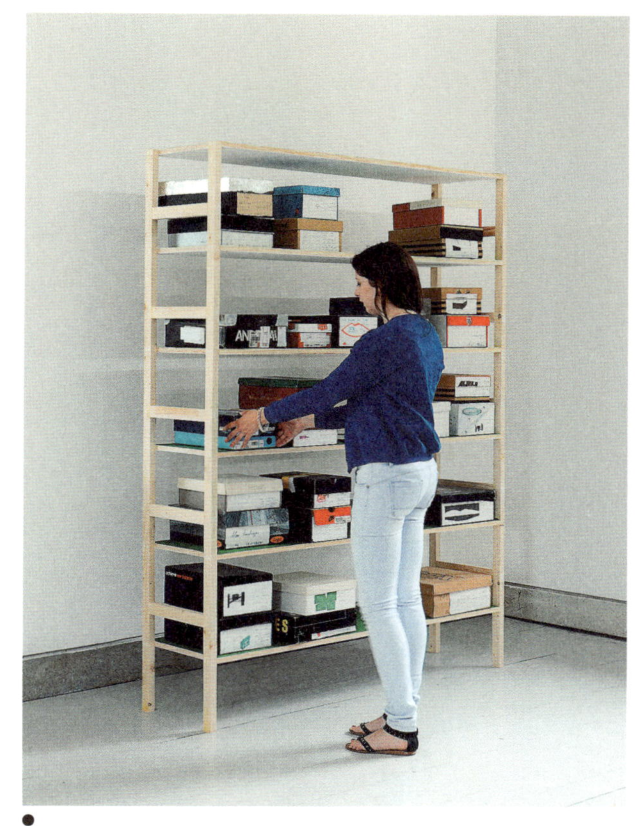

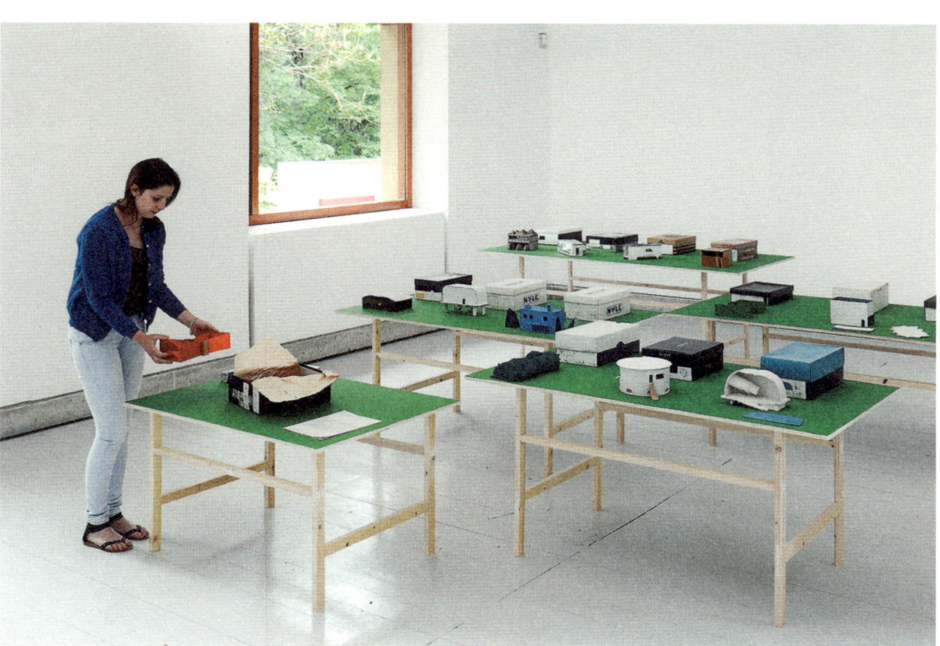

L.A. models, 44 models, various materials and dimensions, 1999–2002.
The models were shown upon demand in the exhibition
breathing house, la maison respire at the Parc Saint Léger, 2012

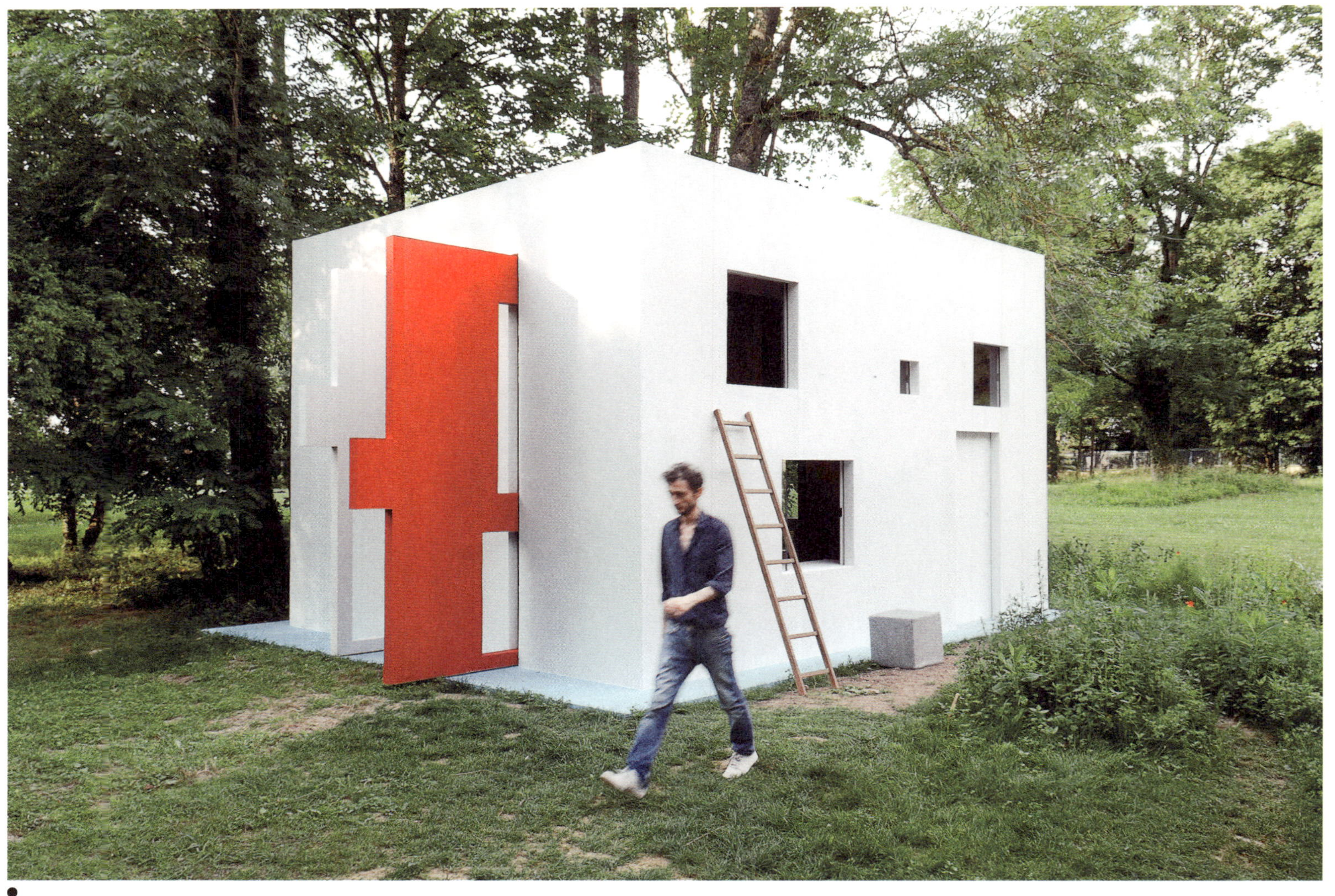

breathing house, Parc Saint Léger, various materials, 3,9 × 6,15 × 4,95 m, 2012

breathing house

2012–
Avenue Conti, Pougues-les-Eaux

The *breathing house* was built in the context of a solo exhibition at the Parc Saint Léger in France. Since then, twenty or so people have been invited by me to live in the house, and most of them have also contributed to a book of texts on the house. It was linked to two other exhibitions, one at Frieze London, the other at the Westfälischer Kunstverein in Münster.

The *breathing house* is a house that breathes. Breathing is the image that describes the relationship that it establishes with the exhibition space next to which it is placed. The exhibition is the extension of the *breathing house* and becomes the fourth living space by aligning itself with the three interior spaces of the house: the living, the sleeping, the working areas. These rooms are parallel and the semantic and architectural partitions that separate them are porous and have openings, allowing for circulation between them. The two interior walls of the house slide and come out of the building. The alignment of the openings changes, modifying the axes of passage. During the exhibition and after it, things and people go from one space to the next, they displace and replace themselves. At night, the daytime furniture—i.e. the table and chairs—were placed in the exhibition space. During the day they were replaced by the night-time furniture—i.e. the bed and the cube—unless the people living in the house crossed over and moved into the exhibition space during the day in order to work ... These are spaces for movements and breezes.

La *breathing house* fut construite dans le contexte d'une exposition personnelle au Parc Saint Léger en France. Depuis, à mon invitation, une vingtaine de personnes y ont habité, et la plupart ont contribué à un livre de textes sur l'habitation de cette maison. Elle fut liée à deux autres expositions, l'une à Frieze London et l'autre à la Westfälischer Kunstverein à Münster.

La *breathing house* est une maison qui respire. La respiration est l'image qui décrit la relation qu'elle établit avec le lieu d'exposition à coté duquel elle se place. L'exposition est l'extension de la *breathing house* et devient le quatrième espace habitable en s'alignant avec les trois espaces intérieurs de la maison; séjour, sommeil, travail. Ces espaces sont parallèles et les cloisons sémantiques et architecturales qui les séparent sont ajourées et poreuses, permettant une circulation facile. Les deux murs intérieurs de la maison coulissent et émergent du bâtiment. L'alignement des ouvertures change, modifie les axes de passage. Pendant la durée de l'exposition et au-delà de celle-ci, les choses, les personnes vont d'un espace à l'autre, elles se déplacent et se replacent. Pendant la nuit, les meubles de jour – c'est à dire, la table, les chaises – étaient placés dans la salle d'exposition. Et durant la journée, les meubles de nuit – le lit, le cube – y étaient déposés. À moins que ce ne soient les personnes habitant la maison qui les traversent, s'installent l'après-midi dans la salle d'exposition pour y travailler ... Ce sont des espaces de mouvements, de courants d'air.

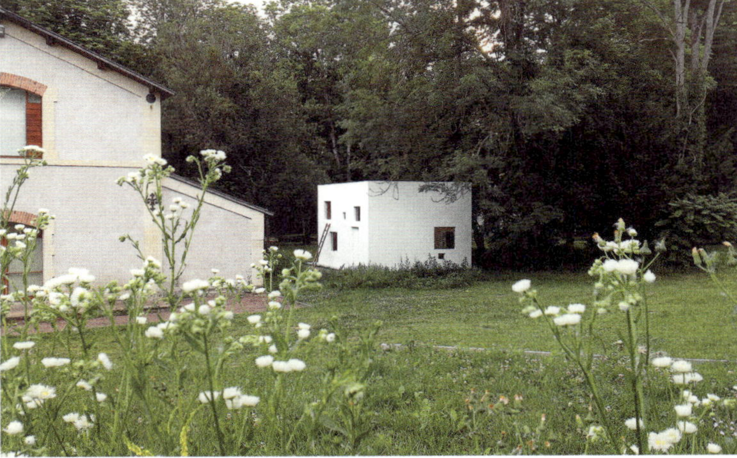

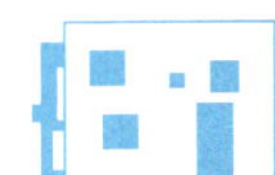

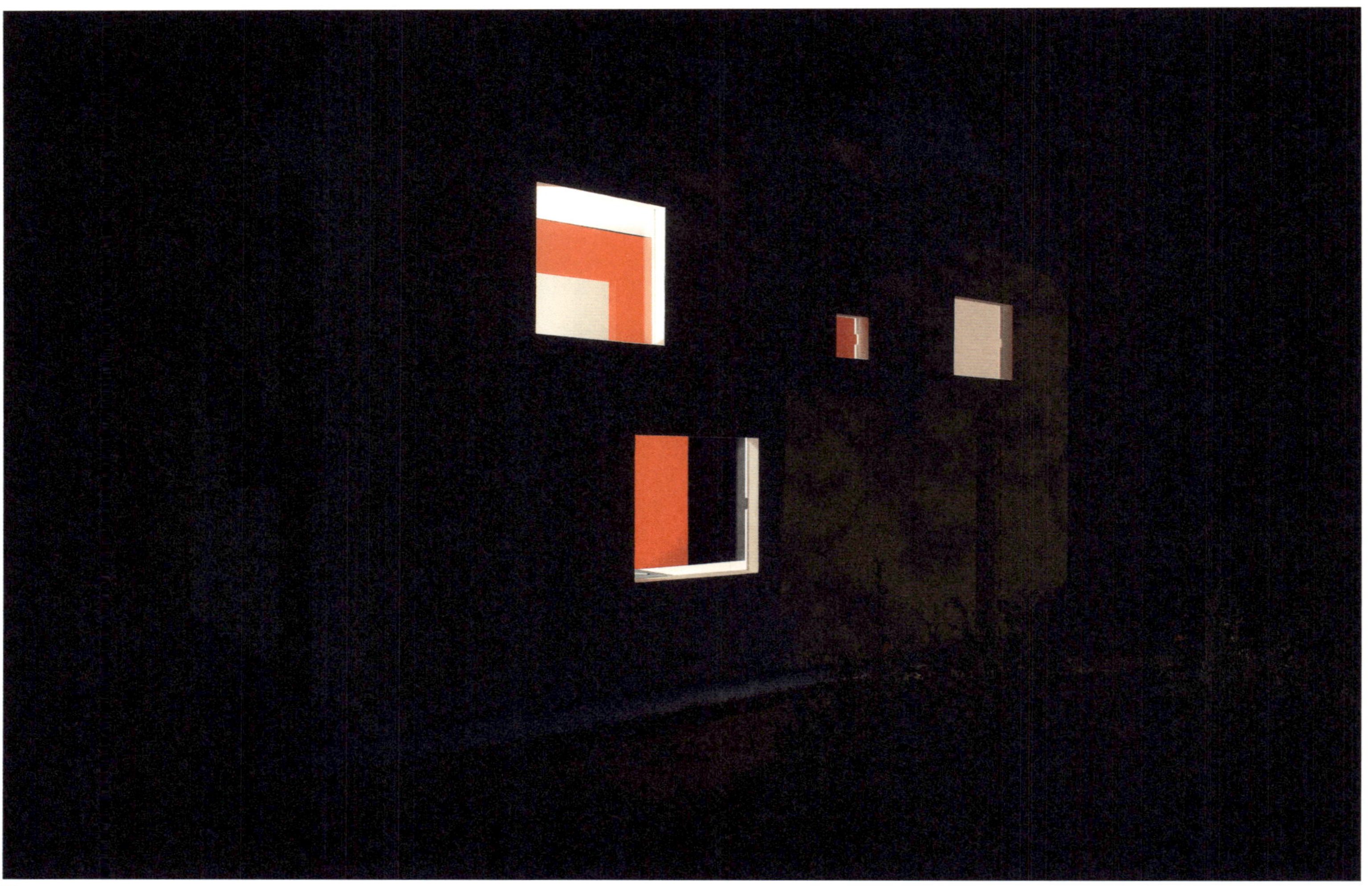

● Night view of the *breathing house*
●● Views of the shifts of the sliding walls of the *breathing house*

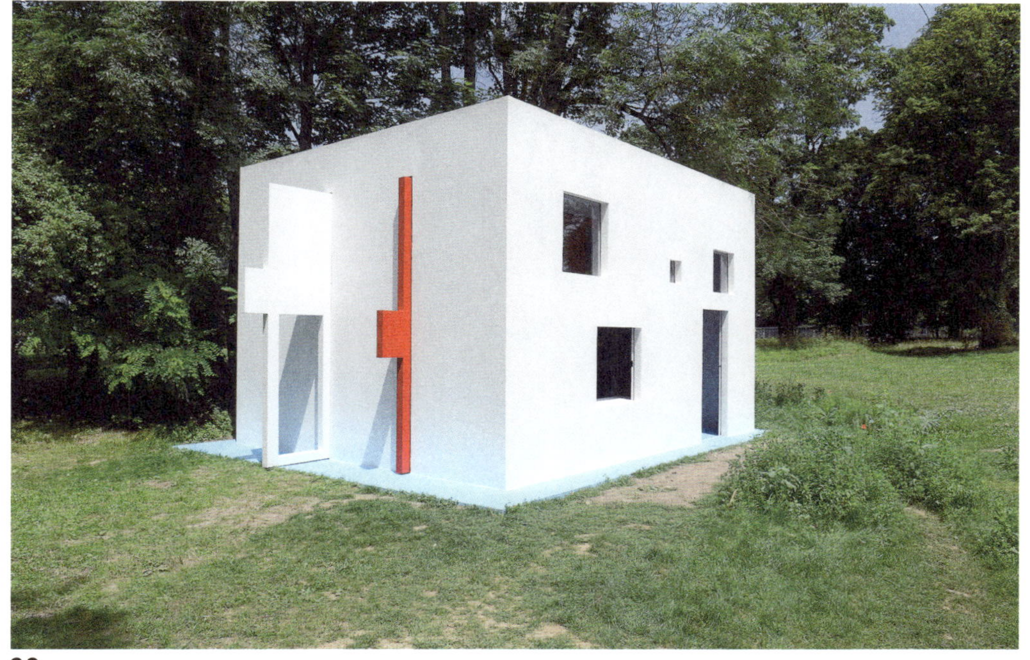

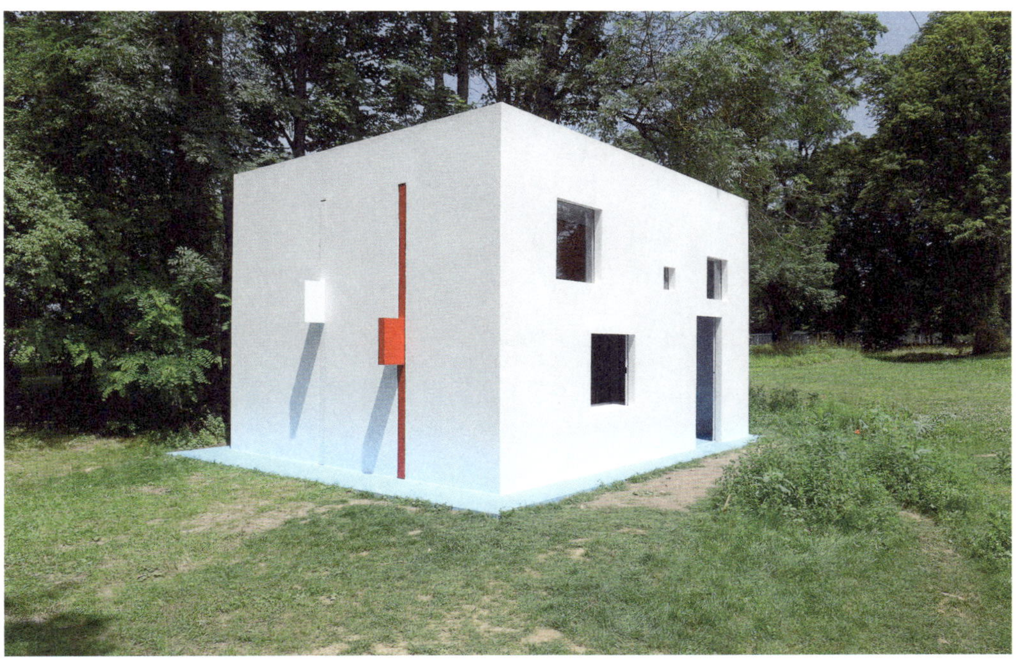

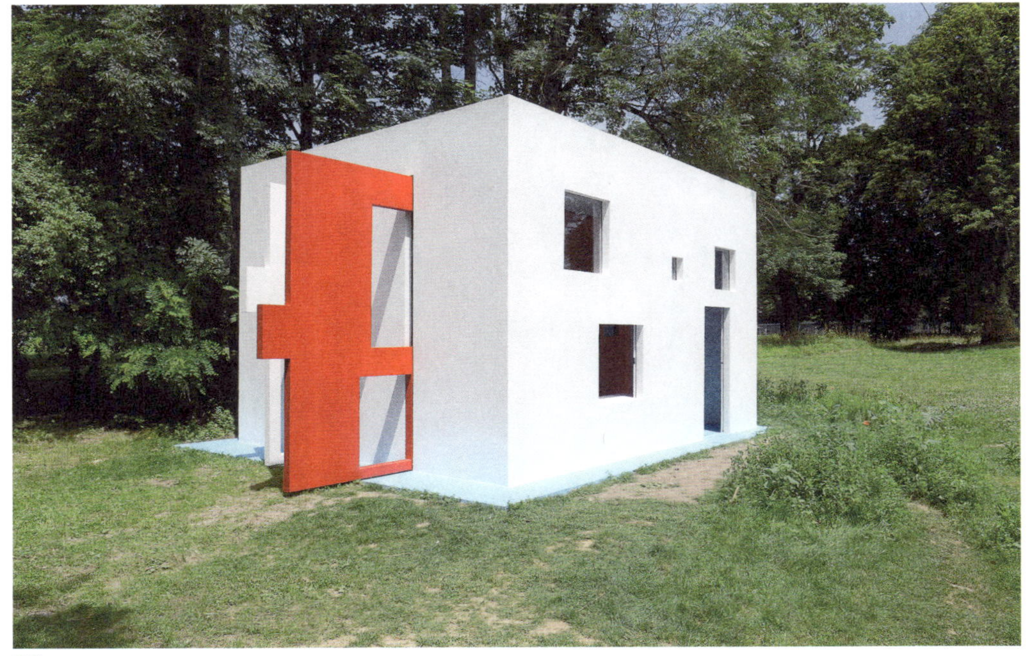

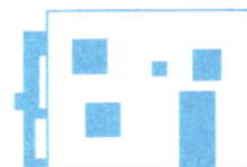

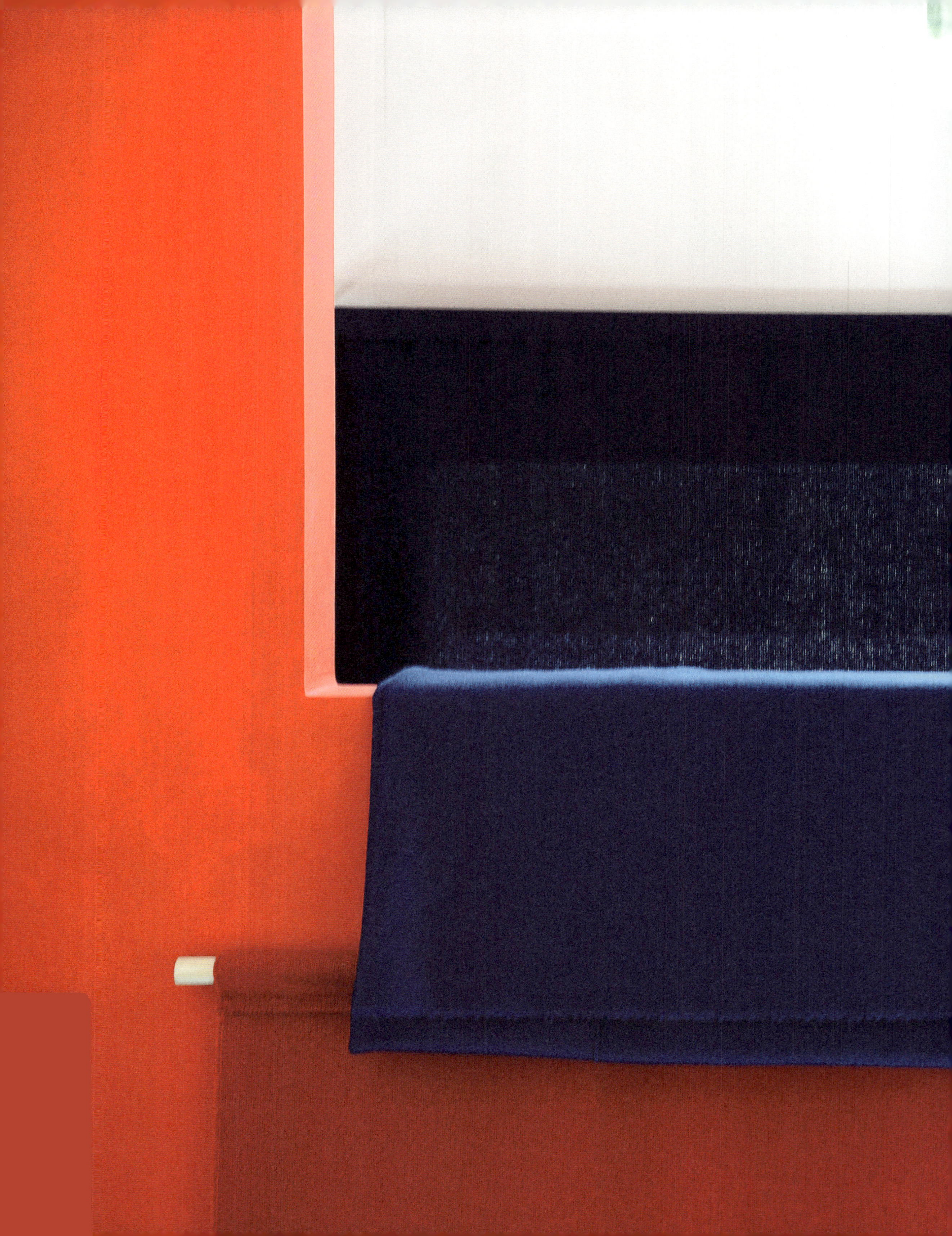

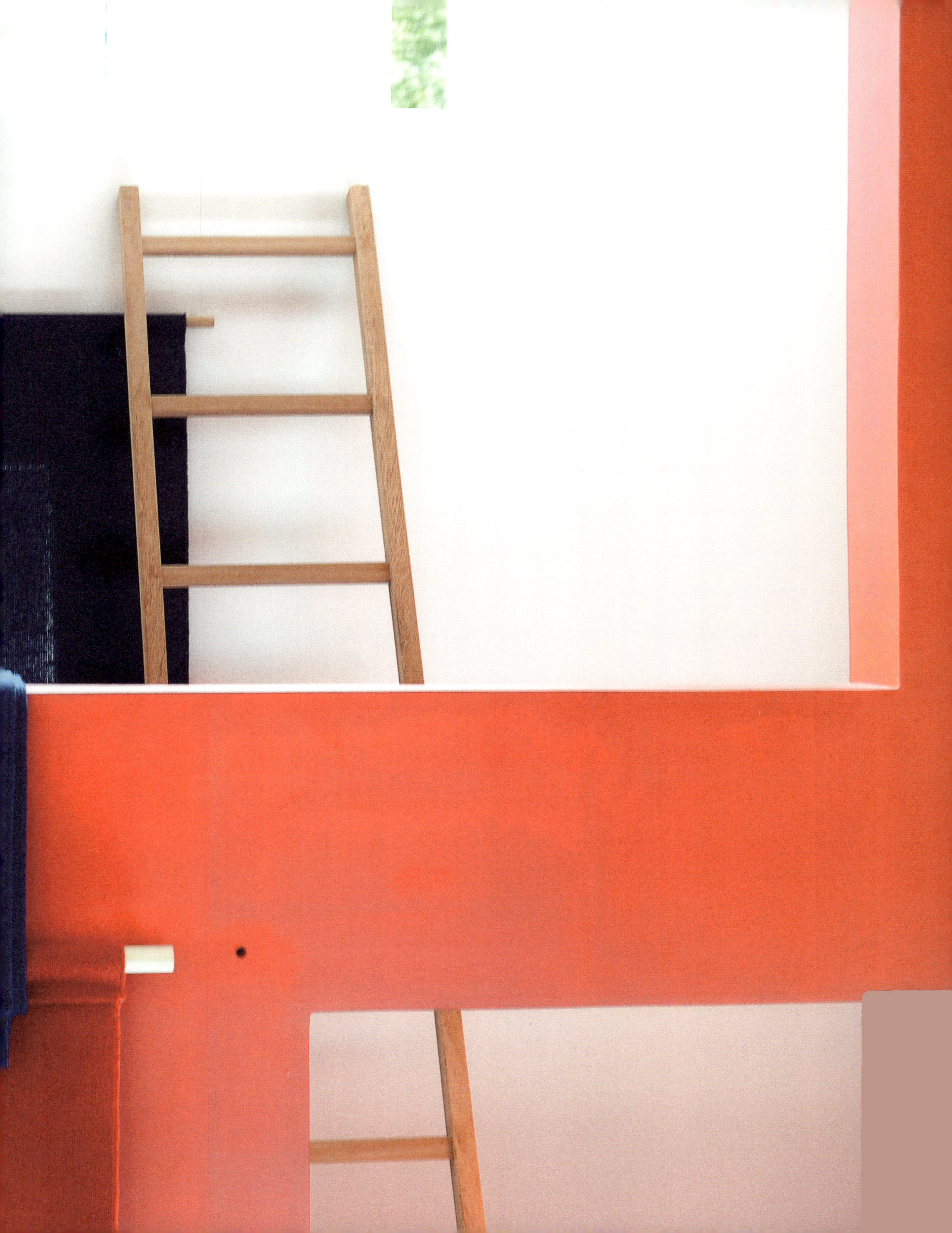

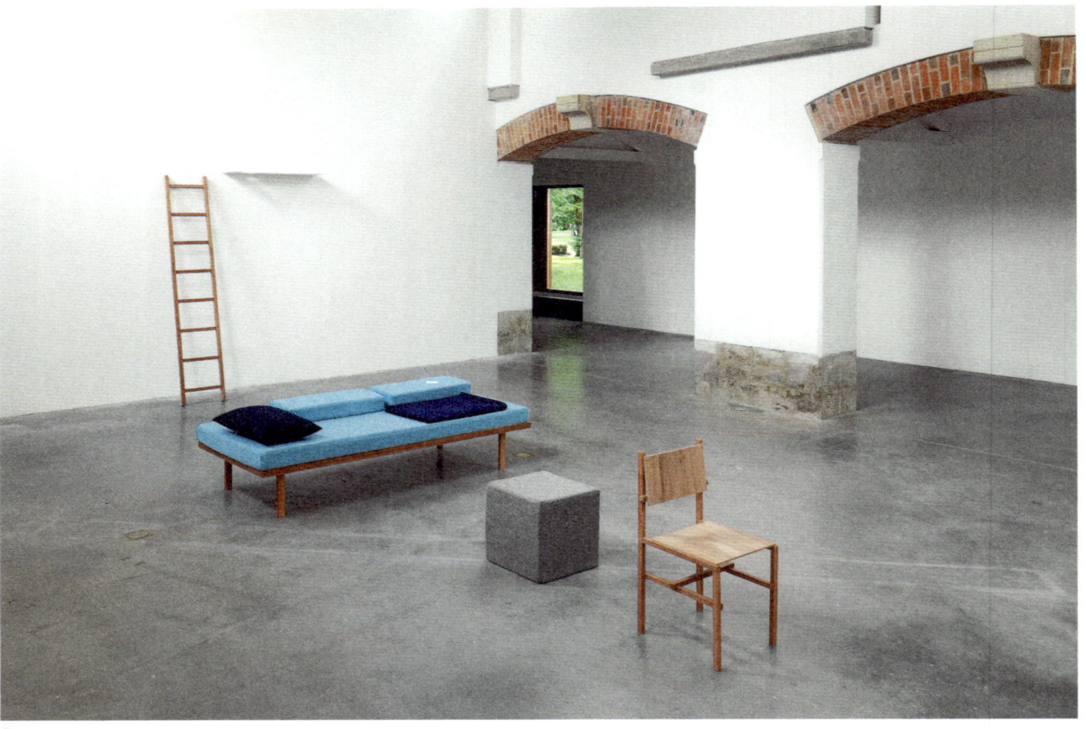

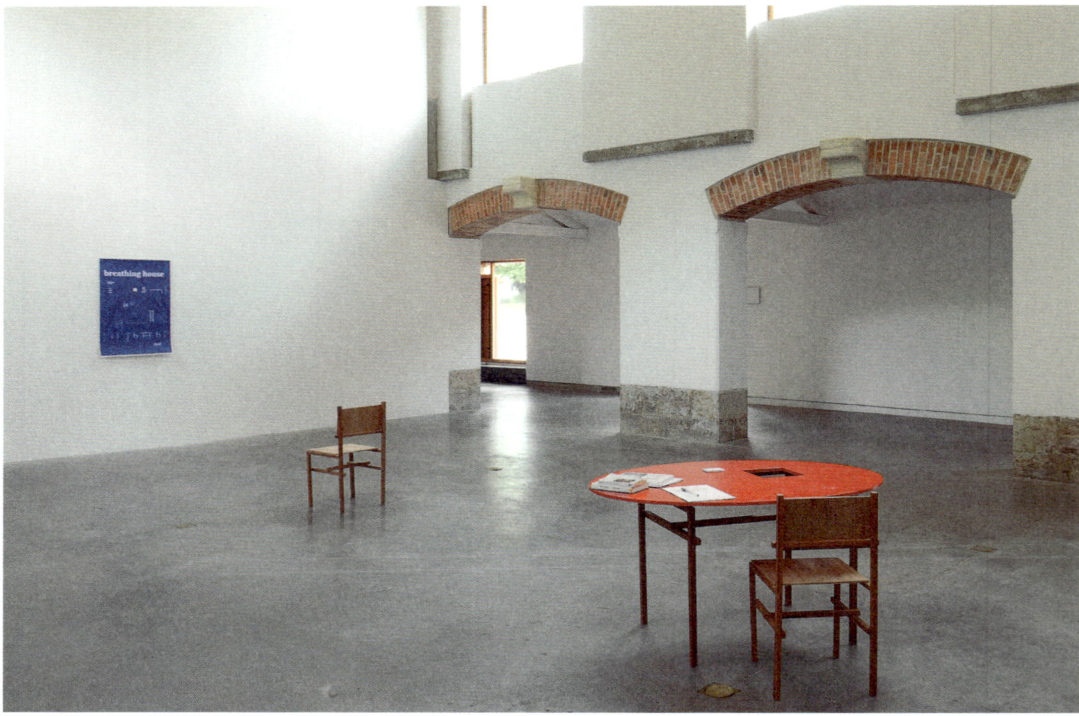

Exhibition views of *breathing house, la maison respire*, Parc Saint Léger, 2012
●● Poster produced for the exhibition, silkscreen print, 100×70 cm, ed. 25+5 AP, 2012

breathing house

Night

ex-
hibi-
tion

a cushion

a cushion

a pillow

parc
saint
leger

exchange
between
what is
needed
at night
and what
is needed
during the
day

the night
breathing
the day
out

a complicated
chair
a chair missed by
its excessive use,
work, addition,
or misplacement

thin air

A second attempt at perceiving the nature of things:

Movement of air – déplacement d'air; it finishes in a current of air. There is a move-ment of air, a wind, a shift of a volume of air from one place to another place next to it, or not to far from it, to a location within sight. The first volume replaces the second. Noth-ing replaces the first, resulting in a hole, a void producing a breeze.

It articulates, places again, as it vanishes in a current of air.

It is an occasion

displacing a volume of air, to take one for another, replacing one by another

i
move
the
chair
from
the
house

bring
the
daybed
back
&

into it
i sleep

to air your
views:
to voice,
make
public,
ventilate,
articulate,
state,
declare

get some
air into
the room
breeze,
draft,
wind;
breath/
blast of
air, gust of
wind

a meeting
(not mis-
sed)
with a
public at
a place
not yet
determi-
nate
with
things be-
ing dis-
placed

a geo-
graphy
of
speeches
&

a breath-
ing and
a reposi-
tioning

DAY

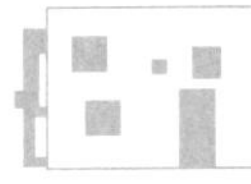

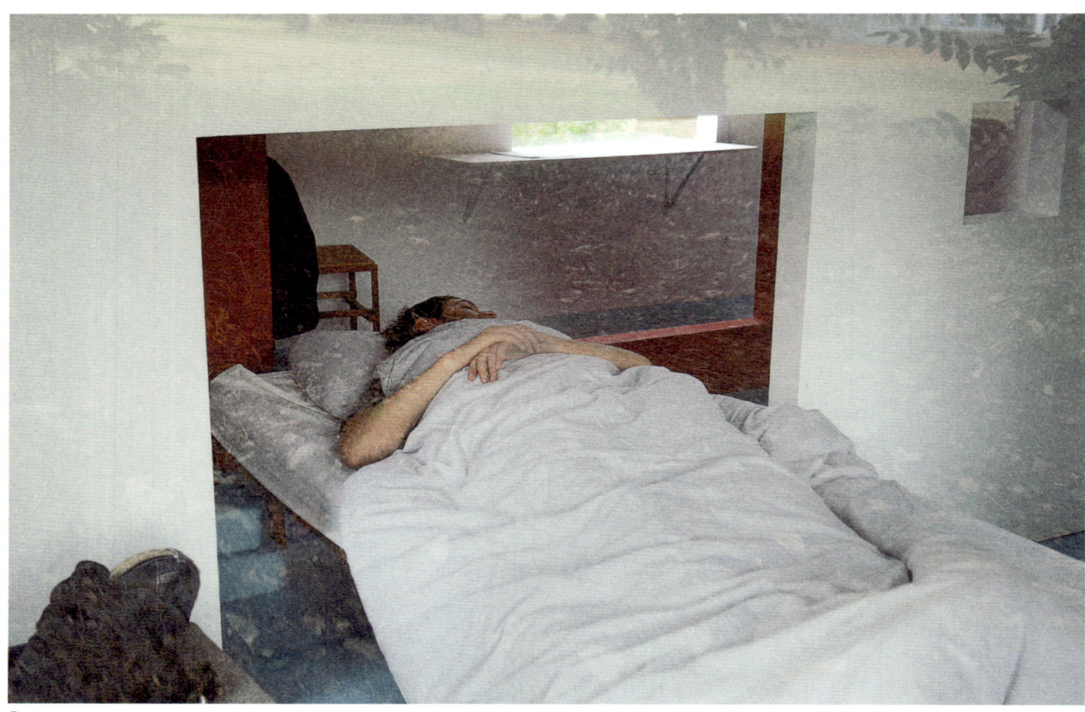

● A guest sleeping across two spaces in the *breathing house*
●● Poster for the entrance of the exhibition, silkscreen print, 174×118 cm, ed. 10, 2012

winds...

comma,
comma,
comma,

i breathe

living and
sleeping,
and...
working
and seeing

to air your views

thin air

displace, or place somewhere else visible

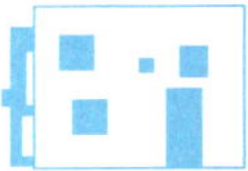

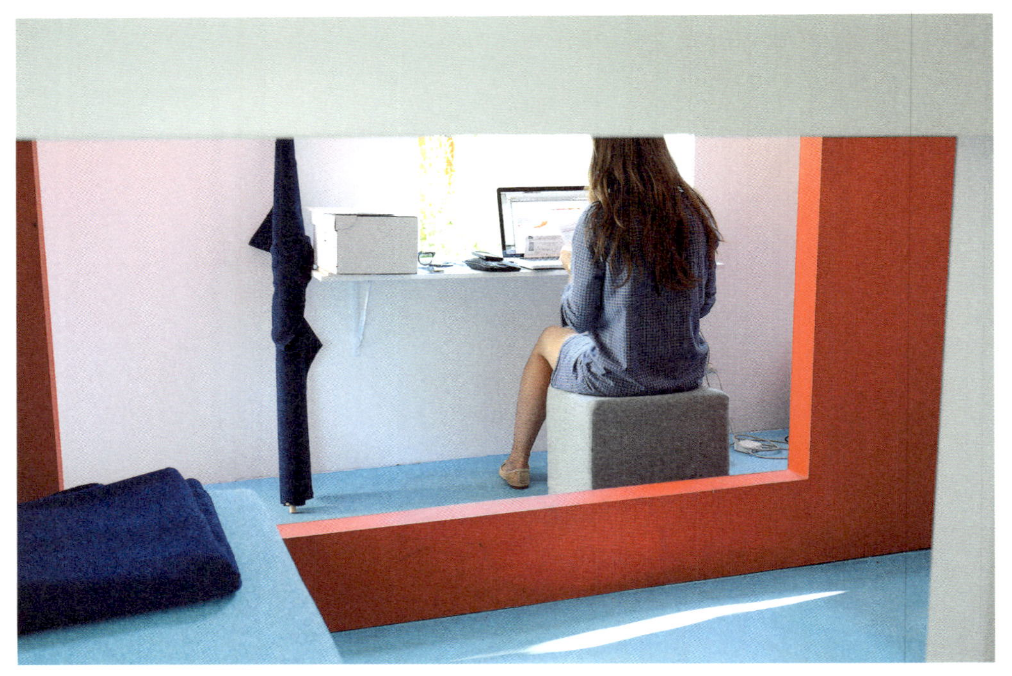

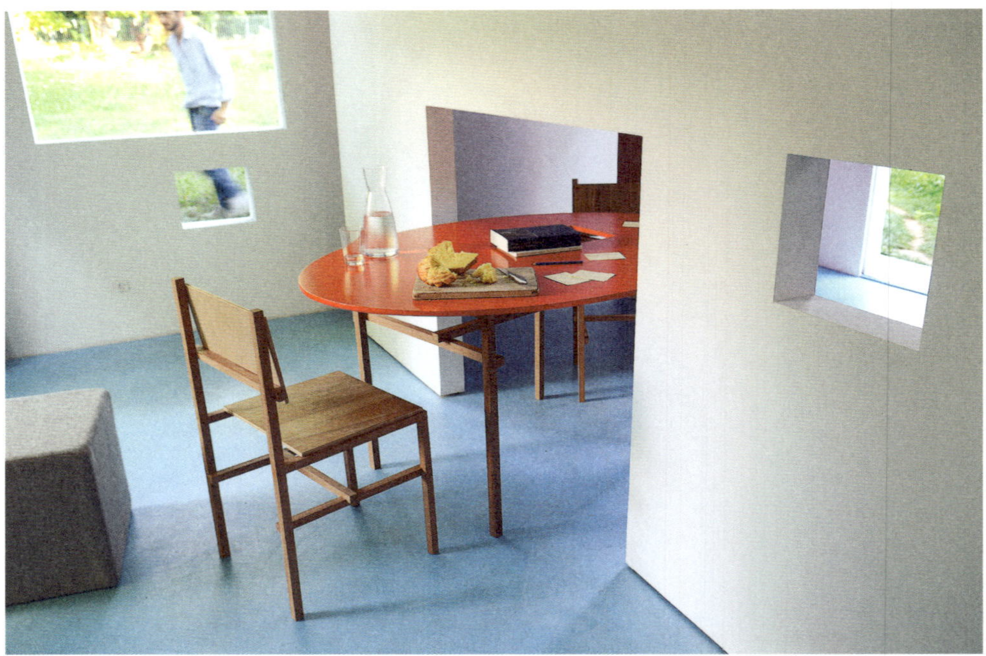

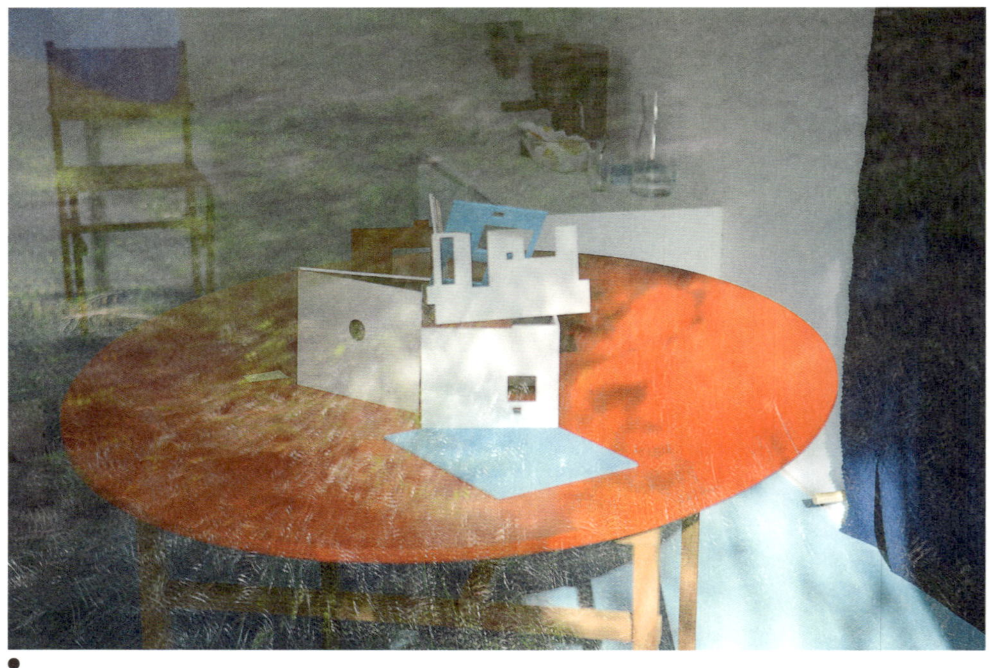

Since the summer of 2012, around twenty people have lived in the *breathing house*. They are its inhabitants, but they are also a distinct and intermediary audience. Among them were: Louidgi Beltrame, Julien Bismuth, Katarina Burin, Marie de Brugerolle, Federica Bueti, Marie Cool and Fabio Balducci, Natalie Czech, Vanessa Desclaux, Övül Durmuşoğlu, Olivier Michelon, Vanessa Joan Müller, Sabine Nielsen, Marc Pérennès, Anri Sala, Matt Saunders, Julia Gwendolyn Schneider, Elfi Turpin, and Jan Verwoert.

Depuis l'été 2012, une vingtaine de personnes ont séjourné dans la *breathing house*. Ils sont des habitants de la maison, mais ils sont aussi déjà un public à part entière, intermédiaire. Parmi eux se trouvaient, Louidgi Beltrame, Julien Bismuth, Katarina Burin, Marie de Brugerolle, Federica Bueti, Marie Cool et Fabio Balducci, Natalie Czech, Vanessa Desclaux, Övül Durmuşoğlu, Olivier Michelon, Vanessa Joan Müller, Sabine Nielsen, Marc Pérennès, Anri Sala, Matt Saunders, Julia Gwendolyn Schneider, Elfi Turpin, Jan Verwoert.

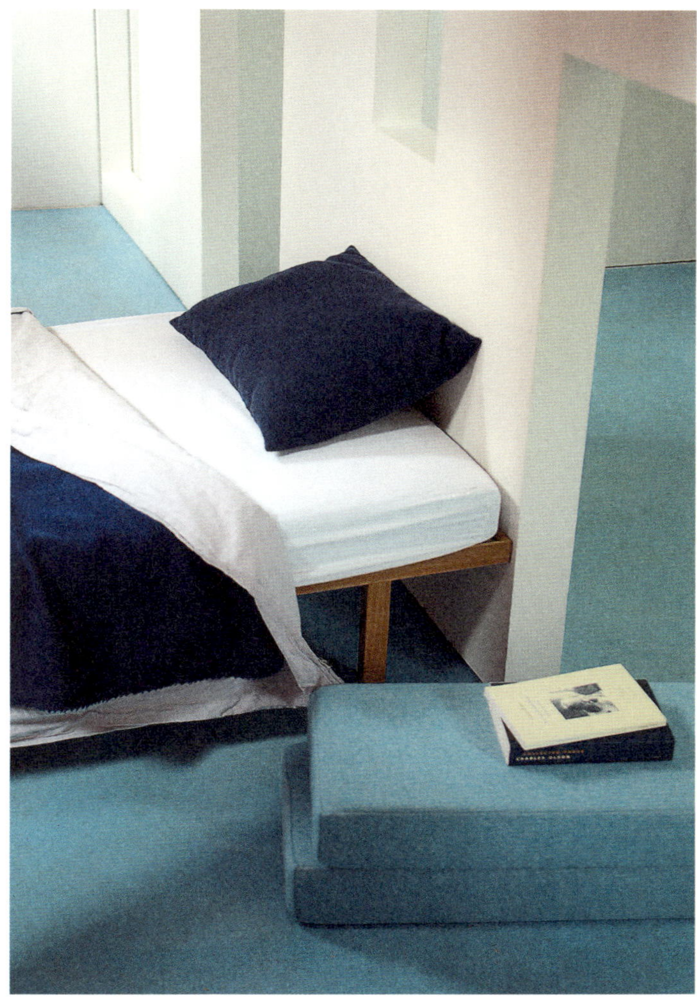

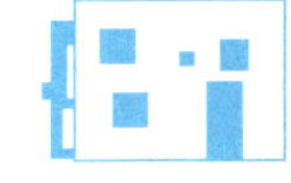

● Model of *breathing house* re-arranged by Yona Friedman, in the living space of the house, painted cardboard, acrylic glass, paper, 30×62×42 cm, 2012

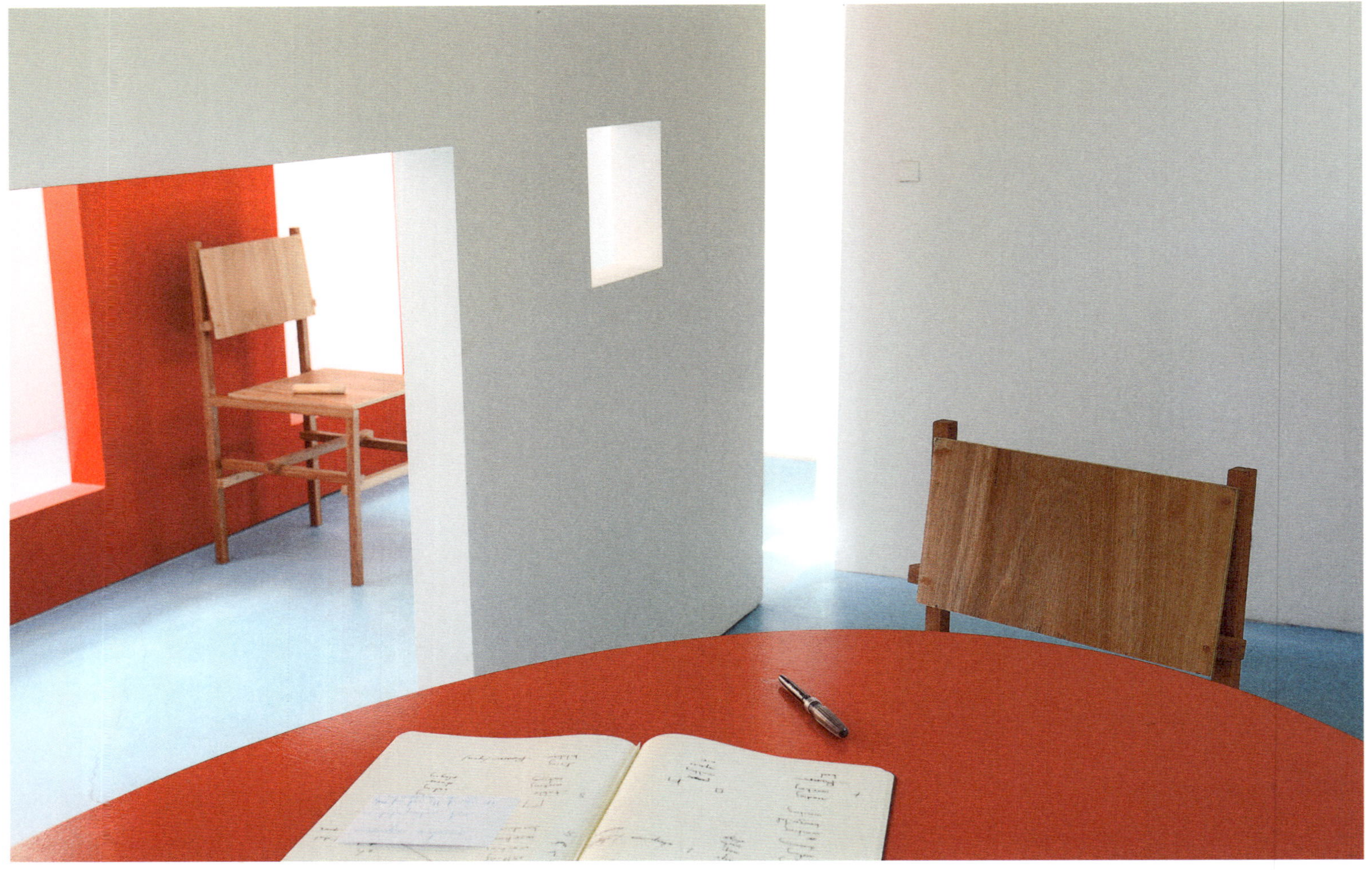

● Guests in the *breathing house*, summer 2012

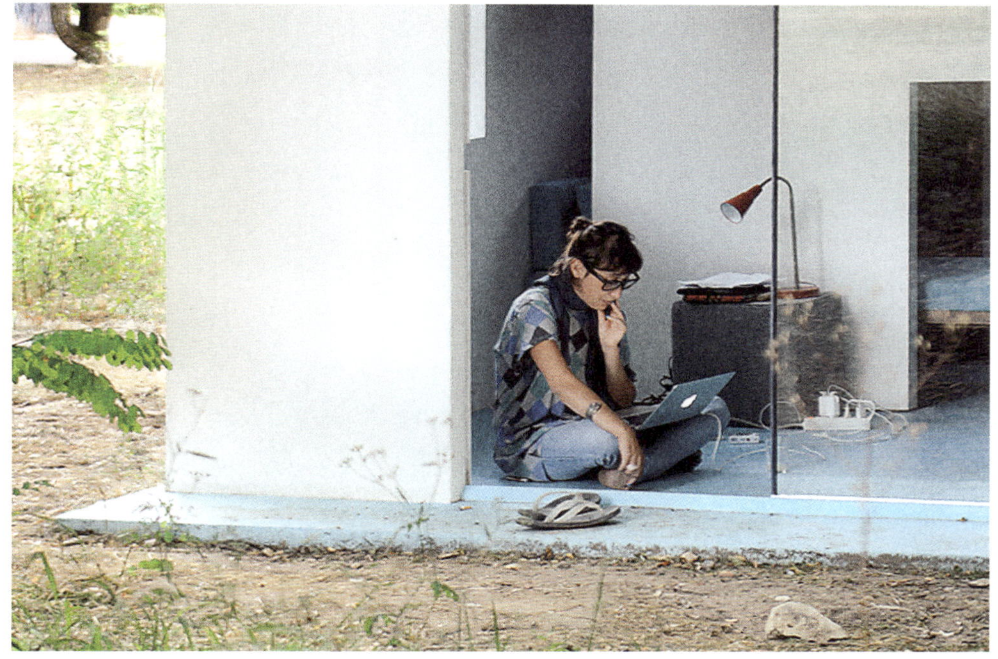

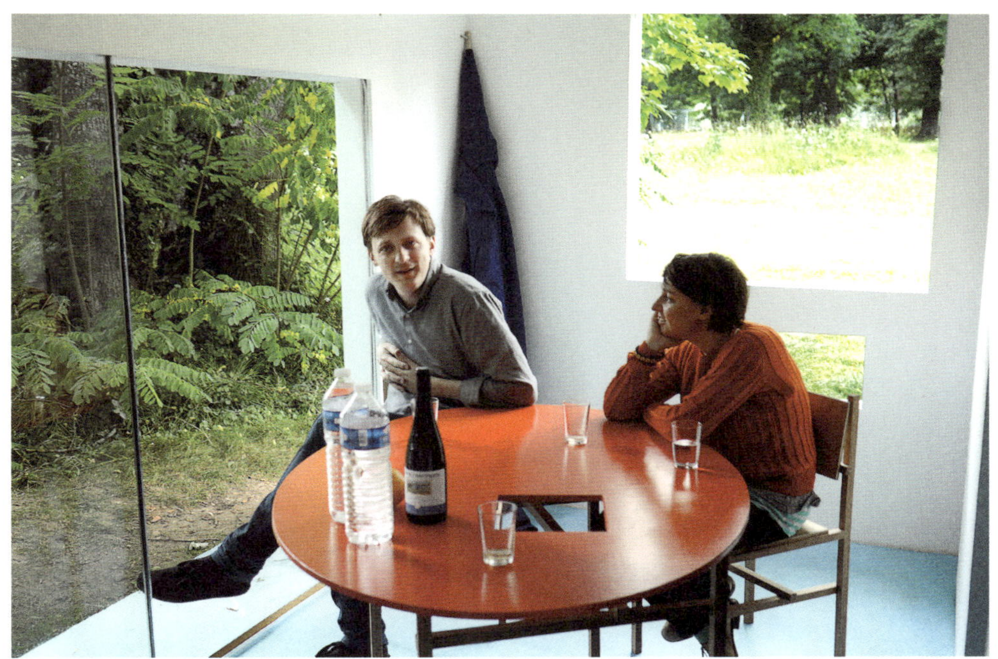

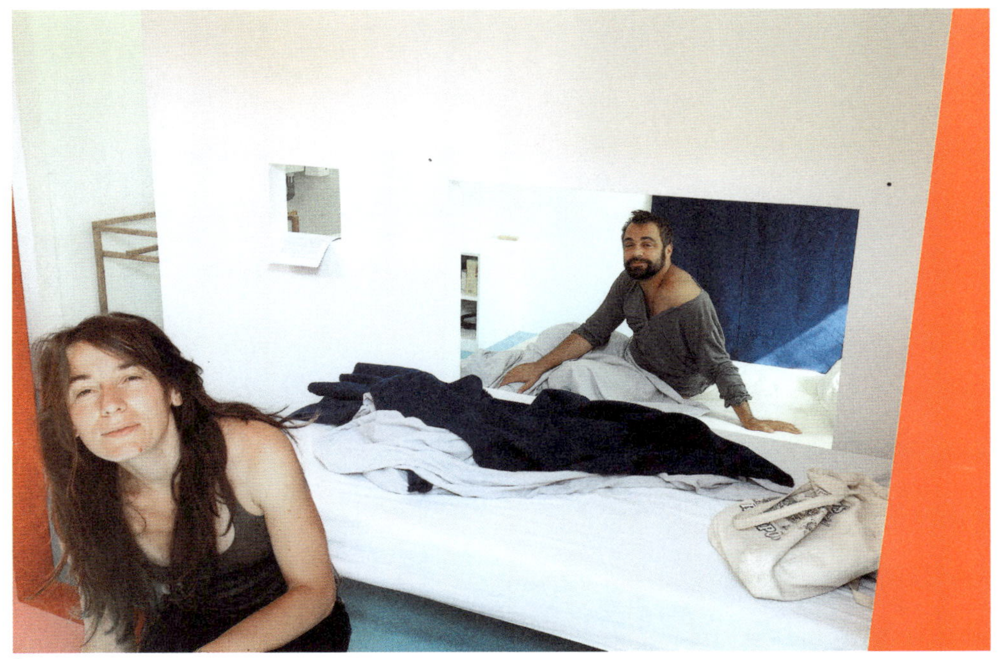

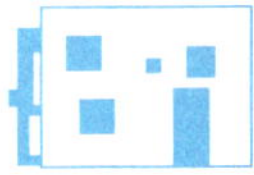

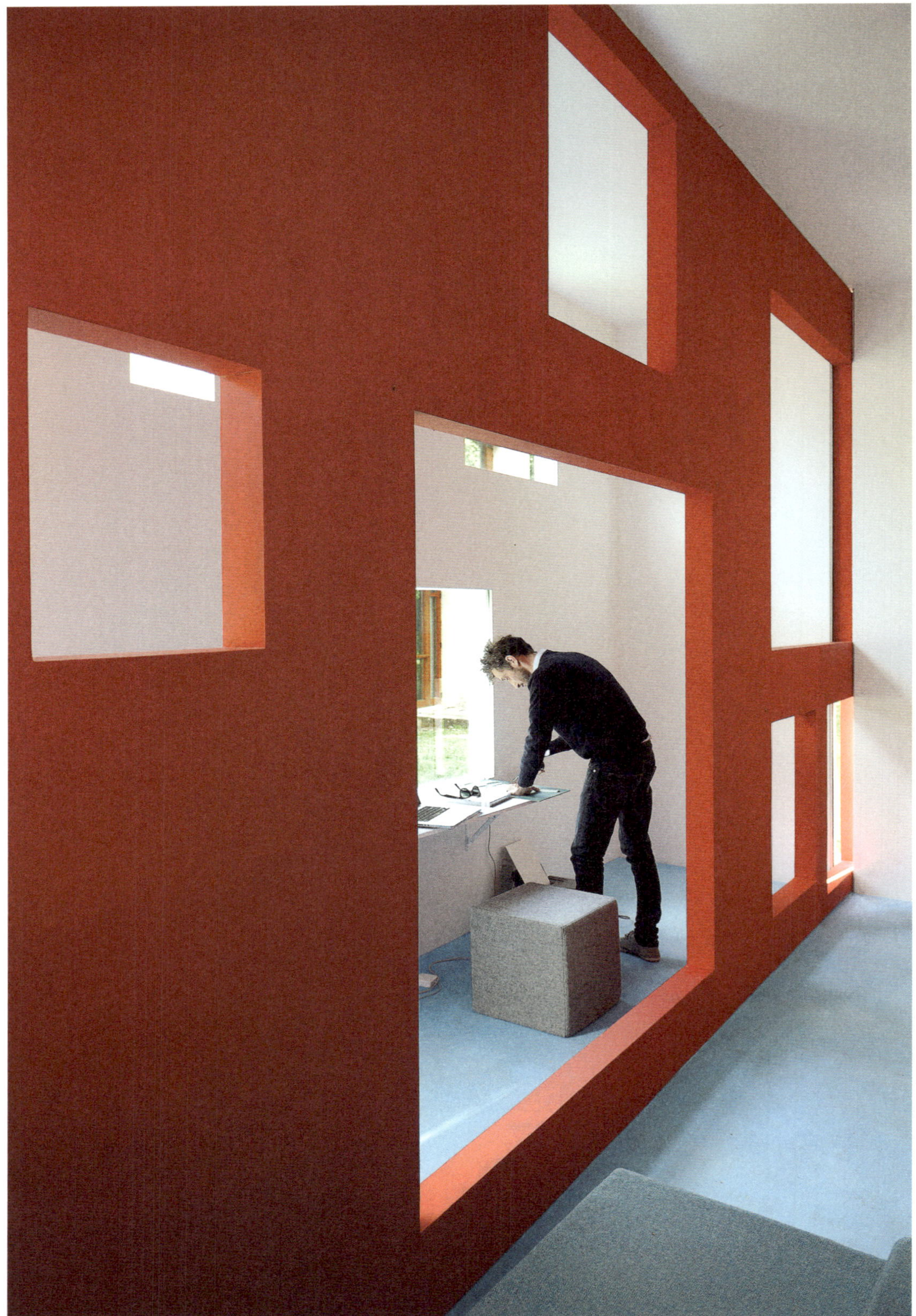

● Jean-Pascal Flavien in the working space of the *breathing house*
●● *breathing house*, custom sink, ceramic
●●● Guests in the *breathing house*, summer 2012
●●●● A guest with a sequence of elements that includes the house
(*a house, a cube, a bed, a chair, a chair*), summer 2012 (next spread)

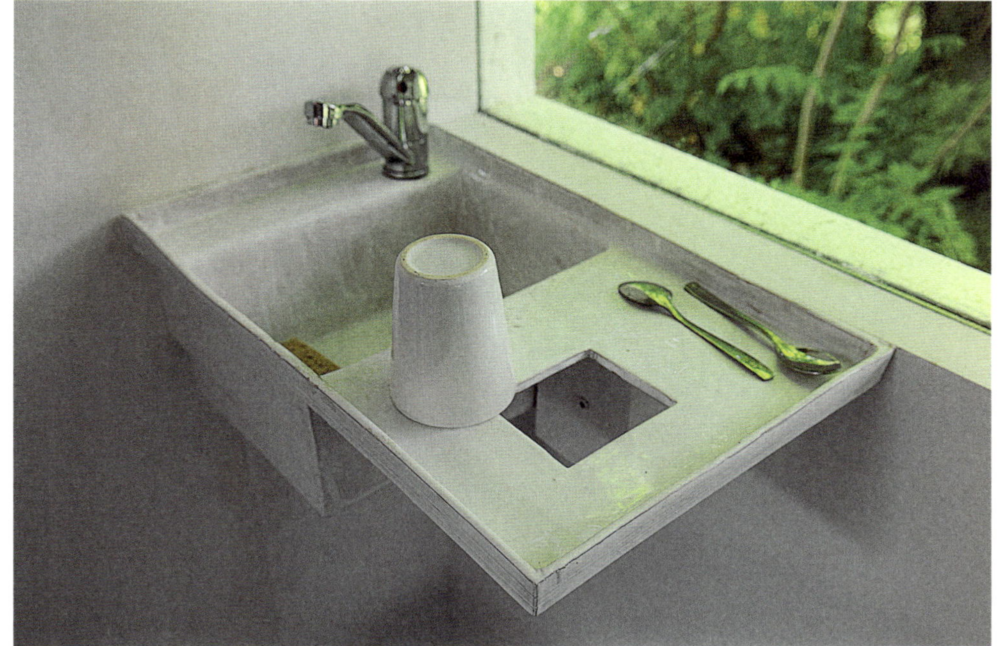

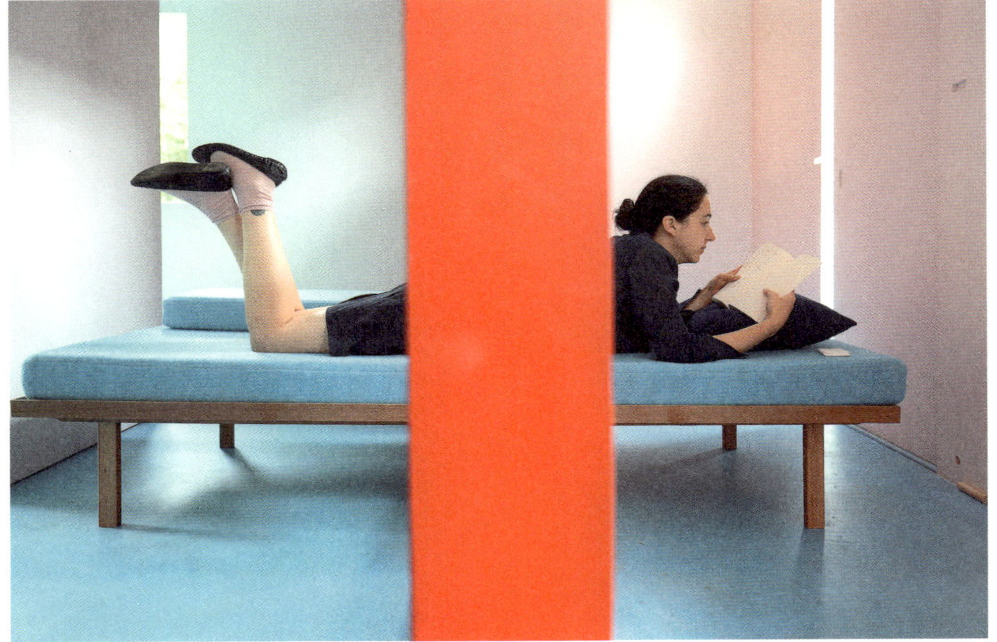

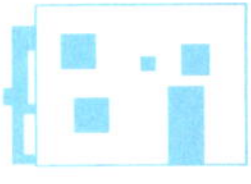

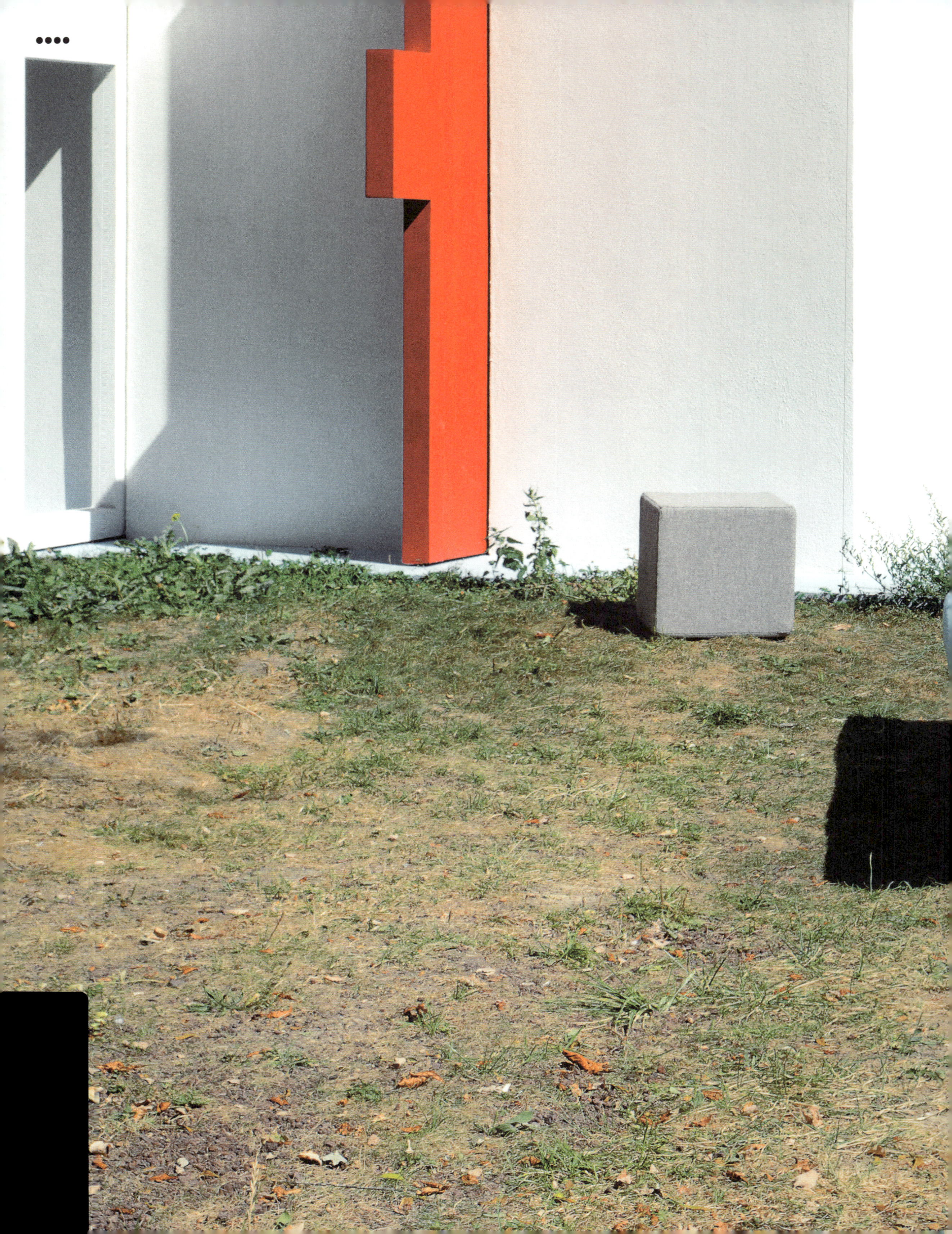

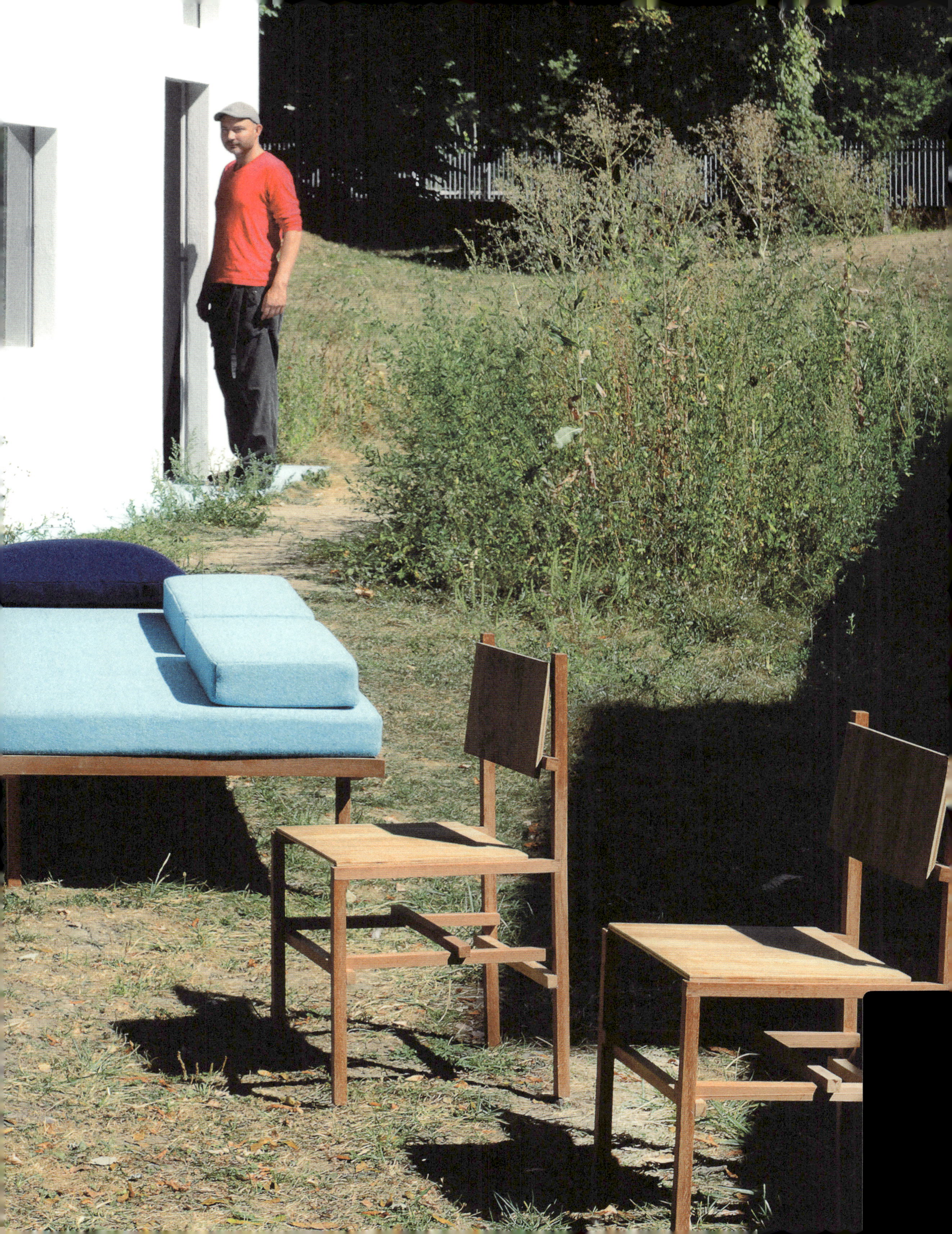

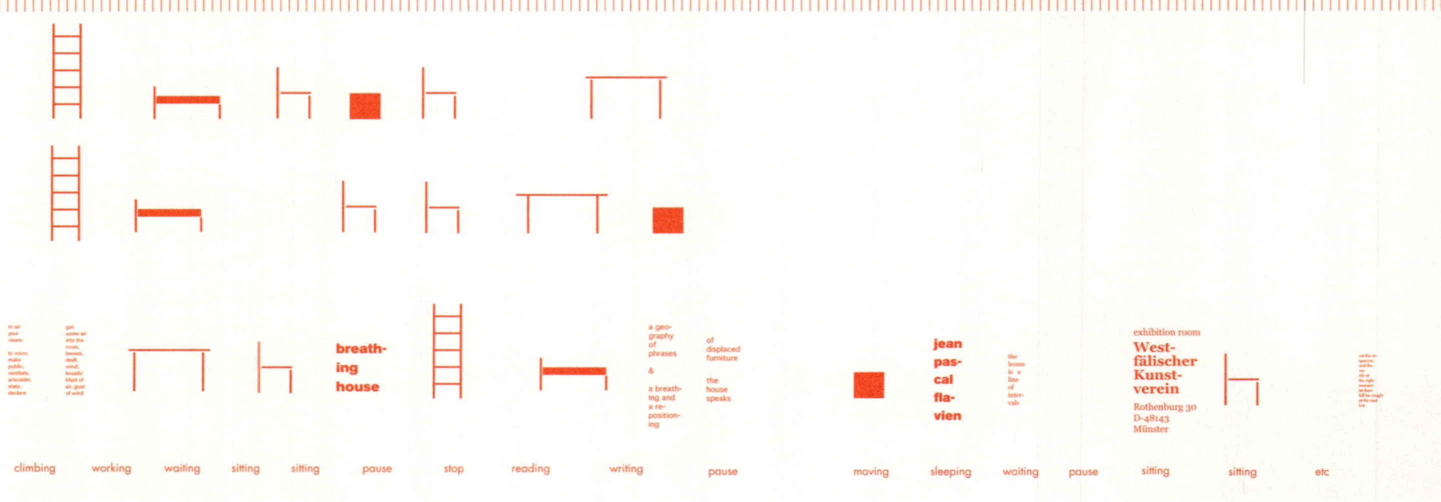

● Poster for the installation, silkscreen print, 76×120 cm, ed. 25 + 5 AP, 2013
●● Exhibition view of *breathing house, sequence or phrase* at Westfälischer Kunstverein, Münster, wood, fabric, paper, various dimensions, 2013

The house speaks. It speaks in sequences and phrases, by linear arrangements of objects placed side by side: sequences of furniture, its furniture, whose paratactic compositions form a grammar of ANDs and COMMAs. The objects neighbor one another, forming an unco-ordinated sequence, without subordination. One morning, a phrase outside set the furniture, the house, and the exhibition space up along the same line:

the house, a cube, a bed, a chair, a chair, the exhibition

The house will continue to speak by arrangements, and sequences, in other exhibition spaces.

La maison parle. Elle parle par séquences ou phrases, par arrangements linéaires d'objets mis côte à côte, de séquences de meubles, ses meubles, dont les agencements paratactiques forment une grammaire du ET et de la VIRGULE. Les objets voisinent, forment une séquence sans coordination, sans subordination. Un matin, une phrase dehors agençait sur la même ligne des meubles, la maison et l'exposition:

la maison, un cube, un lit, une chaise, une chaise, une exposition

La maison continuera à parler par arrangements, par séquences dans d'autres lieux d'exposition.

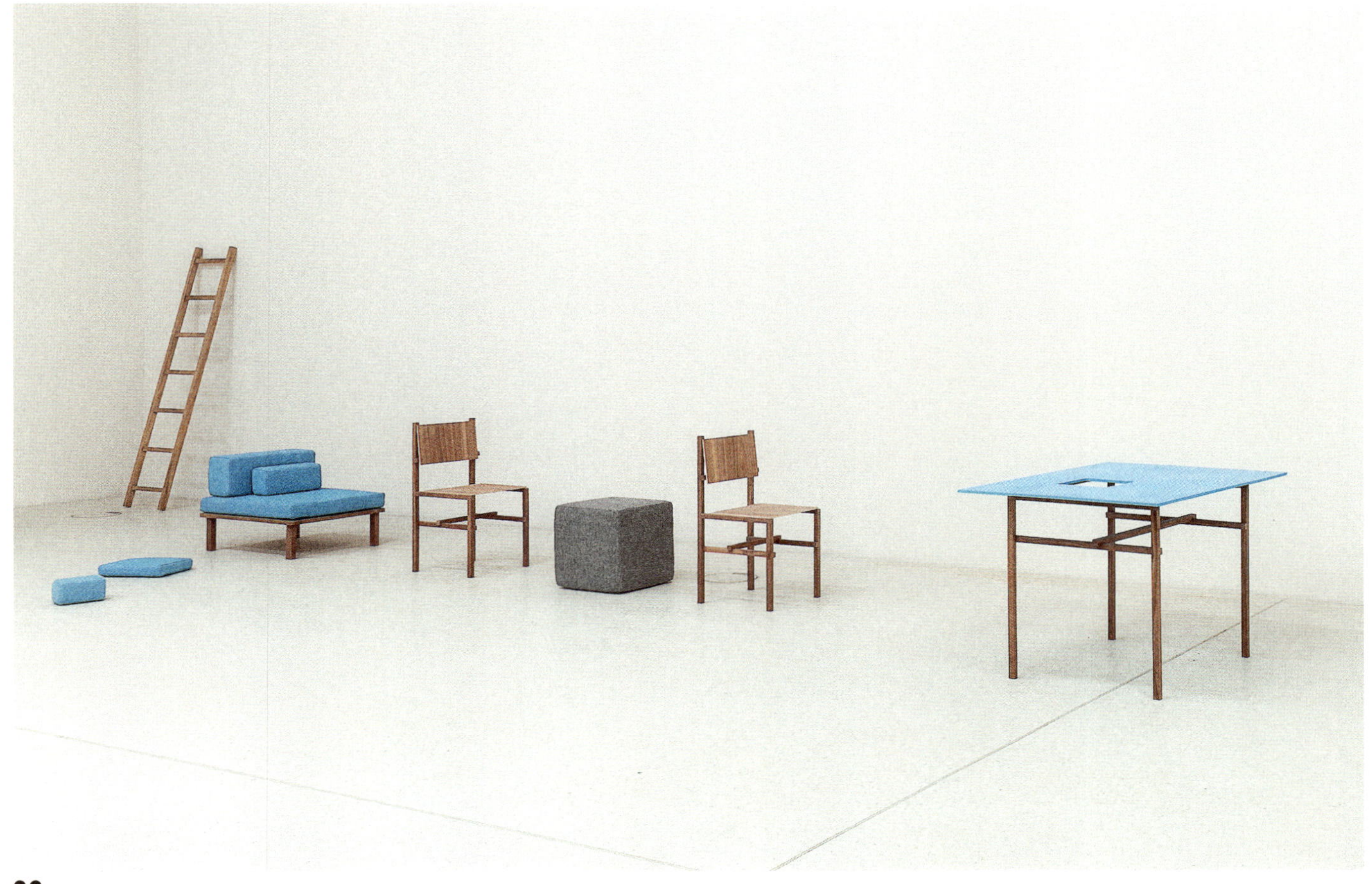

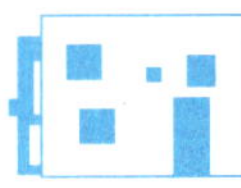

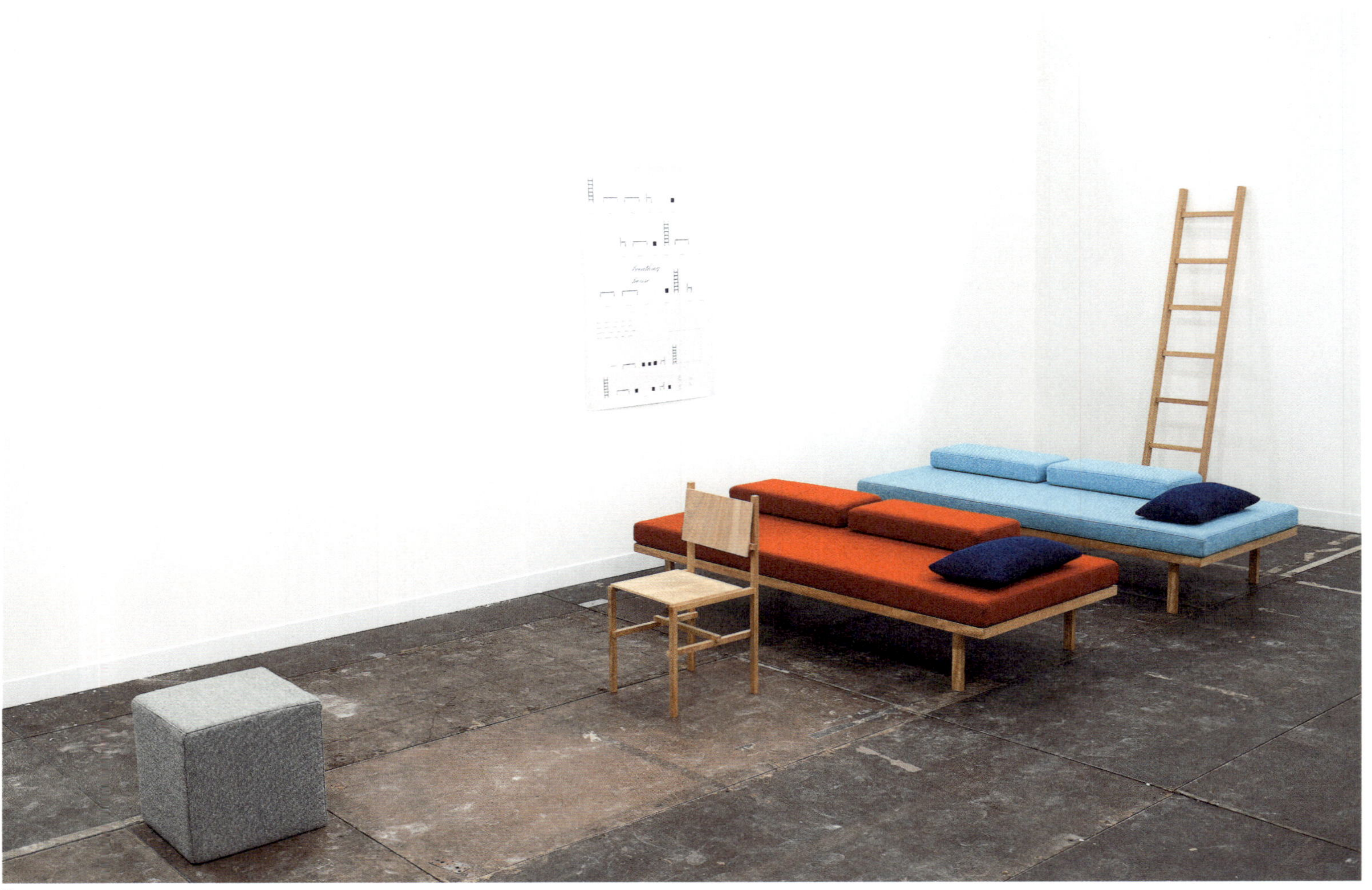

● Exhibition view of *breathing house, sequence or phrase* at Frieze Art Fair, London, wood, fabric, paper, various dimensions, 2012
●● Poster for the installation, silkscreen print, 120×85 cm, ed. 25+5 AP, 2012

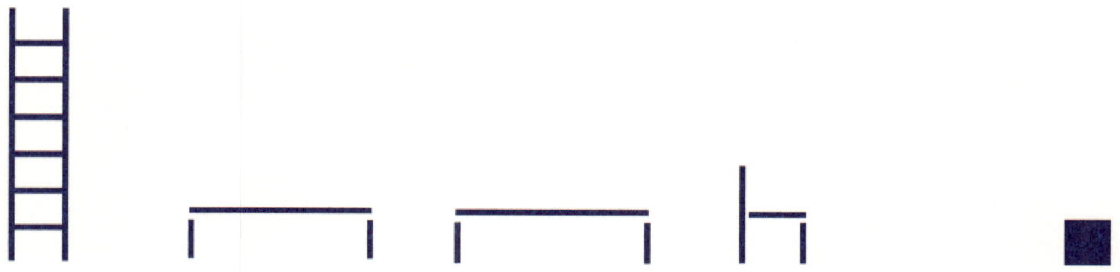

climbing   sleeping   sleeping   sitting   space   sitting

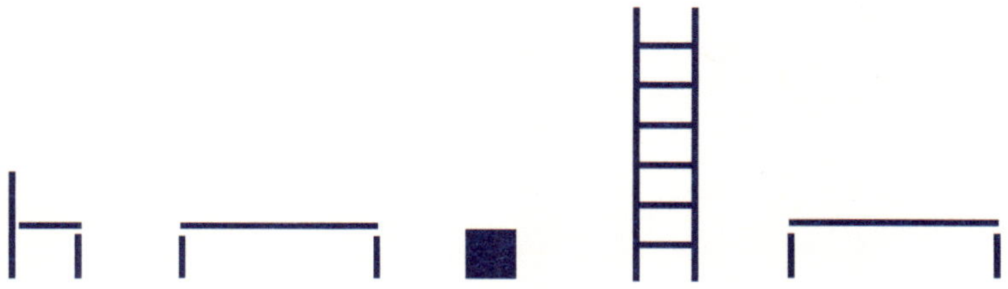

sitting   reading   sitting   breathing   reading   going

breathing

house

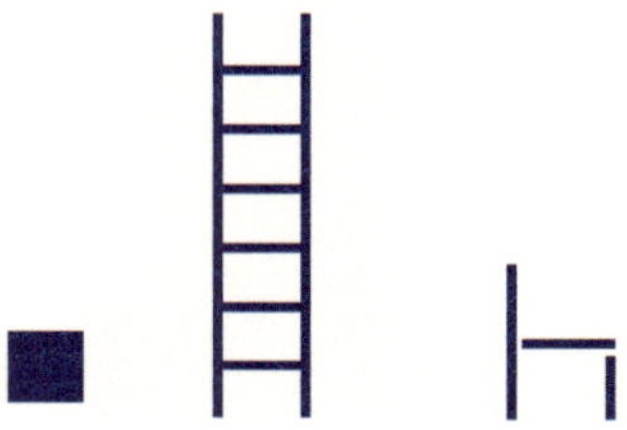

sleeping   sleeping   pause   waiting   sitting   breathing

sleeping   sleeping   waiting   sitting   sitting

reading   working   sitting   waiting   waiting

daydreaming   sleeping   sitting   waiting   sitting

sleeping   repeating   sitting   sitting   going

exhibition

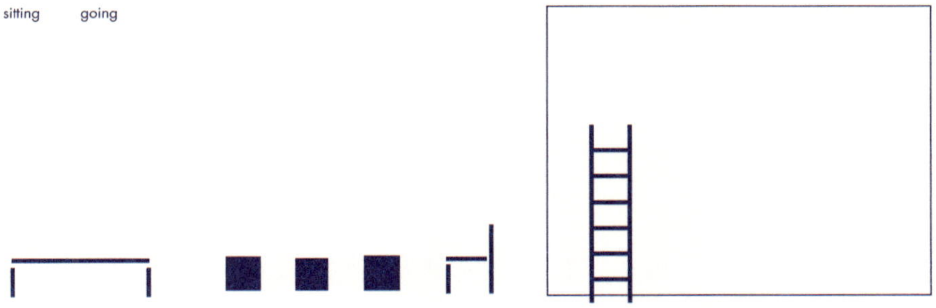

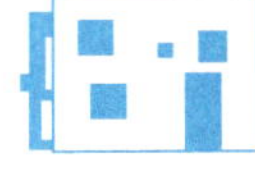

a geo-
graphy
of
phrases

&

a breath-
ing and
a re-
position-
ing

of
displaced
furniture

the
house
speaks

space

pendant...

during...

During the summer of 2006, I visited Raoul Hausmann's three-room apartment with kitchen in Limoges. In 2012, I slept in Jean-Pascal Flavien's *breathing house.*

In 1969, in the opening lines of *Fantastic Architecture*, the anthology of architectural projects that he edited with Wolf Vostell, Dick Higgins writes (with a certain degree of disingenuity) that: "Architecture, to the extent that it is an art, is the last art still in a primitive state. Virtually none of the aesthetic revolutions of the 20th century have touched it."[1] In its abruptness, this preface deliberately ignored the architectural revolutions of the avant-gardes. Finally, the conservatives had won. In a historical hyphen, the Berlin Dadaist Raoul Hausmann (1886–1971) whose contribution to this publication was titled *An Appeal to Fantasy*—a manifesto that aimed to transform the earth into a kamikaze spaceship—perfectly restituted the frontlines between actual progressives and reactionaries: "What is labeled 'urbanism' nowadays is far removed from the initial ventures of the Dutch architects Oud and Rietveld. Present-day urbanism stands under the sway of Le Corbusier, who was inspired by naval construction, by luxury liners. The formula of today's architecture is nothing but the satisfaction of the sedentary and residential needs of the citizen who seeks nothing but peace and quiet and desires a certain level of comfort (central heating, refrigerator, washing machine, TV set, etc.). This is not the goal of a living architecture. Life is fantastic. Let the architectural surroundings of man be equally fantastic. The *minimum vital* is neither fantastic nor artistic. What can we do? Urbanism has to be abandoned and forgotten, it is merely an answer to a need, and not a living action. The beehive system must be abandoned. Man is not a robot-insect. The architecture of free conception has an unusual function, it is something other than a disagreeable misfortune."[2]

For Hausmann, there were thus, on the one hand, the irrigated fantasies of De Stijl, most notably by the Dadaist Theo van Doesburg, and on the other, a poor modern architecture, functional in nature, which was finally not so distant from the concentrationary disgust of large constructions and small pavilions, those housing blocks and "small houses, small lives" that Maurice Pialat describes with such rage in his first short film, *L'amour existe* (1960). When he sent his text to Higgins, Hausmann resided in a small 1950's three-room apartment; but it was from there that he

Pendant l'été 2006, j'ai visité le 3 pièces cuisine de Raoul Hausmann à Limoges. En 2012, j'ai dormi dans la *breathing house* de Jean-Pascal Flavien.

En 1969, en ouverture de *Fantastic Architecture*, le recueil de projets architecturaux qu'il avait conduit avec Wolf Wostell, Dick Higgins écrivait avec une certaine mauvaise foi que l'architecture, « si tant est qu'il s'agisse d'un art est le dernier art dans son état primitif. Virtuellement aucune des révolutions artistiques du XXe siècle ne l'a touchée ».[1] Abrupte, l'avant-propos fermait volontairement les yeux sur les révolutions architecturales des avant-gardes. Finalement c'était les conservateurs qui avaient gagnés. Trait d'union avec l'histoire, le dadaïste berlinois Raoul Hausmann (1886–1971) qui contribuait à l'ouvrage avec son *Appel à la fantaisie* – un manifeste visant à transformer la terre en vaisseau spatial kamikaze – resituait parfaitement les lignes de front entre progressistes réels et réactionnaires : « Ce que nous appelons architecture aujourd'hui est loin des buts initiaux des architectes hollandais Oud et Rietveld. L'urbanisme actuel est marqué par le mouvement de Le Corbusier, ce dernier a été inspiré par des constructions navales, des navires de luxe. La formule de l'architecture actuelle n'est rien d'autre que la satisfaction des besoins sédentaires et résidentiels de citoyens qui ne cherchent rien d'autre que la paix, la tranquillité et un certain degré de confort (chauffage central, réfrigérateur, machine à laver, tv, etc.). Ce n'est pas le but de l'architecture vivante. La vie est fantastique. Laissons l'architecture entourant l'homme être également fantastique. Le minimum vital n'est ni fantastique ni artistique. Que pouvons-nous faire ? L'urbanisme doit être abandonné et oublié. Il est une réponse à des besoins et pas une action vivante. Le système de la ruche doit être abandonné. L'homme n'est pas un insecte robot. L'architecture de conception libre a une fonction inusuelle, c'est autre chose qu'une malchance désagréable. »[2]

Pour Hausmann, il y avait donc d'un côté les expérimentations de De Stijl, irriguées notamment par un Van Doesburg dadaïste, et de l'autre une pauvre architecture moderne, de fonction, finalement pas si éloignée du dégoût concentrationnaire des grands ensembles et des petits pavillons. Ces barres et ces « petites maisons, petites vies » que décrivait rageusement Maurice Pialat dans son premier court métrage, *L'amour existe*, en 1960. Lorsqu'il envoie son texte à Dick Higgins, Hausmann réside à Limoges, dans un petit trois pièces construit dans les années 1950. Mais c'est de là qu'il continuait à vouloir changer le monde,

1 Dick Higgins, *Introduction* (1969), in: Wolf Vostell et Dick Higgins, ed., *Fantastic Architecture* (New York: Something Else Press, 1969), n. pag., traduit par l'auteur.
2 Raoul Hausmann, *An Appeal for Fantasy* (1967), in: Wolf Vostell et Dick Higgins, ed., *Fantastic Architecture* (New York: Something Else Press, 1969), n. pag., traduit par l'auteur.

during…

1 Dick Higgins, *Introduction* (1969), in: Wolf Vostell and Dick Higgins, ed., *Fantastic Architecture* (New York: Something Else Press, 1969), n. pag.
2 Raoul Hausmann, *An Appeal for Fantasy* (1967), in: Wolf Vostell and Dick Higgins, ed., *Fantastic Architecture* (New York: Something Else Press, 1969), n. pag.

continued to want to change the world, by first modifying individual subjectivities. Architecture is finally just a construction like any other; it can only act properly by taking upon itself Hausmann's "eccentric sensoriality," a decentered way of perceiving the world, which he started to promote towards the end of the 1960s. Finishing with occidental rationalism entails surpassing the separation between mind and spirit, thinking with one's organs, revealing the invisible, allowing for animist notions, "the surpassing and enlargement of all of the cellular, nervous, and 'aperceptional' faculties." Starting in 1922, Hausmann, incensed by the failure of the Spartacist revolution, placed all of his hopes for a grand twilight in a disruption of the senses. "And if something new, a new movement, a new organization were to succeed, it would be because an expansion of our sensorial emanations will have taken place," he explained at the time in his manifesto titled *Optophonetic*.[3]

Architecture (like painting, poetry, and sculpture) should have adhered to this new order, and from that point on, ceased to confront itself in the simple function of things, but instead, allow for the emergence of their extensions, their fictions even. Alongside rational modernist architecture, and far earlier than (but also at a complete disconnect from) post-modern thought, it is a truly experimental heritage that we see arising at regular intervals with artists who linked their practices to architectural construction. Works which are thought as extensions of bodies and minds, understood as expansions of their capacities. One thinks of course of Kurt Schwitters's *Merzbau*, the "unitary architecture" of the Situationists, but also of Helio Oiticica's *Parangolé* clothing, his *Penetrables*, and his *Suprasensorial* environments. Less critiques or remakes of a comfort architecture then, but rather eccentric spaces.

en modifiant avant tout la subjectivité de chacun. L'architecture n'est finalement qu'une construction plastique comme une autre, elle ne peut agir proprement qu'en faisant sienne le souhait de cette « *sensorialité excentrique* » que réclame Hausmann à partir de la fin des années 1960, une façon décentrée de percevoir le monde. En finir avec le rationalisme occidental, c'est dépasser la séparation le corps et l'esprit, pouvoir penser avec ses organes, révéler l'invisible, admettre des notions animistes, « le dépassement et l'élargissement de toutes les facultés cellulaires, nerveuses, ‹aperception-nelles› ». Dès 1922, Hausmann, échaudé par l'échec de la révolution spartakiste, replaçait toutes ses promesses de grand soir dans un bouleversement des sens. « Et si quelque chose de nouveau, un nouveau mouvement, une nouvelle organisation réussissait, ce serait parce qu'une expansion de nos émanations senso-rielles se serait réalisée », expliquait-il alors dans son manifeste *Optophonétique*.[3]

L'architecture, tout comme la peinture, la poésie, la sculpture devait obéir à ce nouvel ordre et dès lors ne plus se confronter dans la simple fonction des choses, mais bien en permettre des extensions, des fictions. À côté d'une modernité architecturale rationnelle, et bien avant – et surtout sans relation avec – une théorie post-moderne, c'est ainsi une véritable architecture avant-gardiste, un héritage réellement expérimental que l'on peut voir poindre par intervalles irréguliers chez des artistes ayant lié leurs productions à la construction. Des œuvres qui sont pensées comme des extensions des corps et des esprits, entendues comme expansions de leurs capacités: évidemment le *Merzbau* de Schwitters, l'« architecture unitaire » des situationnistes, mais aussi les vêtements *parangolé* d'Helio Oiticica, ses pénétrables et environnements « suprasensoriels » comme le nommait le Brésilien. Pas tant donc des critiques ou des reprises d'une architecture du confort, mais des espaces excentriques.

3   Raoul Hausmann, *Optophonétique* (1922), dans: *Sensorialité excentrique/Eccentric Sensoriality*, (Dijon / Paris: Les presses du réel, 2002), p. 10–11.

3   Raoul Hausmann, *Optophonetic* (1922), in: *Sensorialité excentrique/ Eccentric Sensoriality*, (Dijon / Paris: Les presses du réel, 2002), p. 110.

during...

Solo Exhibitions and Projects

2014
Galerie Esther Schipper, Berlin
Galerie Catherine Bastide, Bruxelles

2013
NHDT, textes de nuit, Angle Art Contemporain,
Saint-Paul-Trois-Châteaux

2012
Cinonema, no drama cinema, South London
Gallery, London
breathing house, la maison respire,
Parc Saint Léger, Centre d'art contemporain,
Pougues-les-Eaux
Kunstverein Langenhagen
Cinonema, no drama cinema, Galerie Giti
Nourbakhsch, Berlin

2011
night house at daytime, Galerie Catherine
Bastide, Bruxelles
PLAy, HEDAH/Jan van Eyck Academie,
Maastricht
PLAy, Galerie Giti Nourbakhsch, Berlin

2010
two persons house, Capacete/Bienal de
São Paulo
two persons house, Galerie Michel Rein, Paris

2009
no drama house, Galerie Giti Nourbakhsch,
Berlin

2008
Forgotten times and moments, Musée Départe-
mental d'Art Contemporain, Rochechouart
Art Basel Statements, Galerie Catherine
Bastide, Basel

2007
Maricá, Galerie Catherine Bastide, Bruxelles
viewer, Maricá, Rio de Janeiro

2006
Plouf!, with Julien Bismuth, Rio de Janeiro
Devonian Press, A+M bookstore, Milano

2005
Galerie Catherine Bastide, Bruxelles

2004
Galerie Ghislaine Hussenot, Paris, invitation
Catherine Bastide

2003
Museu do Índio, Mostra Internacional
Rio Arquitetura, Rio de Janeiro

2002
Galerie Catherine Bastide, Bruxelles

2000
sculpture noire (exhibition for women only),
Los Angeles

1994
cabin, Chicago

Selected Group Exhibitions

2013
Secret codes, Galeria Luisa Strina, São Paulo
There's no place like home, Wesfälischer Kunst-
verein, Münster
TopoDendroPhilia, Gallery Pilar Corrias, London
L.A. existential, LACE, Los Angeles

2012
Devonian Press, La Vitrine, Frac Île-de-France/
Le Plateau, Paris
La vie des Formes, Les Abattoirs, Toulouse
breathing house, a sequence or phrase, Frieze,
London
The poster show, Galerie Carlier-Gebauer, Berlin

2011
"I was a male Yvonne de Carlo…", MUSAC, León
Melanchotopia, Witte de With, Rotterdam
Anfang gut. Alles gut, KUB Arena, Kunsthaus
Bregenz
Basket—not basket, Galerie Jousse Entreprise,
Paris

2010
Chairs, Galerie Giti Nourbakhsch, Berlin
Sensorialités Excentriques, Musée Départe-
mental d'Art Contemporain, Rochechouart
A Corps Perdu, Frac Bourgogne, France

2009
Drawings, Galerie Max Hetzler, Berlin
Characters, Figures and Signs, Tate Modern,
London
Projections, Carré d'Art, Nîmes
Under cover 1, Barbara Wien, Berlin
L'école de Stéphanie, Utopics, Biennes

2008
Micro-Nation Capacete, Friedrich Petzel Gallery,
New York
Notorious, Frac Île-de-France/Le Plateau, Paris
Can art do more?, Artfocus 5, Jerusalem
Phoenix vs Babel, Fondation d'Entreprise
Ricard, Paris

2007
*L'histoire d'une décennie qui n'est pas encore
nommée*, Biennale de Lyon
Ne pas jouer avec les choses mortes, Villa
Arson, Nice
Pawnshop, e-flux, New York

2005
A show without work, Spazio Lima, Milano

2004
The stars are so big, the earth is so small…,
Galerie Schipper & Krome, Berlin
Closet, Galerie Catherine Bastide, Frieze art
Fair, London

1994
La Figure et le Lieu, Domaine de Kerguehennec,
Bignan

This catalogue is published on the occasion of the exhibitions by Jean-Pascal Flavien at the Parc Saint Léger, Centre d'art contemporain, and at the Kunstverein Langenhagen in 2012

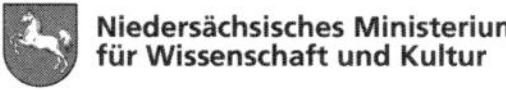

Parc Saint Léger, Centre d'art contemporain
Avenue Conti
58320 Pougues-les-Eaux
France
Tel +33 3 86 90 96 60
Fax +33 3 86 90 96 61
contact@parcsaintleger.fr
www.parcsaintleger.fr

The Parc Saint Léger is supported by the General Council of Nièvre, the Regional Direction of Cultural Affairs of Burgundy (the Ministery of Culture and Communication), the Regional Council of Burgundy and the city of Pougues-les-eaux. The Parc Saint Léger is member of d.c.a. (association pour le développement des centres d'art).

Kunstverein

Kunstverein Langenhagen e.V.

Kunstverein Langenhagen
Walsroderstr. 91A
30851 Langenhagen
Germany
Tel / Fax +49 511 77 89 29
mail@kunstverein-langenhagen.de
www.kunstverein-langenhagen.de

The exhibition at Kunstverein Langenhagen was generously founded by Niedersächsisches Ministerium für Wissenschaft und Kultur with the support of the Bureau des arts plastiques/French Institute and the French Ministry of Culture and Communication.

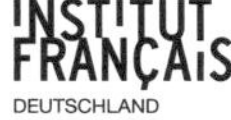

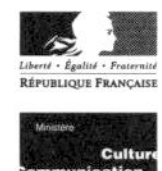

Acknowledgements
Parc Saint Léger, Centre d'art contemporain:
Régis Bertrand, Sandra Patron, Céline Poulin, Thibault Lambert, Léa Merit, Franck Balland, Vincent Valéry, Jean-Philippe Darini

Kunstverein Langenhagen: Ursula Schöndeling, Holger Graab, Eva Schatta, Ilka Schulze, Arno Auer

Galerie Catherine Bastide: Catherine Bastide, Amélie Laplanche, Marie de Gaulejac, Lucille Cocito

Special thanks to Jarbas Lopes, Giti Nourbakhsch, and Carla Zaccagnini for hosting three of the houses on their respective properties.

Helmut Batista, Julien Bismuth, Olivier Michelon, Vanessa Desclaux, Vanessa Joan Müller, Esther Schipper, Pascal Storz, Carsten Humme, Jan Wenzel, Marie de Brugerolle, Anne-Sophie Dinant, Kristina Scepanski, Christophe Wiesner, Saâdane Afif, Alexis Zavialoff, Giancarlo Vulcano, Anri Sala, Françoise Cohen, Anne-Claire Schmitz, Luiza Marcier, Elfi Turpin, Louidgi Beltrame, Marc Pérennès, Katarina Burin, Federica Bueti, Marie Cool and Fabio Balducci, Övül Durmuşoğlu, Yona Friedman, Matt Saunders, Julia Gwendolyn Schneider, Sabine Nielsen, Jan Verwoert, Marc et Josée Gensollen, Sylvie Winckler, Wilfried and Yannicke Cooreman, Cédric Aurelle, Didier Mathieu, Marie-Cécile Miessner, Christoph Schifferli, Clara Gensburger, Dane and Tana Mitchell, Vincent Puricelli, Marion Andrieu, Aude Itting, Isabelle Arthuis, Gérard Alaux, Claire Le Restif, Amilcar Packer, Cathy Larqué, Nina Köller, Dorothée Deyries-Henry, Danièle Orcier, Sebastian Filla, Runo Lagomarsino, Stefanie Lockwood, Marc Pottier, Marie-Claude Beaud, Michel Rein, Lawrence Carroll, John Millei, Erwan Maheo, Denys Zacharopoulos, Jim and Kim Lutes, Dan Peterman, Matt Mullican, André and Madeleine Flavien, and Natalie Czech

Support
This publication was produced with the additional support of Galerie Catherine Bastide, Brussels, and Galerie Esther Schipper, Berlin.

The *viewer* and the *two persons house* were made possible with the support of Capacete, Rio de Janeiro.

The *breathing house* was made possible with the support of the Fondation Nationale des Arts Graphiques et Plastiques, Paris.

Construction and structural works of *no drama house* were supported by archequipe Berlin.

Construction and structural works of *two persons house* were supported by Triptyque São Paulo.

Copyediting
Eva Wilson and Julien Bismuth

Translations
Julien Bismuth

Concept and Design
Pascal Storz and Jean-Pascal Flavien

Typesetting
Fabian Bremer and Pascal Storz

Typeface
Atlas Grotesk

Image Editing
Carsten Humme

Printing and Binding
DZA Druckerei zu Altenburg GmbH

Printed in Germany

© 2013 Jean-Pascal Flavien, Spector Books, Leipzig and the authors

Photo Credits
© 2013 for the reproduced works by Jean-Pascal Flavien
p. 12/13, 16/17: Isabelle Arthuis
p. 23: Helmut Batista
p. 105: Thorsten Arendt

All works are courtesy the artist and Galerie Catherine Bastide, Brussels (except p. 75, 104/105)

Published by
Spector Books
Harkortstraße 10
04107 Leipzig
Germany
Tel +49 341 264 51 012
Fax +49 341 212 24 11
www.spectorbooks.com

Distribution in Germany and Austria
GVA Gemeinsame Verlagsauslieferung Göttingen GmbH & Co. KG
www.gva-verlage.de

Distribution in Switzerland
AVA Verlagsauslieferung AG
www.ava.ch

Distribution in the UK, France and Japan
Anagram Books Ltd
www.anagrambooks.com

Distribution in USA
RAM Publications + Distribution Inc.
www.rampub.com

ISBN 978-3-944669-05-2

imprint

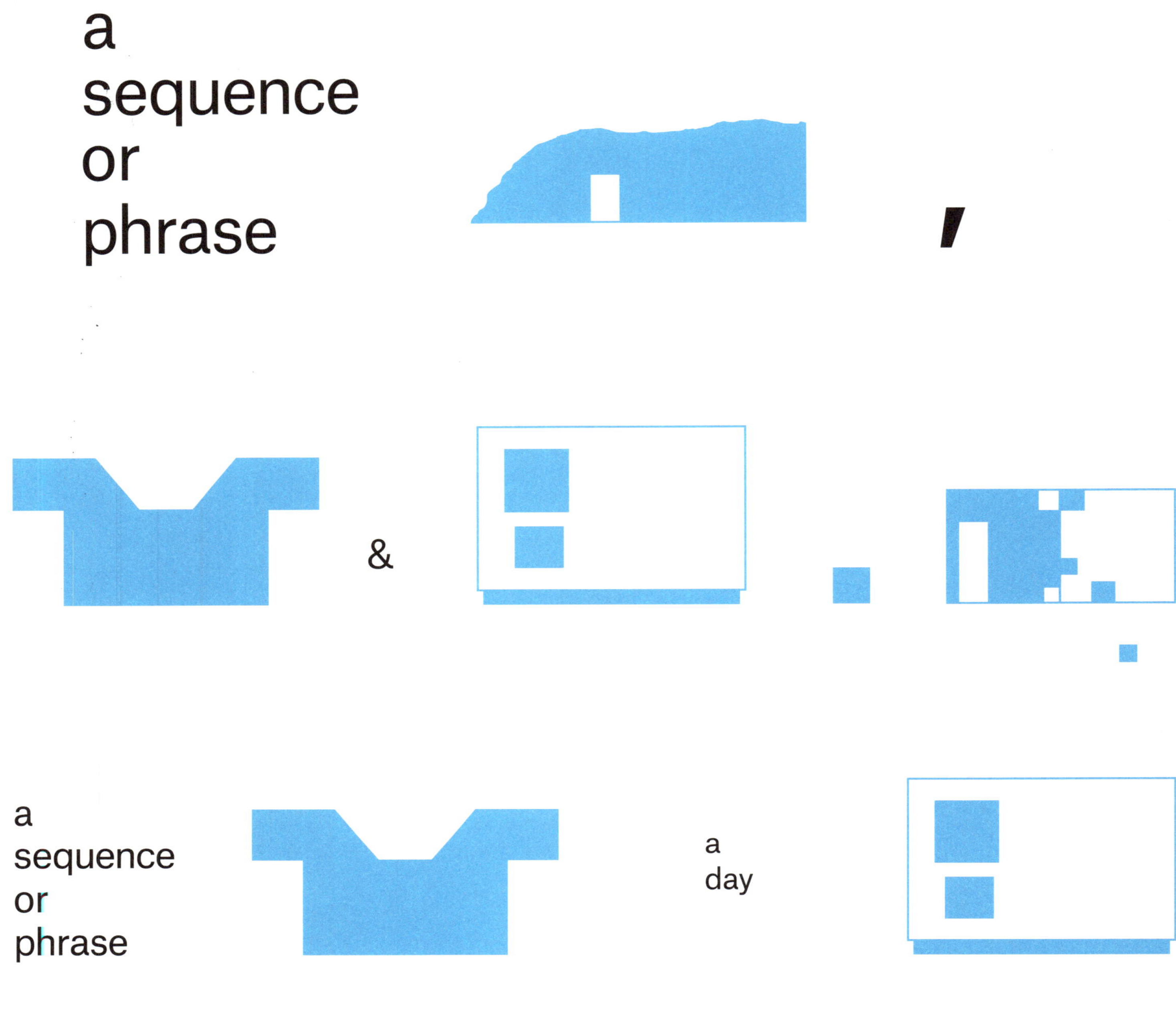

a
sequence
or
phrase

&

a
sequence
or
phrase

a
day

a week

to write
by mak-
ing
a
sequence
or
line,
displac-
ing,
placing,
and
replacing
its ele-
ments,
making
or break-
ing
its inter-
vals